Reverend Rebels

"BLACK SHEEP."

Archbishop Tait dealing with recalcitrant ritualists (from *Punch*, 23 May 1874)

REVEREND REBELS

*Five Victorian Clerics
and Their Fight Against Authority*

Bernard Palmer

Foreword by Bishop Richard Holloway

First published in 1993 by
Darton, Longman and Todd Ltd
1 Spencer Court
140–142 Wandsworth High Street
London SW18 4JJ

ISBN 0–232–52037–2

A catalogue record for this book is available
from the British Library

Cover design by Jeremy Dixon

Phototypeset in 10½/12¾pt Garamond
by Intype, London
Printed and bound in Great Britain
at the University Press, Cambridge

To
the memory of
Martin Fagg,
whose company and conversation
enriched many a Dorset walk.

CONTENTS

FOREWORD by Bishop Richard Holloway   ix

PREFACE   xv

ACKNOWLEDGEMENTS   xvii

1. THE LAW AND THE PROPHETS: 1
   Ritualism under fire

2. CHURCHMAN MILITANT: 19
   George Anthony Denison (1805–1896)

3. ST ALBAN'S MARTYRDOM: 65
   Alexander Heriot Mackonochie (1825–1887)

4. PRISONER OF CONSCIENCE: 117
   Arthur Tooth (1839–1931)

5. SAINT OF THE SLUMS: 159
   Robert William Radclyffe Dolling (1851–1902)

6. MONASTIC PIONEER: 201
   Fr Ignatius (Joseph Leycester Lyne)(1837–1908)

EPILOGUE   245

BIBLIOGRAPHY   250

INDEX   253

FOREWORD

THIS FASCINATING BOOK by Bernard Palmer has given
me occasion to visit some old acquaintances and find them
changed. There was a time when two of the characters in this
book, Father Dolling and Father Mackonochie, were boyhood
heroes, while Father Ignatius fascinated me, and Father Tooth
earned my deepest respect. Even as a boy, however, I found
Archdeacon Denison's brand of theological conservatism
unsympathetic. I was brought up on the legend of the Anglo-
Catholic slum priest and at times sought to emulate it in my
own career. Much of the history I picked up from oral tradition, but I was able to fortify it later by reading biographies
and luxuriating in Compton Mackenzie's novels about the
period. Older now, and possibly a little wiser, I look at the
period with greater objectivity and a desire to find an interpret-
ative key that will help me reappraise the issues that underlay
the Ritualist controversy. The virtue of *Reverend Rebels* is that
it does not force us to accept any particular interpretation of
the events it so vividly describes. The author has an undoubted
sympathy for the subjects under discussion. In fact, we might
well suspect him of carrying a genetic sympathy, since it was
the newspaper founded by his forebears who championed the
cause of the men discussed here with untiring, indeed sometimes hysterical zeal. Nevertheless, Bernard Palmer, while sympathetic, is not uncritical and allows the facts to speak for
themselves.

It is to trivialize the significance of the Anglo-Catholic movement in the Church of England to see it as a struggle for
bells, smells and gold-lacquered candlesticks. Something that

Archdeacon Denison said in an open letter to Bishop Claughton in 1876 captures the real issue with epigrammatic terseness: 'In 1856 I refused to surrender the Doctrine of the Real Presence. In 1876 I refuse to compromise the Doctrine by surrendering the Ritual.'

The ritual that surrounded the Eucharist was re-introduced by the Anglo-Catholics for its own sake, for aesthetic reasons, and partly to make clear the ancient doctrine of the Real Presence. So there was always a doctrinal issue behind the controversies over ritual, but an even deeper issue was the ecclesiastical one. The Fathers of the Catholic movement in the Church of England fought for the autonomy and integrity of the Church. The question they put to the Church of England has not yet been answered. It was put very well by Father Tooth in a letter to his bishop. The bishop had reminded him that he was called upon to administer the law of the Church and the realm, to both of which Tooth had engaged to conform. Tooth replied that he would be happy to place himself '. . . very unreservedly in your lordship's hands for trial and judgment according to the law in primitive use in the Christian Church . . . Your lordship declines to accept the position, and refers me to the Public Worship Regulation Act.' Tooth would have submitted to a properly constituted ecclesiastical court. He refused to submit to 'merely secular proceedings that have not acquired any ecclesiastical force, unless one is to believe that a bishop has super-parliamentary power, and in passing State Law through his hands can alter it and give it something it had not before, a spiritual force, conveying a new character to it'. It was thus the appeal by bishops and the proxies suborned by the Church Association to the secular courts which was the central offence to the Catholic party. It is true that they fought for 'Catholic privileges' for their own sake, but the real and main principle was always the independence of the spiritual from the secular authority.

This is an issue which is still not resolved for the Church of England, still 'by law established'. The genius of the English is to adapt to the challenges of the future by a process of grudging but gradual acceptance. In the case of the Ritualist Controversy it has to be admitted that the Law itself established certain rights for the Anglo-Catholic reformers and this, combined with the revulsion that the people of England increasingly felt for the bullying tactics of the Church Association, resolved the issue practically by refusing to deal with the very principle that was at stake. This ability to operate on the level of pragmatism rather than principle caused equal portions of despair and admiration among sympathetic observers of the English scene. As I write these words a type of replay of the great Ritual Controversy is unwinding before our eyes, though this time the protagonists are reversed. It is the Catholic party that hopes Parliament will rescue the Church of England from innovations of which it disapproves, while the bishops struggle to put together an arrangement that will hold the feuding parties together without fully satisfying any of them. To this affectionate observer of the English scene, the method looks increasingly unpersuasive and creates major doubts about the very fact of Establishment itself.

The other main issue revealed by the Ritualist Controversy is the impotence of negative movements in human, and especially in ecclesiastical history. The text for all these struggles is firmly embedded in one of the earliest documents of the Christian Church, where Gamaliel warned the Sanhedrin not to persecute the Christian movement, because if it was not of God it would not succeed and if it was of God it was futile to oppose it. Zealous reactionaries never learn this wisdom. Invariably, they lose the sympathy of the public with their intense negativity. Ironically, something that *Vanity Fair* wrote about Father Tooth is applicable to them as being 'endowed less with a great power of will than with an enormous power of won't'. Passionate conservatives always refuse to accept the organic nature of the Church in history. They resist all development and change, usually unintelligently, and by their persecution of the new idea or practice breed the very sympathy for it that is so contrary to their own intentions. Again, we are witnessing one of these episodes in the Church of England today. The supreme irony is that, of all the traditions in Anglicanism, the Catholic tradition ought to have learned this lesson best, having won its case against the persecution mounted against it by the Church Association. This great movement that changed world Anglicanism for ever and revolutionized its liturgy is now acting like the Church Association in lace cottas. It is the great negative movement today, opposing developments in the Church's ministry that would make it inclusive of the human race rather than half of it.

It is here that Bernard Palmer's new book offers a salutary reminder. Throughout his account of these great struggles there emerges a theme played under the main tune that becomes increasingly menacing and significant. Charles Gore does not feature as a main character in the drama described in these chapters, but his name crops up from time to time. Gore was a liberal Catholic, open to the intellectual struggles of his day, and he became a hate object to conservative Anglican Catholics like Archdeacon Denison. More strident, if much less intelligent in his opposition, was the exotic Father Ignatius, who followed Gore round like a one man rent-a-mob, screaming at him for his blasphemous attempts to interpret Christianity in a way that would appeal to the intelligences of his day. There has been in the movement from the beginning an element of straightforward anti-intellectual prejudice. It is still alive and kicking.

The final paradox revealed by this engaging book is the deeply Protestant nature of Anglo-Catholicism. The word Protestant can be used in many ways. I am using it here in the sense of protest, in the name of righteousness and truth, against the bullying abuses of authority. The Anglo-Catholic rebels were deeply Protestant in their refusal to conform to the authority set over them, both in Church and State. They always appealed, in a very Protestant way, to a higher authority, that of primitive Catholic Christianity. This was the appeal made by the great Protestant Reformers as well. It was the very Protestantism of the Church of England that, however reluctantly, gave Catholics the space and freedom to make their protests and to win their cause. The intellectual tragedy of Anglo-Catholicism is that it has never acknowledged that it was the very element of Anglicanism it most passionately repudiated

which guaranteed its own right to protest. The publication of
this meditation on long-forgotten battles is entirely apposite.
Those who don't learn from history are condemned to repeat
it. The whirligig of time has brought in another of its revenges.

RICHARD HOLLOWAY
Bishop of Edinburgh and Primus
of the Scottish Episcopal Church

PREFACE

W HEN I WAS EDITOR of the *Church Times* in the 1970s and 80s, I had occasion from time to time to consult back numbers of the paper for special anniversary issues. I soon noticed what a large amount of space in the early numbers was devoted to the Ritual Controversy – to the endless battles between militantly ritualistic incumbents and the authorities of both Church and State. Some of these battles ended in the lawcourts, and even in prison. Those were stirring times in which to be a High Church cleric determined to resist the demands of authority.

The story of this particular epoch in the nineteenth-century Church of England has been told briefly in general histories of the period, and at greater length in specialized studies and in full-length biographies of the principal characters involved. It seemed to me, however, that there was room for a fresh appraisal which, within the covers of a single volume, would tell the eventful story of the ritualists through a series of mini-biographies.

In retirement I have had the leisure to tackle such an assignment; and *Reverend Rebels* is the result. I hope it will fulfil a useful purpose in focusing attention on the lives of five colourful and courageous clerics and on the ecclesiastical context in which those lives were set.

BERNARD PALMER
Charminster, Dorset
June 1993

ACKNOWLEDGEMENTS

I LIST IN THE bibliography at the end of the volume the books I have consulted for the purpose of writing *Reverend Rebels*. I have necessarily drawn heavily on existing memoirs of the five clerics who form the subjects of my book. Among modern biographers I am particularly indebted to Joyce Coombs for her *George Anthony Denison* and for her *Judgment on Hatcham* (Fr Tooth); to Michael Reynolds for his *Martyr of Ritualism* (Fr Mackonochie); and to Arthur Calder-Marshall for his *The Enthusiast* (Fr Ignatius).

I should also like to acknowledge my gratitude to Canterbury Press, Norwich, for allowing me to quote extensively from the *Church Times*; to Canon Alan Wilkinson and the Rev. Tony Shepherd for extending my knowledge of Fr Dolling; to the Headmaster and staff members of St Michael's School, Otford, for sending me material relating to Fr Tooth's later life; and to the late Donald Cormack for letting me see, shortly before his death in December 1992, the chapter on Tooth from his projected history of St Michael's School. Finally I thank my wife for once again turning my imperfect typescript into a fair copy for the publishers and for much-needed encouragement along the way.

B.P.

CHAPTER 1

---◆◆◆---

THE LAW AND THE
PROPHETS

Ritualism under fire

'THIS RITUAL MOVEMENT has by no means reached its
term. It is still in the full vigour of its early years. It appears to
be advancing both extensively, in the work of proselytism, and
intensively, in doctrinal innovation, not always distinctly enun-
ciated but clearly intimated. Its partisans seem to vie with one
another in the introduction of more and more startling novelties,
both of theory and practice.'

This tribute to the growing strength of Ritualism came (as
might be guessed) not from a fervent disciple of the movement
but from a distinctly unenthusiastic episcopal critic. But Bishop
Thirlwall of St Davids was fair-minded, despite his lack of
enthusiasm; and his assessment (given in the course of a charge
to his diocese) was quoted by the Archbishop of Canterbury,
Randall Davidson, in his evidence to the Royal Commission on
Ecclesiastical Discipline which sat from 1904 to 1906. The charge
was delivered in October 1866, at the end of the first of the
three periods into which Davidson divided the modern ritualistic
movement. The second period, from 1866 to 1892, stretched
from the first prosecution of Fr Mackonochie to the trial of
Edward King, Bishop of Lincoln. It was a period of increasing
strife during which five priests were actually sent to gaol – for
conscience' sake or for disobeying the law, according to one's
point of view. It was the period with which much of this book
is concerned. Five individual clerics were in the forefront of the

battle and form the subject of the next five chapters. But why was the battle being fought at all?

By 1866 the Oxford or Tractarian Movement had travelled a long way since Newman's secession to Rome in 1845. The movement's *avant-garde* were no longer willing to rest content with a full sacramental doctrine: they wanted to see its provisions exemplified in the Church's life and worship. This meant rearranging the services, finding room for many more celebrations of Holy Communion, performing the rite with all the traditional adjuncts of music and ceremonial, and giving it the priority over Mattins among the Sunday-morning services. All this was held to smack of Roman Catholicism in the eyes of many men and women in the pews and aroused much opposition. By 1866 the term 'ritualist' was already being used of those priests who had introduced or reintroduced medieval or modern 'Romanist' practices into their services. Soon the rumbling unrest was to develop into open war.

Why then, in the face of much opposition, did Ritualism make such headway so rapidly in the Church of England, and what was so special about it that its practitioners were prepared to endure persecution and to sacrifice all prospects of promotion rather than give in to the demands of the authorities that they should toe the official liturgical line?

One reason was the belief that an advanced ritual (or rather ceremonial) was more likely to attract the working man into attending church. There was a certain amount of truth in this contention. The great 'slum priests' such as Mackonochie, Lowder and Dolling certainly ministered to enormous congregations, though it could be argued that the crowds were attracted not so much by the advanced ceremonial as by the saintliness and charismatic personalities of the priests in question. They were successful just because their lives were so self-denying and their enthusiasm so forceful.

But Ritualism in any event was regarded as much more than a tool of evangelism. The main ritualistic practices were held to have a doctrinal significance. The eastward position of the celebrant at the Eucharist, for instance, was the position of a sacrificing priest. And Mackonochie believed that a 'gorgeously conducted service' underlined a belief in the 'Real Presence' – the idea that, at the Eucharist, Christ's body and blood were actually present under the forms of bread and wine. Such a notion was anathema to Protestants and was to lead to Archdeacon Denison's prosecution for heresy. But it was not only Protestants who objected to ritualistic practices. The older Tractarians looked askance at some of their successors' goings-on. Pusey, for one, discouraged the use of rich vestments on the ground that 'our own plain dresses are more in keeping with the state of our Church, which is one of humiliation'. For their part the new generation of Tractarians tended to look on their elders as (in the words of Dean Church) 'rather *dark* people who don't grow beards and do other proper things.'

At the heart of the dislike of Ritualism that was widespread among the ordinary laity of the Church of England was an innate fear of the Church of Rome. It may have been illogical or unreasoning, but it was there all the same – and it was easy and all too tempting for those who disliked Ritualism for other reasons to play on this fear. In 1837, for instance, in the early days of the Oxford Movement, the Chaplain of New College, Peter Maurice, described in a tract, *The Popery of Oxford*, the 'indescribable horror' he had felt stealing over him on observing a 'plain naked cross' near the communion table in the new church at Littlemore:

> There . . . was the hassock upon which, not long before, a minister of the Reformed and Protestant Church of England had been kneeling. I could not divest my mind of that fond delusion of the man of sin who openly bows down before the image of the Cross and worships the painted wood or cold stone. May my natural eye never fall upon such a degrading spectacle.

Suspicion of the cross as an aid to worship surfaced in a different context in 1854 at Hemel Hempstead, Hertfordshire, when crosses discovered on the book-markers in the Bible and prayer-book of an officiating clergyman led to violent scenes and to 'mobs roving about'.

In 1847 the Bishop of Chichester, A. T. Gilbert, took exception to the 'spiritual haberdashery' on view at Sackville College, East Grinstead, of which the warden was the distinguished Tractarian theologian and hymnologist, J. M. Neale. The day after his visit he wrote a letter condemning 'the frippery with which Mr. Neale has transformed the simplicity of the chapel at Sackville College into an imitation of the degrading superstitions of an erroneous Church.' In 1850 Lady Charlotte Guest confided to her diary her horror at the ritualistic goings-on she had observed during an Ash Wednesday service at Canford. 'It has grieved me, I cannot say how deeply. The more so, as I fear I can do nothing to rescue our people from the contamination of witnessing practices' so redolent of the Church of Rome.

Similar dismay was felt by a retired admiral who had observed a member of a religious brotherhood wearing a habit in public. He complained how the pleasant roads were being darkened by 'these associations of the Inquisition'. Even the humble cassock aroused suspicion. A Hampshire squire grumbled about the 'peculiar clothes down to his heels' being worn by the local parson – 'You could not distinguish whether he had a coat and trowzers on.' The younger Tractarians hardly improved matters when, in imitation of the dress of Roman Catholic priests, they took to wearing what the Evangelicals called 'Mark of the Beast' waistcoats, which carried up to the cravat without dividing, and long straight coats reaching down to the heels. As for the clothes worn by the ritualistic priests in church, the general feeling was summed up by the Rev. J. W. Burgon in a sermon preached in 1873 in the University church of St Mary the Virgin at Oxford. He inveighed against 'their pitiful millinery, their coloured stoles and imported birettas', which would, he claimed, 'betray many unstable souls into the hand of the Church of Rome'.

The popular feeling against Ritualism as aping Roman Catholicism was whipped up in the press, a notorious offender being *Punch*. An inspection of mid-nineteenth-century numbers of that once-famous magazine (which only folded, a shadow of its former self, in 1992) will reveal the bitterness and savagery of the attacks made week by week on the 'Puseyite' – i.e., ritualistic – clergy. Taunts and misrepresentations abounded, and the accumulating torrent of invective must have helped sway the magazine's readers against the ritualists. Typical of the standard of *Punch* references to Puseyism (which were mostly crude, rude and vulgar rather than genuinely witty) was this jingle which appeared in one of the 1850 numbers:

> Though crosses and candles we play with at home,
> To go the whole gander there's no place like Rome;
> We've statues and relics to hallow us there,
> Which, save in museums, you'll not find elsewhere.
> Rome, Rome, sweet Rome!
> For all us Tractarians there's no place like Rome!

Punch carried on its hostility to the ritualists over a long period of years and under a succession of editors. Nine of the first thirteen cartoons published in 1851, for instance, were anti-Puseyite in tone. And over twenty years later, in a comment on a current lawsuit, the magazine commented: 'It is to be hoped that legislation will shortly place the Ritualist and the Reredos thus far on the same footing that the former, if he persists in performing illicit rites in his Church, shall be liable to be, if not straightway demolished, at least summarily removed.'

If *Punch* was a weekly thorn in the Tractarian flesh, there was a less visible but more august opponent: Queen Victoria. Her hatred of the Church of Rome and all that it stood for was notorious – and this hatred spilled over on to its Tractarian imitators. The Queen was fully conscious of her Coronation oath to 'maintain the Protestant Reformed Religion established by law'. She expressed herself in one letter as being 'shocked and grieved' to see 'the higher classes and so many of the young clergy tainted with this leaning towards Rome'. She was determined that something must be done to stem the ritualistic tide. In November 1873 she wrote to the Dean of Westminster, A. P. Stanley, that a *'complete Reformation'* was wanted. 'But, if *that* is *impossible*, the archbishop should have the *power* given to *him*, by *Parliament*, to *stop all* these ritualistic practices, dressing, bowings, etc., and everything of that kind, and, *above all*, *all* attempts at *confession*.' To think was to act. The Queen, with the connivance of Archbishop Tait, put all her influence into persuading the Prime Minister, Benjamin Disraeli, to introduce a Bill into Parliament to put down Ritualism. 'Something must be done', she told Tait in January 1874. Something was done; and the result was the Public Worship Regulation Act (of which more anon). The Queen's anti-Roman and anti-Tractarian views were well known in the nation at large – and played their part in swaying public opinion against the ritualists.

The principal points of issue between them and their opponents were eventually boiled down to six – defined as the Six Points at the annual meeting of the English Church Union in 1875. They were eucharistic vestments, the eastward position of the celebrant at the Eucharist, altar lights (i.e., candles), the mixture of water and wine in the chalice, wafer bread, and incense. A key factor in the endless battles of words in the courts was the precise interpretation of the so-called Ornaments Rubric in the Book of Common Prayer. This laid down that the 'ornaments' of the Church and its ministers should be those in use 'by the authority of Parliament in the second year of the reign of King Edward VI'. The interpretation of the rubric had been a vexed question since its original framing in the sixteenth century. Archbishop Davidson truly remarked of it (in an address to the Convocation of Canterbury in November 1906) that it was a document unlike any other document in history in that it was appealed to on either side in the controversy as conclusive, 'but appealed to with interpretations attached which on the two sides are diametrically opposite. I doubt whether the same number of words in English or in any other tongue have ever stood in quite the same relation as these words stand to a great controversy or to a great epoch in Church life.' The main argument, of course, centred on what exactly were the 'ornaments' in use in the Church of England in the second year of the reign of King Edward VI. Tractarians maintained that they included the traditional eucharistic vestments such as the chasuble; their opponents for the most part proclaimed the opposite. It was the uncertainty on the issue which caused Lord Shaftesbury in 1867 to introduce a Clerical Vestments Bill in the House of Lords, enjoining the use of the surplice for all ministrations in all churches. But his Bill was defeated (twelve bishops voting on his side and seven against).

With the law so ambiguous, it was hardly surprising that recourse should be had to the courts in an attempt to determine which practices were and which were not illegal. The latter half of the nineteenth century was punctuated by a number of major ecclesiastical lawsuits on ritualistic questions. The judgments given often contradicted each other. They almost always went on appeal to the Judicial Committee of the Privy Council – a bone of contention for the ritualists, who denied the Council's competence to pronounce on spiritual matters. They aroused intense feeling on the opposing sides, the successive verdicts being mulled over at length in the newspapers and applauded or denounced in editorials. After the Public Worship Regulation Act had passed into law a number of ritualistic priests were sent to gaol – to the fury of their supporters, the embarrassment of the authorities and the disquiet of moderate-minded churchmen. Some of these cases must now be summarized.

The first important case involving matters of ritual (or, more accurately, ceremonial) was that which resulted in the so-called Knightsbridge Judgment of 1857. The priest involved was the Hon. Robert Liddell, vicar of St Paul's, Knightsbridge. The prosecution was led by one of his churchwardens, an ultra-Protestant named Charles Westerton, who had already proved a menace to Liddell by interfering with the services, complaining to the Bishop of London and publishing numerous tracts to expose the 'meretricious trumpery' at St Paul's and its daughter church of St Barnabas', Pimlico.* He now went one stage further and sued in the Consistory Court for the removal of the high altar at St Paul's with its cross, candlesticks, coloured altar-cloths and credence table. The case continued throughout the spring, summer and autumn of 1855, judgment being delivered on 5 December. The Chancellor, Stephen Lushington, inter-

---

*Catholic hostility to Westerton resulted in an unfortunate incident involving Charles Lowder, then a curate at St Barnabas'. He rashly gave the choristers sixpence to buy rotten eggs with which to bespatter a sandwich-man who was walking the streets of the parish to promote Westerton's candidacy for the office of church-warden. Lowder had to apologize in court for his behaviour and pay the sandwich-man £2 in compensation. *Punch* commented: 'Eggs and stones flung at a man's head from the instigation of a Puseyite curate indicate the animus of Tractarianism.'

preted the Ornaments Rubric in a Protestant sense and ruled against Liddell on nearly every point – to the dismay of the Tractarians, who (in the words of the future Dean Church) deplored the court's 'determination to find a meaning and direction where there is none and to close questions which at the least are open ones'. But all was not lost. Though Liddell's appeal to the Court of Arches, the provincial court of the province of Canterbury, was unsuccessful, he then applied for a further ruling to the Judicial Committee of the Privy Council – which, in a judgment delivered on 21 March 1857, reversed the decisions of the lower courts in all the key particulars. High Churchmen were delighted with a verdict which appeared to confirm their own interpretation of the Ornaments Rubric in a Catholic direction. Although vestments were not specifically covered by the judgment, their use was by implication now permitted. Archbishop Davidson admitted as much in his evidence to the Royal Commission on Ecclesiastical Discipline when he observed: 'After the judgment by the Privy Council in Westerton v. Liddell, vestments began . . . to be introduced in various churches . . . In the series of five or six years that succeeded the judgment the usages undoubtedly became more frequent'. Davidson went on: 'The bishops, most of them, felt the awkwardness, to say the least, of seeming to be repressing usages which they knew to be under the more or less explicit sanction of the only court of law to which an appeal had been made.' But, regrettably for the peace of the Church, any belief that the last word on the subject had now been said was an illusion which before long was to be rudely shattered.

*   *   *

First, however, came a prosecution not over allegedly illegal ceremonial but over allegedly heretical doctrine. The defendant was Archdeacon Denison, and the case is described fully in the next chapter. It ended in Denison's acquittal on a legal technicality – to his regret, in that he would have preferred to have been acquitted specifically of the charge of heresy. In fact the orthodoxy of his teaching on the Real Presence was implied as a result of a similar case involving the Rev. W. J. E. Bennett, vicar of Frome Selwood in Somerset. Bennett published an open letter to Pusey in 1867 in which he argued that the body and blood of Christ were actually (and not only figuratively) present in the sacrament of Holy Communion. He was accused of heresy by the Church Association, a Protestant body founded in 1865 to fight Tractarianism through the courts, but was acquitted in 1870 by the Dean of the Arches, Sir Robert Phillimore (who was Denison's brother-in-law). The Church Association appealed against the verdict to the Judicial Committee of the Privy Council, but in 1872 the Committee also ruled in Bennett's favour. As a result (in the words of a later historian, G. M. Young) 'the Privy Council had rendered it so difficult for a Churchman to be a heretic that prosecutions for heresy almost ceased, and the public mind turned with the greater avidity to the persecution of ritualism.'

The first and most prolonged 'persecution' was that of the Rev. A. H. Mackonochie, vicar of St Alban's, Holborn, which is described at length in Chapter 3. But, just as 'Martin v. Mackonochie' was getting into its stride, the 'lazy, snug and well-paid ecclesiastics' of the Church Association (as the *Church Times* dubbed them) struck again. Their victim this time was not a priest like Mackonochie toiling in the slums, but the incumbent of a 'mere proprietary chapel in a fashionable watering-place' (the *Church Times* again) – the Rev. John Purchas, vicar of St James's, Brighton. He was charged with no fewer than thirty-five illegal practices. The most significant of these were adopting the eastward position at the altar, wearing eucharistic vestments, using wafer bread for communion, and mixing water with wine in the chalice; the least significant was suspending over the altar a stuffed dove supposed to be symbolic of the Holy Ghost. The Court of the Arches met to hear the case in November 1869, and Sir Robert Phillimore delivered his judgment in February 1870. He ruled against Purchas on most points (including incense and altar lights, which had already been declared illegal in the Mackonochie case); but he allowed vestments, the eastward position, wafer bread and a non-ceremonially mixed chalice.

At this stage the ritualists were disappointed but not too

dismayed. However, the Church Association, true to form, now appealed to the Judicial Committee of the Privy Council, which in 1871 reversed the Arches verdict in respect of the four key practices allowed by Phillimore. In fact the Committee's decision in the Purchas case had been widely forecast in the light of its latest judgment in Martin v. Mackonochie, which had again reversed a decision by the Dean of the Arches; and the English Church Union (the Tractarian counterpart of the Church Association) had even declined to assist Purchas with funds to retain Counsel for the hearing before the Judicial Committee, on the grounds that his cause was too forlorn to be worth defending. Nevertheless, whatever they may have thought privately, the ritualists lost no opportunity in publicly deploring the Purchas Judgment. Their organ, the *Church Times*, in a leader for 3 March 1871 headed 'The Last Straw', assured its readers that the whole series of ritualistic judgments over the past few years had formed part of an organized conspiracy. The Privy Council had been guilty of injustice for the purpose of 'gratifying partisan bias'. The paper claimed that the latest verdict was in no sense a true representation of the law, and that obedience to the law meant disobedience to the Judicial Committee. The clergy could not therefore comply with its findings without violating their own ordination vows and incurring the contempt of the laity. 'Things have come to this pass now: Protestantism has given up trying to argue with us. . . . It has fallen back on fraud and violence.'

All this was heady stuff, but undoubtedly the Purchas* Judgment marked a significant stage in the fight against ceremonial in church services. Up till now a number of the key practices objected to by the Church Association and their allies had been regarded by many churchpeople as at least conforming to the letter of the law. The latest judgment, however, branded ritual-

---

*The unfortunate Purchas died prematurely, aged fifty-one, in the year following the judgment. The *Church Times*, in its issue of 25 October 1872, commented: 'This sad event was proximately caused by an attack of inflammation of the lungs; but there can be no doubt that it was really attributable to a long-standing heart disease aggravated by worry and anxiety occasioned by the proceedings of the Church Association.'

ists as law-breakers – and, as a result, was widely disregarded. From 1871 onwards the aims of the revivers of ceremonial crystallized into the restoration of the Six Points – the four allowed by the Court of Arches but disallowed by the Privy Council, plus the two (incense and altar lights) forbidden by both courts. These were formally adopted by the English Church Union at its annual meeting on 15 June 1875 as matters upon which, 'without wishing to go beyond what recognized Anglican authorities warrant as to their use . . . there should be no prohibition . . . when desired by clergy and congregations'.

In the eyes of a large and growing number of churchpeople the Purchas Judgment discredited the Judicial Committee of the Privy Council as a final court of appeal in ecclesiastical cases. The Anglo-Catholic historian S. L. Ollard compares it to the judges' decision in the matter of John Hampden and Ship Money under Charles I: 'resistance to it became a duty to those to whom constitutional government, whether in Church or State, was dear'. The Royal Commission on Ecclesiastical Discipline recognized this when it conceded, in its report of 1906, that the judgments of the Judicial Committee 'cannot practically be enforced'.

*   *   *

The next stage in the battle to curb the ritualists was the passing of the Public Worship Regulation Act in 1874 after a prolonged struggle in Parliament and as a result of the unholy alliance between the Queen, the Prime Minister and the Archbishop of Canterbury to which reference has already been made. The purpose of the Act was unashamed: to suppress the growth of Ritualism in the Church of England – or, as Disraeli put it to the House of Commons, to destroy 'the Mass in masquerade'. It changed not so much the law regarding worship as the machinery for enforcing it – by shortening the procedure before a case reached the provincial court, and by amalgamating the two provincial courts of Canterbury and York under a single lay judge. The Bill, originally drafted by Archbishop Tait, was significantly amended in a more Protestant and Erastian direction during its passage through Parliament. Tait did, however, manage to secure, in the teeth of fierce opposition, the crucial provision for a bishop to be able to veto proceedings under the Act against priests in his diocese. It was this power of episcopal veto which was eventually to turn the Act into a dead letter. Seventeen out of twenty-three attempted prosecutions were to be vetoed by the diocesan bishops concerned, though the remaining handful of cases proceeded to court. Monition (or warning) could under the Act be followed by suspension, with the possibility of imprisonment for contempt of court – though the implications of this last-resort penalty seem not to have been properly thought out by the framers of the Act. Undoubtedly it was Tait's success in securing the bishop's right of veto which minimized the Erastian nature of the Act.* Five clerics were sent to gaol under it; but only one of these, S. F. Green, served for any length of time, the other four being released after very short spells in gaol because of irregularities in the committal proceedings. The imprisonment of these five priests, however, resulted in a swing of public opinion in favour of the ritualists and against the Act.

The first move under the Act, however, resulted not so much in the culprit's imprisonment as in his eventual agreement to toe the line. The priest concerned was the Rev. Charles Joseph Ridsdale, incumbent of St Peter's, Folkestone, a district chapelry which happened to lie within Tait's own diocese of Canterbury. The Church Association, which had been formed specifically to resist ceremonial innovations by legal action and to counter the 'idolatrous adoration of the elements in the Lord's Supper', persuaded a number of parishioners to complain that Ridsdale was indulging in twelve objectionable practices – including eucharistic vestments and the eastward position, which had already been declared illegal under the Purchas Judgment. Tait declined to veto the proceedings, and the case was to set the pattern for later disputes.

---

*Tait's original plan was to have had in each diocese a board of assessors, clerical and lay, to whom the bishop would have referred complaints and on whose advice he would have acted. Appeal would have been to the archbishop of the province, whose judgment would have been final.

The first hearing came before the new court set up under the Public Worship Regulation Act. It was presided over by James Plaisted Wilde, Baron Penzance, a retired judge (and amateur rose-grower) who had made his name in the Divorce Court – a fact which added insult to injury in the eyes of his opponents. Penzance, needless to say, ruled against Ridsdale on all twelve points. Ridsdale, whose costs were met by the English Church Union, appealed to the Judicial Committee of the Privy Council on four of these (vestments, the eastward position, wafer bread, and a crucifix and candles on the rood screen). In its judgment, delivered on 12 May 1877, the Committee confirmed that all four practices were unacceptable in the Church of England – a verdict denounced by the *Church Times* as the 'craziest of a series of so-called legal decisions which have seriously impaired the credit of English jurisprudence'. This accusation was not quite so wild as it sounded, a minority on the Committee having dissented from a decision which on the surface had appeared unanimous. One of the dissentients, Sir Fitzroy Kelly, described it as a 'judgment of policy, not of law'; another, Lord Justice Amphlett, called it 'flagitious'; a third, Sir Robert Phillimore, could hardly have subscribed to it in that, as Dean of the Arches in the Purchas case, he had already affirmed the legality of vestments, wafer bread and the eastward position – the very practices which a majority of his colleagues on the Judicial Committee now wanted to pronounce illegal. In fact the Committee's ban on the eastward position had not been a total one. In an endeavour to mollify High Church susceptibilities it had conceded that it was a permissible option *provided* that it did not conceal the priest's manual acts from the congregation. But this gesture failed to satisfy the ritualists. The *Church Times* described it as a 'mere trap for fresh persecutions'.

Gladstone called the prosecution of Ridsdale 'unjust and unwise'. Liddon thought the result likely to be 'fatal to the conqueror'. Dean Church drew up a memorial signed by seventy-seven clergymen (including four deans, eight archdeacons and thirteen canons) asserting that no authority would be considered binding on the clergy unless it proceeded from the Church as well as from the State. Fortunately for the powers-that-be, Ridsdale by this time had had enough. He had recently married, and was unwilling to risk the possible loss of his livelihood by carrying on a campaign of civil disobedience – even though such a course would have turned him into a martyr in the eyes of his more militant fellow-ritualists. He informed Tait that his 'conscience' favoured carrying on according to the rubrics (i.e., in particular, the Ornaments Rubric), but that he would ignore its promptings if Tait, as his spiritual superior, would grant him the necessary dispensation. Tait was happy to oblige. He granted Ridsdale a 'complete dispensation from the obligation under which you believe yourself to be'. All was well, and Ridsdale soldiered on at St Peter's, Folkestone, for over thirty more years.

The Archbishop was not to get off so lightly in the next case, that of Arthur Tooth at St James's, Hatcham. Tooth, as described in Chapter 4, was the first priest to be sent to prison under the Public Worship Regulation Act. Four others were to follow him. Three of these were released fairly soon on technical grounds. The Rev. Thomas Pelham Dale, rector of St Vedast's, Foster Lane, in the city of London, was freed with the aid of a writ of *habeas corpus* after fifty-six days in Holloway Gaol (30 October – 24 December 1880); Richard William Enraght, vicar of Holy Trinity, Bordesley, in the diocese of Worcester, was released after fifty-one days in Warwick Gaol (27 November 1880 – 17 January 1881), on the ground that the writs had not been opened in the presence of justices of the Queen's Bench;* the Rev. James Bell Cox, vicar of St Margaret's, Toxteth Park, in the diocese of Liverpool, spent only sixteen days in Walton Gaol (5 – 21 May 1887) before his conviction was quashed by the Court of Queen's Bench on the ground that Penzance had pronounced sentence through a proxy.

The most notorious gaoling under the Public Worship Regulation Act was that of the Rev. Sidney Faithhorn Green

---

*A particularly unpleasant feature of the Enraght case was the pilfering of a consecrated wafer from Holy Trinity by an agent of the Church Association to be used in evidence at the court hearing – the so-called 'Bordesley sacrilege'. The wafer was eventually 'consumed reverently' by Archbishop Tait.

(1841–1916), vicar of St John's, Miles Platting, in the diocese of Manchester. At the prompting of the Church Association Green was accused by three parishioners of introducing eleven allegedly illegal ceremonial practices into his church. He was summoned to appear before Penzance's court, but declined to do so. In November 1880 he was found guilty of contempt of court and on 19 March 1881 committed to Lancaster Gaol, where he was to languish for no fewer than 595 days – one year and seven months – to the acute embarrassment of the authorities of both Church and State. In every issue of the *Church Times* from 25 March 1881 to 3 November 1882 the following announcement was printed in bold type above the first leading article: 'ARRESTED MARCH 19TH 1881. The Prayers of the Church are desired for SIDNEY FAITHHORN GREEN, Priest. IN PRISON FOR OBEDIENCE TO THE CHURCH'S LAW.' This helped to keep the issue before the High Church public, though in fact churchpeople of all schools of thought were shocked by Green's imprisonment, however misguided his views might have seemed to them. Eventually his benefice became void under the terms of the Public Worship Regulation Act; Green resigned rather than wait to be expelled; and he was finally released from gaol on 4 November 1882. But his long spell behind bars had played a large part in the discrediting of the Act.*

In the early days of the Act, however, the pundits of the Church Association were much exercised by the number of priests who escaped their net. Seventeen out of twenty-three attempted prosecutions under the Act fell foul of the episcopal veto. It almost seemed as if the bishops had agreed to disallow ritual prosecutions as a matter of policy, though Tait denied this when challenged on the point in the House of Lords. All schools of thought were represented among those who applied the veto. Bickersteth of Exeter, for instance, an Evangelical, remarked that 'in the present state of the law I fear that prosecutions in the courts on such matters of ritual only aggravate the evils

---

*Public opinion had been particularly outraged by the enforced sale of Green's household goods and personal belongings to pay his opponents' legal costs, although they were bought back by the English Church Union and restored to him.

they are intended to suppress'. And Tait himself vetoed the prosecution of the charismatic Charles Lowder of St Peter's, London Docks, after hearing from the Bishop of London, John Jackson, that, if Lowder went to prison ('which he will with the greatest pleasure'), he doubted whether the Public Worship Regulation Act, unamended, could ever be put into force again. Defending his attitude, Tait declared that he had looked into the man's work and would not allow the prosecution to go ahead. And, in a memorandum he drew up on the ritual difficulties, he said he had come to believe that there should be as little interference as possible in churches where the parishioners were satisfied with the ceremonial and where 'hearty work' was being done, even though in some respects the incumbent might be stretching the law beyond its proper limits. This was indeed a near-deathbed conversion.

The officials of the Church Association, however, were not prepared to give in without a struggle. They were unimpressed by the peace-at-any-price policy apparently being exercised (despite official denials) by the bench of bishops. They determined that, if the bishops would not prosecute erring incumbents of their own accord, they should be *made* to do so. The target they selected for a test case was Canon Thomas Thellusson Carter, the saintly vicar of Clewer, near Windsor, in the diocese of Oxford. Acting through a doctor of medicine named Julius who spent much of his time in Egypt but who claimed that he had been driven away from Clewer church by the ritualistic acts that assailed his eyes there, they urged the Bishop of Oxford, J. F. Mackarness, to prosecute Carter. The bishop at first played for time, remarking that recent cases had had 'a tendency to cover all persons concerned in them with ridicule' and to bring the Church itself into contempt. When he eventually refused to permit Carter to be prosecuted either under the Public Worship Regulation Act or under the Church Discipline Act of 1840, the Church Association applied to the Queen's Bench for a writ to compel him to do as it wanted. Mackarness, in his defence, insisted that the law must surely be intended to allow a bishop discretion even when an offence had been committed. The court was unimpressed and, in March 1879, ruled against him. It maintained that he had no discretion in the matter and *must* allow the prosecution of Carter. The Church Association was jubilant. But two months later the verdict against Mackarness was overturned by the Court of Appeal; and his victory was confirmed by the House of Lords in March 1880, to the immense relief of the ritualists. Even Carter's resignation at this point to avoid the possibility of further trouble could not disguise the awkward fact that a bishop's right to veto a particular prosecution was now legally unassailable. The Church Association might (and did) carry on its campaign against individual ritualists, but it had to fight hard in each case to secure a prosecution. And the writing for the Public Worship Regulation Act was now well and truly on the wall.

But I am running ahead of my main theme, which is a consideration of how these stirring events affected the lives and careers of a handful of well-known clerics of the period. So I pass on to the series of mini-biographies which form the body of the book. The revulsion of public feeling which followed the imprisonments, and the eventual triumph of the ritualistic cause, at least in so far as external observances were concerned, will be the subject of a brief epilogue at the end of the volume.

Archdeacon Denison: man of principle

------◆◆◆------

CHAPTER 2

CHURCHMAN MILITANT

George Anthony Denison
(1805–1896)

GEORGE ANTHONY DENISON may be said to have typi-
fied the Church militant here on earth. He fought the good
fight in a literal sense. Indeed, his ministry of over fifty years
at East Brent in Somerset witnessed an endless succession of
battles on behalf of one ecclesiastical cause or another. To
Denison everything was a matter of principle; and, whenever
he waged a particular war, he did so regardless of possible side-
issues and of the havoc that might result from his actions. He
had no use for the pussy-footed diplomacy of the Church
authorities. Tact was never his strong point and, if he thought
a thing wrong, he never hesitated to say so. He interpreted
literally the words of our Lord, 'I am come not to bring peace,
but a sword.' As his niece remarks in her preface to the collected
edition of his letters, *Fifty Years at East Brent*: 'He never
allowed himself to be drawn by the opinion of others one hair's-
breadth to the right or the left of the path which he had marked
out for himself and which he considered to be the right one.'
To his foes he might seem impossibly bigoted. To his friends
he was a man whose ceaseless battles for the faith once delivered
to the saints transformed him into a latter-day crusader of heroic
proportions. But if he had no use for the biblical injunction that
the soft answer turneth away wrath, he never bore a grudge
against his opponents once the battle was over. A conspicuous
example of his charity in this respect was the way in which,

once he had been finally cleared of the charge of teaching false doctrine brought against him by a neighbouring incumbent, Joseph Ditcher, he immediately sent round a note to Ditcher asking to be allowed to resume 'our old friendly relations' – a request which was cordially granted by his erstwhile opponent. But in action he was a formidable figure: and the *Church Times* put it in a nutshell when, in an editorial after his death, it remarked: 'The nature of the great Archdeacon of Taunton was as a magnificent mountain, the beauties of which can only be adequately realized at a distance.'

*   *   *

George Denison was born at Ossington Hall, near Newark, Nottinghamshire, on 11 December 1805, two months after the Battle of Trafalgar. His father, John Wilkinson, belonged to the landed gentry, and changed his surname to Denison in order to inherit the wealth of two uncles who had made a fortune in cloth-manufacturing. He entered politics, becoming MP successively for Colchester and Minehead and owning a town house in London. He married twice. By his first wife, Maria Horlock, a wealthy heiress, he had two daughters. By his second wife, Charlotte Estwick, daughter of a fellow-MP, he had no fewer than nine sons and three more daughters.* George was the fourth son of the second marriage, but he was not the only one in the family to carve for himself a notable career. His eldest brother, John Evelyn, rose to be Speaker of the House of Commons and was later ennobled as Viscount Ossington; Edward, the next oldest, was Bishop of Salisbury from 1837 to his death in 1854 (and presented George to both his livings); and William, the third brother, served as Governor-General first of Australia and later of India. Of George's younger brothers, Frank did well in the Navy and Charles in the Army; Henry became a Fellow of All Souls', Stephen Deputy Judge-Advocate and

---

*To add to the confusion John Denison unimaginatively named *two* of his daughters Charlotte (one by each of his wives). Charlotte I married Charles Manners Sutton, son of the Archbishop of Canterbury; Charlotte II married Robert Phillimore, QC, who defended his brother-in-law in the courts in 1856 and ended up as Dean of the Arches.

Alfred a lawyer who ended up as private secretary to his brother the Speaker.

According to George there was no 'petting and coddling' in the Denison household. At the tender age of six he left home with his brother William to attend a boarding-school at Sunbury, Middlesex. There were two curious bits of discipline at the school. One was that any boy who misbehaved himself during the week received no mutton pie on Saturday. The other was that, when a boy committed a really grave offence, the whole school was made to suffer for it: each boy had to write a penitential letter home to his parents in identical terms (and of course at their expense, the postage on a letter being then eight pence). George gives an example of the prescribed epistolary style: 'My dear Parents, We have committed a great sin. For William Denison spat on the usher's back as we went to bed. I remain, Your affectionate Son . . .' When William went on to Eton, George was transferred to a 'grammar-school of much repute' at Southwell, which was near his home. He acquired, he tells us, 'a good deal of Latin and some Greek' at the school – but also a Midlands accent which had to be eradicated when he followed William to Eton in 1817, aged eleven and a half. The school at that time was in a state of near-anarchy under its would-be reforming headmaster, John Keate. George says that he was very happy there; but the atmosphere was so unruly that his parents removed him from the school after only two years. When he took leave of Keate, he was required by tradition to tip him a ten-pound note. In his nervousness he dropped the note, but Keate put his foot on it to make sure it remained with the recipient.

For the next four years George continued his education at home under a private tutor, Charles Drury, son of the Head-master of Harrow. Discipline was strict but effective. George reports having been flogged by Drury for an error in Greek grammar, but he would have been used to such a punishment by now. He had been flogged at Southwell for throwing a brass candlestick at the usher's head, and at Eton for pretending to Keate that he had not been bathing when an obviously wet towel was evidence to the contrary. But George took such ordeals in his stride. 'All honour to judicious flogging', he remarks in his autobiographical *Notes of My Life*. 'We lived under a real good despotism.' George was required to report to his tutor at eight o'clock each morning to recite fifty lines of *Paradise Lost* till he had learned the whole poem by heart. But it was not all hard work. There were intervals for hunting, shooting and fishing; and the younger Denisons were allowed, as soon as the hounds were heard in the woods, to throw aside their books and rush off to the stables for their horses.

The period of home tuition laced with country pursuits came to an end in the autumn of 1823, when George matriculated by signing the book at Christ Church, Oxford. He came into residence the following January, his tutor being C. T. Longley, the future Archbishop of Canterbury. He did well at university, graduating with a first in classics at Michaelmas 1826. Longley evidently thought highly of him, describing him on one formal occasion as *simplex iste et modestus iuvenis* ('that simple and modest youth'). Many years later, when he was Archbishop of York, George reminded him of this unsolicited tribute, whereupon Longley retorted: 'It's quite impossible: I never could have said that of *you!*'

In 1828, on the strength of his degree, Denison applied for a fellowship at Oriel College, Oxford, then at the height of its fame. He failed to answer the scientific questions in the preliminary examination, but pulled off the fellowship on the strength of his classical expertise. After an extended trip on the Continent with Charles Drury which lasted nearly a year, he began work as a tutor at Oriel in January 1830.

The college common-room at that time abounded in talent. Edward Pusey had recently left to take up the professorship of Hebrew at Christ Church, but the remaining Fellows included the leading Tractarians John Henry Newman, John Keble and Richard Hurrell Froude; Richard Whately, the future Archbishop of Dublin; Thomas Arnold, the future Headmaster of Rugby; and Renn Dickson Hampden, the future (and allegedly heretical) Bishop of Hereford. The dons belonged mainly to two rival ecclesiastical camps, Tractarian and Broad Church; but Denison occupied a neutral ground, not being prepared at this stage to identify himself wholly with the Tractarians but finding the Whig politics of the Broad Churchmen anathema. He thought the common-room a dull place socially and its occupants 'stiff, and starched, and afraid of one another'. But he had set his sights on ordination and soon managed to free himself from the restraints of the college. On Trinity Sunday, 1832, he was ordained deacon by Bishop Bagot to a title at Cuddesdon, a village a few miles outside Oxford where the bishop had his palace and was nominally the incumbent. Denison was priested at Christmas of the same year. He retained his Oriel tutorship for his first four years as a curate, commuting between Cuddesdon and Oxford on horseback, but in 1836 exchanged it for the treasurership of the college, the duties of which could be carried out mainly in his home.

There is a glorious air of amateurism about Denison's own account of his Cuddesdon curacy. Among other achievements he managed almost to kill off one of his parishioners with an overdose of 'physic' from his mother's medicine-chest; and to set fire to the church thanks to his unorthodox method of heating it. But he seems to have been well liked in the parish. It was towards the end of his time there that he fell for the local MP's daughter, Georgiana Henley. She was only nineteen to Denison's thirty-two; but it was a genuine love-match, and they remained devoted to each other throughout the fifty-eight years of their marriage, which was sadly unblessed with children. There was no trouble for George, in those nepotistic times, over maintaining Georgie (as she was known) in reasonable comfort. His brother Edward, who had been appointed Bishop of Salisbury in 1837, presented him both with the living of Broadwindsor,* Dorset, and with a prebend of Salisbury Cathedral, together worth £750 per annum, a largish sum for those days. Denison was instituted to Broadwindsor on 4 April 1838 and married Georgie exactly five months later.

*   *   *

Broadwindsor, near Beaminster in west Dorset, was six miles

---

*Denison always spelt it 'Broadwinsor'.

from the sea. The parish covered an area of fifteen square miles and had a population of about 1500. Most of the adult parishioners were either farm-hands or workers in the local sailcloth factory. Wages were low and living conditions primitive. Even the vicarage was uninhabitable – at least by the vicar and his young bride. But Denison managed to rig up three rooms in it for his curate, Edward Tufnell, a future Bishop of Brisbane. For the first two years of his incumbency he and his wife lived in temporary lodgings at Waytown, in the neighbouring parish of Netherbury, while a new, Tudor-style vicarage was being built for them at a cost of £3000. Denison had to meet this from his own pocket (with the aid of a £2000 loan from Queen Anne's Bounty), but he left the parish well-endowed in this and other respects. He spent £1000 on building a chapel at the west end of the parish and another £1000 on the church schools. He says in his *Notes* that, as a result of his lavish expenditure at Broadwindsor, he had been 'half-ruined' ever since. Certainly he was reduced to taking in private pupils to supplement his clerical stipend.

The schools were one of his great interests and sowed the seeds for his passionate concern with education. His involvement was a practical one, he and his wife teaching the children on weekdays and the often-illiterate adults and adolescents on Sundays. He insisted on retaining control of the syllabus and curriculum rather than delegating it to a committee, and on having a 'tight' constitution with the schools' trust-deeds vested solely in the parson. Denison had a profound suspicion of State interference in education, which he looked upon as the rightful province of the Church. And it was at Broadwindsor that he had his first brush with the Privy Council's Committee on Education. This was set up in 1839 to support a policy of undenominational education which to Denison was anathema. Its first secretary, James Kay-Shuttleworth, a one-time Dissenter with a social conscience, defined its role as being to 'prevent the successful assertion on the part of the Church of a purely ecclesiastical system of education'. The Committee attempted to enforce a 'loose' constitution on Denison's schools – but 'I told them I would have nothing but a tight one, and they gave way'. To Denison the Committee was 'the abomination of desolation', condensing into itself all the evil of the times. 'I have had to do with many official people', he says in his *Notes*, but 'with none for whom I have had throughout so deep a dislike, amounting to a shrinking from all contact, as "the Committee of Council on Education".' Small wonder, then, that he should have devoted so much time and effort to attempting to thwart its wishes.

Most of his educational campaigning was done, however, from a new base: the vicarage at East Brent, Somerset, to which he was appointed, again by his brother Edward, in 1845. This second piece of episcopal nepotism had been made possible by the failing health (in George's words 'incapacity') of the Bishop of Bath and Wells, G. H. Law. The elder Denison, as bishop of the adjacent diocese of Salisbury, was put in temporary charge of Bath and Wells; and when the living of East Brent fell conveniently vacant in 1845, was able to present it to his brother. It was superior to Broadwindsor both financially and in the amenities it offered. The stipend of £1000 per annum was a third more than Denison had been getting in his former cure, and he was able to exchange his Salisbury prebend for one at Wells. The vicarage was palatial, with beautifully laid-out grounds and ample outbuildings. The parish was accessible to such larger centres as Bath and Bristol: in the words of Denison's friends, it was 'much nearer to civilization'. He was able to report shortly after his arrival: 'I am quite in good heart about the place, and I trust very thankful.'

His first impressions had not erred on the side of optimism. He liked East Brent so well that he was content to spend the rest of his life and ministry there – over fifty years in all. It was to be a memorable ministry. In spite of his constant preoccupation with national Church issues and occasional forays to London in pursuit of them, Denison remained firmly based at East Brent. Most of his letters were addressed from the vicarage, and he rarely left the parish except on official business. He seldom took a holiday. He revelled in the simple life of a country parson. He rose early – in summer often about four or five a.m.

– and would work in his garden or greenhouse until it was time for morning service in church at eight.

The village itself is set in the flat pastureland of west Somerset between the steep, isolated hill of Brent Knoll and the M5 motorway. The advent of the motor car has had an inevitable effect on the character of the village in the hundred years that have elapsed since Denison's death, and the vicarage in which he lived was turned into an independent girls' school. From the summit of Brent Knoll an extensive view is bounded on the north by the Mendip Hills, on the south by the Quantocks and on the west by the Bristol Channel. In Denison's day the parish had a population of only four hundred, a quarter the size of Broadwindsor's. Many of the inhabitants worked on the half-dozen large farms in the parish, while the vicarage itself absorbed a fair amount of labour. On the surface it seemed an idyllic rural community, and its health was greatly improved after Denison had introduced a new and purer water supply.

At the time of his arrival in the parish there was a certain amount of ecclesiastical unease. The former vicar, William Law, a nephew of the Bishop of Bath and Wells, was a follower of the Tractarians (and was eventually to go over to Rome). His allegedly ritualistic practices, such as preaching in a surplice, had alarmed the villagers, so that Denison had first to dispel any suspicion that he was a bird of the same colour as Law. This was fortunately not difficult, as at that time he was in no sense a ritualist. Although, under the influence of his nephew Henry, he later became much more sympathetic to their cause, he valued ritual only in so far as it was an expression of doctrine and enjoined by the Prayer Book rubrics. He never attached as much importance to it as did many of his friends; and his chief concern was lest the thing signified should be lost sight of in the outward symbol. From the start, however, he conducted Morning and Evening Prayer daily in church, and there were increasingly frequent celebrations of the Eucharist; a daily cele-bration was begun in 1874. In his early days at East Brent 'a large part of my time was given to looking after my people'. It was only as he became more and more engrossed in central

Church issues that he had necessarily to delegate much of his pastoral work to a curate.

One of the first extra-parochial chores he was to take up was an examining chaplaincy to the Bishop of Bath and Wells. Law had died in 1845, a few weeks after Denison's arrival at East Brent; and his successor was none other than Richard Bagot, translated from Oxford by Sir Robert Peel and of course well known to Denison. Before accepting Peel's offer Bagot sent for Denison and asked his opinion. 'I told him I thought he had better accept.' Bagot then asked Denison to be his examining chaplain, to which he agreed. He held his chaplaincy for nine years, resigning shortly before Bagot's death in 1854 because of his threatened prosecution over a doctrinal issue. 'I wanted to keep myself clear to fight my own battle.' Although his relations with Bagot were to be soured in the closing months of the bishop's life because of the impending lawsuit, for most of the time they got on well; and Bagot was only too relieved to be able to pour out his worries into a sympathetic ear. Nor did he mince his words when talking to Denison about his ecclesiastical superiors. He referred to J. B. Sumner, who had succeeded Howley as Primate in 1848, as 'Archbishop Soap Suds', and, in one of his frequent letters to Denison, complained: 'The ArchB-ish. is quite the most wishy-washy Primate we ever saw or read of, nor have I power of mind to conceive a greater ass.' Bagot's letters to Denison invariably began 'My dear George' and ended 'Ever yours' or 'Yours affectionately'; and the warmth of their relationship was cemented by Denison's frequent visits to the palace. His duties included dealing with the ordinands at the newly-founded theological college at Wells; and it was this that was to involve him in grave difficulties with the authorities and to lead to an eventual rift in his relationship with the bishop. But that was in the future, and all to begin with was sweetness and light. So much so that, in 1851, Bagot appointed Denison to the vacant archdeaconry of Taunton – which had once been held by Archbishop Cranmer. 'Many people were astonished,' Denison recalls. 'Some were amused at the bravery of the Bishop. The Bishop was indeed as brave and straightforward a man as I have ever known, or he would never have made me

Archdeacon.' Perhaps it was just as well for Bagot's peace of mind that he died three years later – and so escaped many of the problems that his unruly archdeacon was to set for his successors. But, at the time of his appointment, Denison was very much the blue-eyed boy on whom Bagot was prepared to lean, in the words of Denison's biographer, Joyce Coombs, 'nearly to breaking-point . . . Bagot's relationship with Denison was the dependence of a failing man on a younger and more vigorous one. Its rupture in 1854 was painful and decisive.'

By and large, Denison proved a good archdeacon, retaining the confidence of his clerical brethren even when he was undergoing prosecution in the courts. He conducted annual visitations at Taunton, Crewkerne, Bridgwater and Dunster and delivered occasional magisterial charges on burning issues of the day. He never allowed the judicial side of his visitations, however, to mask their essentially pastoral aspect and he dealt faithfully with such perennial clerical problems as curates, churchyards and church rates.

*   *   *

Throughout his first twenty-five years at East Brent Denison was in the forefront of the battle against State involvement in education. Up till the Forster Act of 1870 the responsibility for education was largely in the hands of the Church. A system of voluntary schools covered the country, most village schools being Anglican at least in theory. Following the establishment of the Privy Council Committee on Education in 1839, an attempt was made to improve standards at the national level. The government offered schools a subsidy in exchange for a management committee and the right of inspection. Most incumbents were happy to accept both the cash and the conditions. Not so hard-liners like Denison, who led the opposition to what he regarded as the replacing of 'Church schools' by 'State schools'. He castigated the feeble attempts of the Church authorities to stem the tide of 'Indifferentism' which he saw sweeping the land: 'The paring down Religious duty to the level of social and political exigency is the plague spot of our Ecclesiastical position.' He accepted that church schools had not been perfect before 1839, but contended that the cure was worse than the disease: 'What was wanted was amendment and improvement; what has come is ruin.'

Denison attempted to stem the tide, or at least to crystallize the opposition, at the annual meeting in June 1849 of the National Society for Promoting the Education of the Children of the Poor, of which he was a leading member. The eight-hour meeting was held at the Society's headquarters in Westminster; and the hundreds of members who attended included prelates, peers and politicians. Gladstone was there, as were 'Soapy Sam' Wilberforce, who had succeeded Bagot as Bishop of Oxford; Denison's brother Edward, Bishop of Salisbury; and Henry Manning, still Archdeacon of Chichester and an Anglican. In the chair was Bagot's 'wishy-washy' Primate, Archbishop 'Soap Suds' Sumner. With Wilberforce and Manning Bishop Denison led the opposition against his brother, who proposed a motion that would effectively have ruled out the imposition of management committees on schools as a condition of State assistance. In a speech of excessive length he inveighed against the new system of education with which they were threatened – 'an experiment not devised by the Church at all, but by a section of a Government which has no distinct Church character'. He declared that the greatest evil was that Churchmen should be content to receive State assistance 'without the largest and most definite security that no damage will be caused thereby to the dogmatic teaching and the apostolic discipline of the Church of England'. But the high-ups of the National Society were unwilling to confront the government head-on and endeavoured to water down Denison's motion. This they did through an amendment put forward by Manning which, while technically in agreement with the motion, effectually (in the words of Manning's biographer, E. S. Purcell) 'turned Denison's denunciation of the Committee of the National Society for the betraying of the cause of Church Schools into a vote of confidence in the Committee and for its policy of compromise with the Government'. The meeting was so bemused by now after nearly eight hours of speech-making that Sumner had to count the votes twice before deciding that Manning's amendment had won the day.

In spite of the similarity of the rival resolutions Denison was in no doubt that *he* had lost. 'From that hour,' he recalled in his *Notes*, 'I date the ruin of "Church Education" in England at the hands of Churchmen.' He went on:

> Most of my supporters congratulated me and themselves, thinking we had done very well. I knew better; I knew that the battle was virtually lost that day, and I reproach myself for having accepted the amendment. . . . I ought to have fought it out there and then, and not have concerned myself with the immediate issue; but I was comparatively young then in my experience of these things.

Although Manning wrote Denison a friendly letter after the debate justifying his 'wrecking' amendment, Denison remained unconvinced of his good intentions. In a letter sent in 1889 for inclusion in Purcell's biography he wrote: 'What the Cardinal may regard the cause I contended for now to be, I have no concern with; all I know is that it was *first* by his hand that the Church School in England was destroyed.' He had earlier summed up his educational philosophy in a letter to a friend in Scotland a few months after the great debate:

> It appears to me that the time is fully come when all those who hold that there is such a thing as objective truth – that there are such things as religious doctrines – that these have a real existence – and that the maintenance of them in all their integrity is vital to religion – should be prepared to combine for the purposes of a steady and uncompromising resistance to the whole system and operations of the Committee of [the Privy] Council on Education. That system goes, and by a very direct path, to the establishment amongst us, in place of any distinctive religious teaching whatsoever, of the comprehensive methods of German theorists. The inevitable and not distant result of permitting the establishment of the comprehensive method would be the Socinianising* the great mass of the

---

*Relating to the doctrines of the sixteenth-century Italian rationalist theologians Laelius and Faustus Socinus, who denied the existence of the Trinity and the divinity of Christ.

people of this country. It is therefore, as it seems to me, quite impossible to overrate the magnitude of the present crisis.

But of course such views were derided in many quarters. The Broad Church Frederick Denison Maurice, for instance, dismissed Denison as a 'vulgar Church agitator using the most sacred phrases for claptraps, and throughout confounding the right of the clergy to have their own way with Church principles'.

Denison's dislike of educational innovations was not confined to theory. His opposition could be practical as well, as when he refused to allow a government inspector to inspect the parish school at East Brent. 'I said to Bellairs thereupon, – "My dear Bellairs, I love you very much; but if you ever come here again to inspect, I lock the door of the school, and tell the boys to put you in the pond." ' The inspector prudently stayed away, and for many years the school remained immune from prying government eyes. When another inspector – 'my dear friend Tinling' – eventually did turn up, Denison was not quite so militant. 'I said, "Oh, come by all means. I shall never ask for a sixpence of their money, and I think them quite as mischievous as I ever did; but pray come if you like, always very glad to see you." ' Unfortunately, during the inspection, the children were allowed to sing a comic ditty which poor Tinling thought was aimed at him personally. So he never repeated his visit – and indeed the offending ditty was even quoted in the House of Commons.

The climax of Denison's educational struggles was his battle against the Education Bill introduced in 1869 by W. E. Forster, President of the Board of Education in Gladstone's first government. The Bill established a national system of education, making full use of the denominational schools and requiring a board school to be set up only where a need could be shown to exist. A 'conscience clause' permitted parents to withdraw their children from church schools during periods set aside for denominational religious instruction. To Denison the Act itself was a 'national sin'; and it was the conscience clause that drew forth his especial strictures: 'The Parish Schools ceased to be

A.D. 1870 with consent and advice of the Episcopate. In their room we have – 1. Schools Secular, both in name and reality; 2. Schools Secular in reality, but not in name.' Denison was insisting that a Church school subject to the conscience clause could no longer properly be called a Church school: ' "Church School" means *only* a school into which no child is admitted but the child baptised, or being prepared for Holy Baptism.' In a letter to Gathorne Hardy, Gladstone's Home Secretary, he claimed that a 'conscience clause' was 'a principal instance of combined secular, financial, religious tyranny and violation of Conscience'. The case for such a clause, he told Hardy, rested on two 'violent' assumptions:

1. That 'Secular Education' is a necessity; but that 'Religious Education' is not.
2. That, 'Secular Education' being a necessity, if the religious scruples of Church-people come in the way of giving it, or allowing it to be given, in Church schools, the religious scruples of Church-people must be put aside if such Church-people are to have any share in the Parliamentary Grant.

About the same time he was writing to a fellow-cleric in Somerset: 'I see no possible safety for the Church in making any Concordat with the Civil Power which shall admit the latter into any manner of partnership with the Church in matters of Religion.' But the battle was now all but lost. Since only a handful of Dissenters chose to take advantage of the provisions of the conscience clause and deprive their children of Church teaching, the old arguments about the clause's alleged iniquities rapidly faded. But Denison, who had resigned from the National Society in May 1870 because of its failure to support him, continued to fly his lone flag. Seventeen years after the passing of the Act he declined to sign a memorial in praise of elementary education on the grounds that it included the words 'under the direction and with the assistance of the State'.

My mind is exactly where it was in 1842. I have lived to see the iniquity first hatched in 1833 carried out to its only possible issue by the act of 1870, and the successive development thereof. . . . This development of the astute and unostentatious policy of 1833 had not till 1870 thrust its dark face into the Tableau of Indifferentism in the matter which is still, in the exercise of an unique hardihood, called Education in the principles of the Church of England.

In 1887 Denison's mind was thus 'exactly where it was' forty-five years earlier. That was his great strength – or weakness. He could not or would not move with the times.

*   *   *

Nine months after Manning's successful torpedoing of Denison's motion at the annual meeting of the National Society, the event occurred that was to drive the future cardinal into the arms of the Church of Rome. This was the 'Gorham Judgment' of 1850, the climax of one of the nineteenth century's most famous lawsuits. Although Denison declined to follow Manning out of the Church of England, his outcry against the judgment was such that a question was actually asked in the House of Commons about his loyalty to the Crown.

The basic facts about the Gorham case are well known: that the Rev. G. C. Gorham was refused institution to the living of Brampford Speke by the Bishop of Exeter, Henry Phillpotts, on the ground of his allegedly heretical views on baptismal regeneration; that Gorham took proceedings against the bishop in the provincial Court of Arches and lost his case; that he then appealed to the Judicial Committee of the Privy Council, which reversed the Arches decision; and that the effect of the Privy Council judgment was to cause a number of prominent Anglicans such as Manning to abandon the Church of England for the Church of Rome. What is not so well known is that Gorham was *already* a priest in the diocese of Exeter at the time he accepted the living of Brampford Speke; and that he had been instituted to his previous living of St Just-in-Penwith by that same Bishop Phillpotts who now had such grave doubts about his doctrinal orthodoxy.

George Cornelius Gorham was a man of parts, achieving

modest fame both as an antiquary and as a botanist. He was ordained in 1811, but the bishop who ordained him, Thomas Dampier of Ely, is said to have been dissatisfied, like Phillpotts afterwards, with his views on baptism. After holding four cura- cies in succession (broken up by a thirteen-year 'sabbatical' during which he pursued his antiquarian studies), Gorham was instituted by Phillpotts in 1846 to St Just, a Cornish mining village at the extreme western end of the diocese. The following year he had a dispute with the bishop over his advertisement for a curate who should be 'free from Tractarian error' – which hardened Phillpotts's growing doubts about his orthodoxy. Brampford Speke, near Exeter, was in fact a much poorer living financially than St Just; and the purpose of the exchange was to give Gorham a less onerous charge in his declining years (he was sixty in 1847) and to afford him better facilities for educating his children. He must have seen the writing on the wall, how- ever, when Phillpotts insisted on subjecting him to a lengthy pre-institution examination on doctrine. This consisted partly of a verbal interrogation extending over fifty-two hours, partly of a series of 149 written questions. Gorham's answers on baptis- mal regeneration failed to satisfy the bishop, who declined to institute him to his new living.

Gorham was an Evangelical, and he differed from Phillpotts, a High Churchman, over whether the sacramental grace con- ferred in baptism was given conditionally or absolutely. Gorham contended that regeneration would not automatically follow baptism unless the sacrament was rightly received – though he conceded that in the case of infants, who were born in original sin but could hardly be said to be in a state of faith and repent- ance, God *might* perform an act of prevenient grace which washed away the sin. Phillpotts maintained that the act of bap- tism conferred regeneration on the recipient and washed away his sin whatever his age and merits might be. Gorham's view of baptism (necessarily presented here in simple terms) was adjudged by the bishop to be 'contrary to the true Christian faith, and the doctrines contained in the Articles and Formularies of the United Church of England and Ireland'. Gorham appealed against the bishop's ruling and, after losing his case in the Court of Arches, took it to the Judicial Committee of the Privy Council, which quashed the Arches verdict – and, in the cynical words of the *Oxford Dictionary of the Christian Church*, 'attributing to him [Gorham] a view which he did not hold, declared it to be not contrary to the doctrine of the Church of England'.

The judgment provoked a furious controversy and the publication of over sixty books and pamphlets. High Churchmen especially were incensed: not only because a baptismal theory of which they disapproved had been judged to be doctrinally sound, but, more importantly, because the judgment had been pronounced by a court consisting entirely of laymen. A body of lawyers appointed by the Crown thus appeared to have the legal right to formulate the religious doctrine of the Church of England. Protests and denunciations rained down. Denison, who had been present in the Council-chamber to hear the delivery of the judgment on 8 March 1850, was in the forefront of the protesters. As he put it in a letter to a friend:

> Mr. Gorham has formally denied the Catholic doctrine, and yet, say the Supreme Court of Appeal, he may lawfully be instituted to a cure of souls. Where will be, I ask, the authoritative teaching of the Church of England? . . . Our teaching then would resolve itself into a mere exercise and assertion of private judgment . . . such a decision [of the Judicial Committee] would take away from the Clergy the power to teach anything in respect of the Sacrament of Baptism as necessarily true.

He reacted in typically Denisonian fashion. He drew up two formal declarations of protest which he read out to his churchwardens and other leading parishioners in the vestry of his church on the Sunday following the Privy Council judgment. The first declaration protested against the state of the law which empowered the Judicial Committee to 'take cognizance' of matters of doctrine and pledged that he would use 'all lawful means within my reach' to prevent the continuance of such a situation. The second declaration protested specifically against the Gorham Judgment; warned his parishioners 'to beware of allowing themselves to be moved or influenced thereby in the least degree'; and pledged that he would again use all lawful means 'to assist in obtaining, without delay, some further formal declaration, by a lawful Synod of the Church of England, as to what is, and what is not, the doctrine of the Church of England in respect of the Holy Sacrament of Baptism'.

It was not to be supposed that such a semi-public gesture of protest would escape the notice of the pro-Gorham camp. Copies of Denison's declarations filtered through to the House of Commons and resulted in an anti-clerical Scottish MP, Joseph Hume, giving notice of a question to the Prime Minister, Lord John Russell, concerning Denison's loyalty to the Crown. Denison hastened to defend himself, sending to Russell a statement claiming that he had neither denied the Queen's position as Supreme Governor of the Church of England nor impeached any part of the Royal Supremacy. The statement went on: 'But I humbly conceive that the Constitution does not attribute to the Crown, without a Synod lawfully assembled, the right of deciding a question of Doctrine; and this – although disclaimed by the Lords of the Judicial Committee of Her Majesty's Privy Council – is what, as appears to me, has been done, indirectly indeed but unequivocally, in the late case of "Gorham v. the Bishop of Exeter".' On 18 March Hume put his question to the Premier in the Commons. Having read out Denison's two declarations, he asked what notice the Government intended to take of a protest 'impugning the judgment of Her Majesty's Council . . . and denying the Supremacy of the Crown as head of the Established Church'. Russell neatly defused a potentially explosive situation by reading out Denison's statement and adding that, though he entirely dissented from Denison's view of the case, 'I should be most reluctant to take steps against any men who give what they conceive to be the conscientious expression of their views with regard to the Church.' Any such act, he feared, would only tend to disturb still further the harmony of the Church. The Government, he told Hume, was therefore 'not prepared to take any steps with regard to the Protests'.

Denison had by no means shot his bolt with regard to the Gorham controversy. He played an active part in drawing up a set of nine 'resolutions' which were published in *The Times* of

20 March. Besides Denison the fourteen eminent signatories included Pusey, Keble and Manning; six of them afterwards seceded to Rome. The resolutions castigated Gorham's view of baptism as erroneous, and urged the vital need for the Church to pronounce an authoritative declaration of the Catholic doctrine of baptism impugned by the Gorham judgment. Protest meetings were held up and down the country; but much of the wind was taken out of the protesters' sails by the feeble attitude of the bishops, who kept a low profile throughout the controversy. No bishop was willing to take the chair at a great public meeting held in London on 23 July, though Bagot of Bath and Wells did turn up to repudiate the Privy Council judgment. The Archbishops of Canterbury and York had in fact sat in on the Judicial Committee's deliberations as assessors and had concurred in the judgment. In the words of a modern Church historian, A. O. J. Cockshut, 'instead of protesting, they had acquiesced in a state-controlled Christianity and a state-tailored doctrine'. Denison was so incensed at this particular aspect of the affair that he dashed into print with an impassioned 25,000-word pamphlet, *Why Should the Bishops Continue to Sit in the House of Lords?*, which ran into three editions. Individual secessions to Rome continued, but the controversy gradually died down. The case had at least drawn attention to the limitations of the Judicial Committee of the Privy Council as a final ecclesiastical court of appeal.

*   *   *

The first rift in the lute between Bagot and his new archdeacon occurred in May 1852, when the bishop's health was beginning to fail. Denison had just delivered his first official charge to the clergy of his archdeaconry – and had inadvertently been guilty of what Bagot termed a 'grave offence against decency and good breeding'. What his 'dear George' had been rash enough to do was to deliver a charge lasting no less than two hours. Bagot protested that 'an affliction of two hours upon any gathering especially of educated men is an infliction not to be borne as men are at present constituted'. No doubt the reproof was intended to be taken with several grains of salt; but it was an earnest of things to come.

The real trouble began, and Denison's own doctrinal ortho-doxy was first called into question, when Bagot's deteriorating health* led to his having to delegate the task of conducting confirmations to George Spencer, a former Bishop of Madras then resident in the diocese of Bath and Wells. Spencer was an Evangelical and considered Denison a Puseyite, so was naturally suspicious of his views. The row arose because Denison, in his role as chaplain, was accustomed to examine the candidates for priest's orders at Wells before presenting them to the bishop for ordination. It was the nature of some of the questions about the Eucharist which he asked at those examinations that caused the difference of opinion with Spencer. The questions concerned the doctrine of the Real Presence – whether Christ's body and blood were actually present in the Sacrament at the Eucharist, or only present symbolically or figuratively. This was a matter on which Denison held strong views. Indeed, on the actual day on which the Gorham Judgment was delivered, he had remarked to the Sub-Dean of Westminster, Lord John Thynne, as they came down the steps of the Council Office, 'Well, what do you think will come next?'

> He said, 'I suppose you mean something about the other Sacrament?' 'Yes,' I said, 'and it will come very soon!' I did not think, when I said it, that it would come in my own person within four years from that day.

The basic point at issue between the High Church Denison and the Low Church Spencer concerned the reception of the Sacrament by the unworthy. Denison held that Christ was really and spiritually present in the Sacrament; that all who received the Sacrament, both 'those who eat and drink worthily' and 'those who eat and drink unworthily', received the body and

---

*A friend wrote to Denison in April 1852 concerning Bagot: 'There was a vacancy of manner about him at one time and an *irritability* at another so unlike his former self that it was impossible not to be painfully conscious of the inroads of disease upon him.'

blood of Christ; but that those who ate and drank unworthily 'purchase to themselves damnation, as St. Paul saith'. Spencer, on the other hand, took the line that Christ's real presence was in the heart of the faithful receiver only, and not in the conse-crated bread and wine. Taking his stand on Article XXIX, he maintained that those who ate and drank unworthily 'in no wise are partakers of Christ'. Such a belief Denison considered totally unsound. He took *his* stand by the exhortations and rubrics in the Book of Common Prayer.

His first brush with Spencer concerned his right to examine ordinands. But within four years he found himself standing before the Archbishop of Canterbury in a Church court at Bath charged with propagating false doctrine. The wheel had come full circle. The ultra-traditionalist Denison, who had raged at the failure of the Church authorities to prosecute Gorham for heresy, now found himself falsely tarred with a similar brush.

Spencer's commission to stand in for Bagot in no way author-ized him to take part in the examination of the candidates for ordination. This task was reserved to Denison, as examining chaplain, under a special form of 'direction and authority' from Bagot issued in September 1852. Spencer was authorized merely to ordain those presented to him by Denison. The brush between the two men occurred shortly before the Advent ordi-nation service in the same year. Spencer claimed that Denison had 'invited' him to speak privately to the candidates. Denison maintained that he had done nothing of the sort, but had reluc-tantly agreed to a proposal to speak to them put forward by Spencer. Encouraged by the bishop's implied invitation to con-fide in him, one of the candidates who had been made deacon at Advent, W. F. Fisher, wrote to Spencer on 27 January 1853. He told the bishop that he understood that he was unlikely to be priested unless he agreed to meet Denison's wishes by acquiescing in a 'certain peculiar explanation of our Church's doctrine of the Holy Eucharist':

> That, in the holy ordinance referred to, the body and blood
> of Christ are, first, really present 'objectively' and 'subjec-
> tively', and, secondly, are verily and indeed 'received' and

'partaken of' by the wicked and such as be void of a lively faith, yet only to their damnation.

Fisher told Spencer that he considered such an explanation contrary to the Articles and Liturgy of the Church of England. He asked for Spencer's 'wisdom and guidance' – which the bishop proceeded to give him in a lengthy exegesis of the Evangelical doctrine of the Eucharist. Giving *his* version of the incident twenty-five years later in his *Notes*, Denison maintained that Fisher had completely misunderstood him, 'and had assumed that it was my purpose to impose a new test of admission or rejection of candidates upon my own authority . . . it was absurd to suppose that I could state such purpose.' A ding-dong battle of words then ensued, with Spencer threatening not to ordain any candidates holding Denison's doctrine of the Real Presence and Denison on his side threatening not to present any candidates if they had then to undergo a doctrinal counter-examination by the bishop. At this stage in the proceedings, when an impasse appeared likely, Denison thought it politic to inform the ailing Bagot what was happening. At first Bagot backed his examining chaplain. 'I entirely approve of *everything* you have said and done in this disagreeable business,' he wrote on 29 April. 'You are right in Doctrine, and it is the Doctrine of the Church; and you are also as clearly right in your view of what should pass between a Bishop and his Examining Chaplain.' A few days later Spencer sent in his resignation as Bagot's commissary. He put the blame for it 'on the avowed opinions of your examining Chaplain on a most important point of gospel truth and his refusal to allow me in any way to examine the candidates for holy orders'. Before quitting, however, Spencer agreed to ordain the candidates presented to him by Denison. The ordination took place in Wells Cathedral on 1 May 1853. Spencer then published the correspondence that had taken place between him and Denison – which caused a seeming change of heart on the part of Bagot. Denison had already sent copies of the key letters to the palace, but the bishop appears not to have read them at the time. It was only when, on a visit to London to consult his brother-bishops, he was shown the published correspondence that he realized the full extent of the row. He wrote Denison a letter from Wells on 3 June of which the key sentence read: 'It pains me to say that I cannot hold the Doctrine of the Real Presence to the extent that you there go.' On receiving the letter Denison rode off to Wells in a huff and resigned his examining chaplaincy on the spot. It soon appeared, however, that Bagot had not meant what he had said. He explained to Denison: 'When I said I could not go so far as you did with regard to your statement of the Doctrine of the Real Presence, what I meant was, against its being imposed upon the candidates as a *sine qua non*.' Denison says in his *Notes* that, had he realized what Bagot really meant, he would never have resigned his chaplaincy. 'But it was never so put till it was too late.'

The next act in the drama was a series of sermons on the Eucharist preached by Denison in Wells Cathedral. It was the first two of these addresses that eventually put him in the dock. The initial sermon was preached on 7 August 1853 and concerned the doctrine of the Real Presence. It was an unashamedly propagandist address, in that Denison was anxious for the doctrinal charge against him to be brought into the open. He demanded that Spencer 'should lay the charge publicly made against me before the Bishops of the Church of England in Sacred Synod assembled [i.e., in the Convocation of Canterbury, revived in 1852] and to request the Synod to pronounce sentence thereon'. The second sermon was delivered three months later, on 6 November; its theme was the Church of England's claim to be a part of the Catholic Church and not a quasi-Protestant sect.

Denison's implicit invitation to a would-be prosecutor was soon taken up. The neighbouring incumbent at South Brent, Joseph Ditcher, challenged him on 16 January 1854 to retract the dogmatic statements contained in his two sermons. Denison naturally declined to do so, and Ditcher requested Bagot to take legal proceedings against him. The bishop first called on Ditcher to state formally his specific charges; and, after some delay, Ditcher accused Denison of teaching doctrine contrary to that of the Church of England. The archdeacon responded by sending Bagot a series of eight 'propositions' summing up the doc-

trine of the Holy Eucharist and the Real Presence contained in
his two cathedral sermons (both of which had been published).
The great concern of the authorities at this early stage of the
proceedings was to prevent the case from ever coming before
the courts. To this end the advisers of the now-dying Bagot
persuaded him to put his signature to a vague mish-mash of
admonition and quasi-censure which Denison admitted was
'very kindly meant as towards myself personally' by steering
the issue clear of the courts. He declined to believe, however,
that his old friend Bagot could possibly have been responsible
for the 'judgment' or for the correspondence that had preceded
it. 'His name was used ... I am obliged to say, I think not
legitimately. The letters themselves bear no mark of the Bishop's
mind and hand, both for so many years familiar to me.' They
may well have been the work of the Bishop of Oxford, 'Soapy
Sam' Wilberforce. Denison recognized the desire behind the
letters as being to 'get rid of the business', but thought it misguided.

The bishop's 'judgment' acquitted Denison of having maintained any doctrine either condemned or censured by the
Church of England, but pronounced that there were certain
errors in his manner of teaching. In respect of such errors the
judgment 'passed a sentence of admonition upon me and
enjoined me to be more cautious in future'. But Bagot's well-
meant efforts were to no avail, as Denison found himself unable
to concur with the terms of the judgment. A week or so after
learning this Bagot conveniently died, leaving the position wide
open. But the State authorities were as anxious to calm things
down as were those of the Church. The Prime Minister, Lord
Aberdeen, in translating Lord Auckland from Sodor and Man
to Bath and Wells, stipulated that Bagot's successor should
refrain from prosecuting Denison. Auckland did his best to
comply with the Downing Street behest. In spite of three appli-
cations from Ditcher he declined to prosecute, but Ditcher then
applied to the Court of Queen's Bench for a mandamus to
compel Archbishop Sumner to issue a commission under the
Church Discipline Act. The legal wheels had now begun to
turn; and nothing could stop them.

The lawsuit, with its consequential appeals, lasted for well over three years, the lawyers on either side employing every technical and procedural device, in addition to mere rhetoric, to secure a favourable verdict for their client. The general High Church view of the case was reflected by Gladstone in a letter ⁀M he wrote to a friend in August 1854:

> I fear if he [Denison] can build a brick wall to break his head against he will do it; but it moves one's indignation to see the judicial arm raised against him by the Archbishop, whose own words plainly disclose (I am far from saying conscious) unbelief in the sacrament of the Eucharist.

Denison himself, writing in his *Notes* with the benefit of hindsight, claims that the promoters of the prosecution (Ditcher had the support of the Evangelical Alliance) were straining every nerve to secure a conviction. 'I know well that what was aimed at in my person was the branding with "heresy at law" the Catholic Doctrine of the Blessed Sacrament. I knew that the prosecution had left, were leaving, and would leave, no stone unturned to get condemnation of me.' In a letter to Keble written in 1854 he maintained that the rumpus had been provoked not by himself but by the 'unfaithfulness' of the bishops and clergy in 1850 and since (i.e., following the Gorham Judgment):

> The Bishops who could stand by and not repudiate collectively, on behalf of the Church, the decision of 1850, in respect of the Holy Sacrament of Baptism – the Clergy who could stand by and not press for such repudiation by the Bishops with all their energies of body and soul – have no cause to complain that a very few years have sufficed to bring up a formal and deadly assault upon the truth of the Holy Sacrament of the Lord's Supper.

In a letter to the new Bishop of Bath and Wells, Lord Auckland, Denison claimed that the Archbishop was endeavouring to strain the law for the purpose of eliminating the Catholic character of the Church of England. 'I contend, openly and unreservedly, for entire and unquestioned liberty to teach all Catholic Doctrine, as a Priest of the Church of England, because I know of no Catholic Doctrine which is not embodied in the formularies of the Church of England.'

Throughout the period leading up to the trial Denison was able to rely on the support of leading Tractarians. Pusey, in a letter to *The Guardian*, the most influential Church newspaper of the day, pointed out that it was the doctrine of the Real Presence that Denison's opponents were attacking. 'They seem to wish to exterminate out of the Church of England the school which believes as good Bishop Andrewes and Cosin and Wilson [all notable Anglican divines] believed.' And Keble enlarged on this point in a letter to the same paper: 'The question is not whether we agree with the Archdeacon on every point, but whether or not we concur with his accusers in desiring to cast out of the Church all who hold the doctrine of a Real Objective Presence as inherited by our Church from antiquity, taught in our Catechism, maintained by our great divines and implied, while it is guarded from abuse, in our Articles.'

The commission which Archbishop Sumner had been manoeuvred into setting up to enquire into the charges against Denison met under his presidency in a hotel at Clevedon at the beginning of January 1855. The principal charge was that the doctrines set forth in Denison's two cathedral sermons with reference to the Real Presence in the Eucharist 'are unsupported by the Articles in their literal and grammatical sense and are contrary to the doctrines and teaching of the Church of England'. Denison declined at this stage to admit authorship of the sermons. On being refused permission to make a statement on his own behalf he withdrew from the hearing, only reappearing to hear the commissioners' verdict. This was to the effect that there was sufficient *prima facie* ground for instituting further proceedings. Those proceedings eventually took place at Bath in the summer of 1856: both Denison and Ditcher had objected to the case being heard outside the diocese. The Archbishop was forced to preside himself because, under the terms of the Church Discipline Act, the diocesan, as patron of the living held by Denison, was precluded from hearing the case. Sumner was assisted by assessors, the chief of whom was the Dean of Arches,

Stephen Lushington. Denison's defence counsel was his brother-in-law, Robert Phillimore. Lushington and Phillimore were to cross swords again in the first Mackonochie trial a dozen years later.

For all the passions aroused, the Denison trial had its bizarre moments. The prosecution had first to prove that the sermons published and objected to really were the ones Denison had preached during 1853 in Wells Cathedral. The witness on whose evidence they chiefly relied was a local grocer called Everett; and there was much merriment in court as the Archdeacon of Wells recalled discussing the sermon in the grocer's shop ('I deal with Mr. Everett as my grocer'). He assured the court, however, that Everett was a man of good character and accurate memory and that he was well informed for his position in life. The closing speeches by the opposing counsel included rival strings of quotations from eminent authorities. Phillimore spoke for over five hours on Denison's behalf, with numerous references to the New Testament, the Fathers, the sixteenth-century Reformers, the Caroline divines and even the Tractarians. His eloquence was to no avail. Denison was found guilty of teaching false doctrine and stripped of all his ecclesiastical preferments. In a declaration of several hundred words read out to the court on 12 August by Lushington on the Archbishop's behalf the key sentence read: 'His Grace, with the assistance of his Assessors, has determined that the doctrines in the said passages are directly contrary and repugnant to the 28th and 29th of the said Articles of Religion mentioned in the aforesaid Statute of Queen Elizabeth.' Denison was given until 1 October to 'recant'. He declined to do so, stating in a written paper the grounds on which it was 'not in my power' to make the revocation required of him. The court took three weeks to digest this piece of information and reconvened on 21 October. The next day, after hearing further arguments from Phillimore, Lushington declared that Denison's statement, far from being a retraction, was a reiteration of what had been said before. Then (in Denison's words) 'the learned Judge proceeded to deliver the Judgment of the Court: depriving me of my Vicarage and Archdeaconry'.

Denison at once gave notice of appeal to the provincial Court of Arches.

He was optimistic as to the outcome. In a letter to his mother written on the day of the verdict he said that he had never expected anything else – 'nor has dear Georgie, nor, I think, any one who had the means of knowing all the case. That the sentence will be reversed upon Appeal I have as little doubt – that is, no doubt.' His friends took up the cudgels on his behalf. A weighty declaration signed by fifteen leading Tractarians (including Keble, Pusey, J. M. Neale and Isaac Williams) was sent to the Archbishop in protest against the judgment – or at least against those parts of it which implied that Denison's views, to which the signatories themselves subscribed, were 'repugnant to the Doctrine of the Thirty-nine Articles'. His Grace acknowledged the declaration but took no action on it. Both Keble and Pusey were spurred by their indignation over the judgment to champion Denison's views in print. A treatise by Keble, *On Eucharistical Adoration*, was published in 1857; it was dubbed by Liddon as 'perhaps the most beautiful of his contributions to the theological treasures of the Church of England'. A companion treatise by Pusey, *The Real Presence*, which appeared in the same year, claimed that this particular doctrine was the teaching of the English Church.

Meanwhile Denison himself sat tight at East Brent. And, in April 1857, the Court of Arches reversed the Bath judgment on the technical ground that the suit against him had not been begun within two years of the commission of the alleged offence (i.e., the sermons in Wells Cathedral). Ditcher appealed to the Judicial Committee of the Privy Council, the final court of appeal in ecclesiastical cases; but, in a judgment delivered on 6 February 1858, the Committee upheld Denison. This brought the legal proceedings to a close, with Denison still in possession of his living and archdeaconry. He was not, however, all that pleased by the manner in which he had been enabled to retain them. His lawyers had had other cards up their sleeves with which to contest the judgment if the ground of out-of-dateness had failed; one of these was that the Archbishop had been wrong in deciding Denison's teaching to be heretical. According to Sir

Walter Phillimore, son of Sir Robert, Denison wished to rely on the last point only and to fight nothing but the question of heresy, but was overruled by his legal advisers. He was acutely conscious, however, of the imputation by his opponents that he had wriggled out of his just deserts through a legal quibble – 'when, if I had been an honest man, I ought to have waived all such things and gone at once to "the merits". I despised the imputation as dishonest: I laughed at it as ridiculous. If there had been so much as the shadow of a shade of a decently fair tribunal . . . competent to pronounce in a matter of Doctrine . . . I might possibly have considered about taking the case *simpliciter* upon its "merits". But fairness and competency were alike lacking.' Denison ended the account of his trial by remarking: 'I was not sorry when the supposed tragedy, but real farce, was played out, and I was left to go back to my proper work.'

His parishioners at East Brent were delighted by the news of his final acquittal. When he and Georgiana returned to Somerset after the Privy Council judgment they were met at Highbridge station by 'every man, woman, and child of the parish that could come' and, after hearing a congratulatory address, escorted in triumph back to East Brent. The address itself was framed in suitably grandiloquent terms. Anxiously, it declared, his parishioners had watched the case:

> We regretted it ever arose; we regretted its long-protracted infliction; but, now that you stand freed by the highest Court in the land, we can never regret the display of Christian fortitude and Christian forbearance you have manifested to us during those four years and a-quarter. Not one of your parishioners can tax his memory with having heard you use an unchristian, an unkind, or an ungentlemanly expression, against those who unfortunately were your accusers. Meekly have you borne the Cross, meekly may you wear the Crown.

At the bounds of the parish the horses were taken from the carriage, which was then drawn by stalwart male hands the mile and a half to the church, where a service of thanksgiving was held. The next day Denison displayed a fine example of Christian forbearance by sending round a note to Ditcher at South

Brent asking to be allowed to resume 'our old friendly relations'. He and his wife were 'very kindly received' by Ditcher – who proved a staunch ally many years later, when the Athanasian Creed was under fire.

*   *   *

Freed from his clash with authority over doctrine, Denison was now able to devote at least a part of his time to his 'proper work' in the parish – though his reputation as a doughty defender of the faith ensured his involvement in many of the major Church controversies of the day. But he always had one foot firmly planted in the Somerset soil of his parish, which remained his base. His concern for its welfare was intensely practical. One of the earliest boons he conferred on the parish was the improvement of its water supply. In place of the unhealthy drainage ditches from which the inhabitants had been accustomed in the past to draw their drinking water he built a system of wells and reservoirs which ensured a copious supply of pure water. As a result East Brent escaped the ravages of cholera and other dangerous diseases spread by an impure water supply. Denison was also a champion of the local Cheddar cheese against an American rival. In a letter of 1879 he tells his brother-in-law's son, Walter Phillimore, that he has been eating a cheese eighteen months old but 'as sound and sweet as the day it was made . . . But then it was never dried by any artificial process for the sake of turning money quick.' For his efforts on behalf of local cheese-makers he was elected a member of the West of England Agricultural Society. Another of his innovations was the 'Harvest-home', which he introduced at East Brent in September 1857 – 'It was not only a holiday for all classes alike, but a holiday which all classes kept and enjoyed in close contact with one another.' The Harvest-home at East Brent was much more than a sedate parish supper. Denison describes the 1883 event in a letter to one of his sisters: 'Steam Merry-go-round, fortune-telling, various other amusements; teetotal drinks only – football, etc.; two grand Balls, 1000 people in tent on Tuesday night, 500 Wednesday night; had food over on Tuesday enough for poor parishioners' second meal Wednesday. . . . Our attraction was so great that the Landlord of Brent Knoll Inn says he lost £10 or £12 by us.' Denison was above all a genuine countryman, never happier than when digging in his garden or pottering about the farm attached to the vicarage.

But his leisure for such rustic recreations was necessarily limited. As a renowned controversialist he found himself inevitably drawn into the forefront of the major ecclesiastical battles of the day. He was a leading opponent of *Essays and Reviews*, a collection of essays by seven authors who advocated free enquiry in religious matters, and were dubbed heretics for their pains. He chaired a committee of the Lower House of the Convocation of Canterbury which issued a report condemning the book. Nine years later he opposed the nomination by Gladstone of Frederick Temple to be Bishop of Exeter on the ground that he had been one of the essayists. After Temple's consecration (in the face of nationwide opposition) he only agreed to withdraw a motion asking Convocation to register its objection to the appointment after hearing that Temple was withdrawing his essay from future editions of the book.

Denison threw himself with equal vigour into the battle against Gladstone's attempt to disestablish the Church of Ireland – united with the Church of England since 1801 and an obvious symbol of the English yoke in possessing privileges which Irish Roman Catholics, far more numerous than Irish Anglicans, bitterly resented. Although many English churchmen opposed Irish disestablishment, few did so to such an impassioned degree as Denison. He opposed it, he told the Earl of Carnarvon, because 'it makes the State to be of no religion . . . thus handing over the people to all the licence of private judgment in its wildest excess, and, in effect, handing them over either to Roman Catholicism or to Infidelity'. To claim that the Church of Ireland should cease to be the national Church because it was not the Church of the majority was, said Denison, to 'separate Truth and Religion and to put in its place man's disbelief or man's corruption as the rule of the National Life' – whatever that may have meant. Denison organized a 'Church and State Defence Society' which sent to all incumbents and church-wardens copies of an address for signature to be forwarded to

the Crown as a protest against disestablishment and disendow-
ment. The response was disappointingly poor. One of Denison's
arguments against disestablishment was the inviolability of the
Queen's Coronation oath to defend the established Church. He
therefore persuaded the Lower House of Convocation to
approve an address to Her Majesty protesting in extreme tones
against disestablishment. He urged the House of Lords to reject
the Bill and, even after the Bill had been enacted, questioned its
validity. He did have the grace, however, to confess afterwards
that, had he realized in 1868 how Low the outlook of most
Irish churchmen was, he would not have fought so vigorously
on their behalf.

*   *   *

The next controversy in which Denison found himself involved
was to be much nearer home – and to involve the sacking of his
two curates because of alleged ritualistic goings-on at East Brent.
On Ritualism itself he had undergone a conversion experience
inspired partly by one of the curates, his nephew Henry. He
admitted that it was 'the one question of my life, as Priest of
the Church of England, upon which I have changed my mind'.

For his first twenty-five years in the parish Denison added
little to the outward symbols of worship which he had inherited
from his predecessors. As late as 1866 he went into print to
affirm:

> I am not a 'Ritualist'. I am no advocate for the revival of
> vestments or rites long disused. . . . I earnestly deprecate such
> revival. . . . I believe that I can teach the Doctrine better in a
> surplice and stole than I could in 'the vestments' – without
> incense than with it; in the simple form and manner in which
> I have been used for more than thirty years to administer the
> Lord's Supper.

Denison made this avowal in the course of an open letter to the
Bishop of Gloucester and Bristol, C. J. Ellicott, who, in a
sermon in Bristol Cathedral, had identified ritual with the doctrine of the Real Presence. Denison, as a non-ritualistic cham-

pion of that doctrine, felt in honour bound to deny that the two were necessarily connected.

What caused his change of heart? According to his own account, given in his autobiographical *Notes* of 1878, 'I went on, gradually seeing more light, but stumbling all along over the stones of the old foundation, which I had helped to pull out, till my illness in 1870–71. I then for the first time grasped all the principles of the case.' More specifically, he had been profoundly shocked by the attempts of the Church Association to invoke the law to put down ritualists – attempts which reached their apogee in the protracted prosecution of A. H. Mackonochie of St Alban's, Holborn. Denison felt that many of those who accused others of breaking the law were themselves law-breakers and were 'comforting their consciences by abusing their less easy brethren'. Moreover, observing the comparatively slow process of his teaching among his own parishioners, he came to feel that the ritualistic practices being introduced by a younger generation of priests might prove the most effective means for bringing Catholic truth home to the understanding of the simple churchgoer. All in all, it was beginning to dawn on Denison that (in his own words), 'though my antecedents did not dispose me to high Ceremonial, after all I might be quite wrong upon first principles of Worship . . . inasmuch as a costly and magnificent Ceremonial . . . was the natural accompaniment and exponent of the teaching of the Doctrine of the Real Presence.'

He had the leisure to sort through his ideas in the course of the long illness to which he refers in his *Notes*. The breakdown in his health in 1870 was not caused primarily by his age (he was then sixty-five) or by definite physical symptoms so much as by the emotional and psychological tensions that must have accompanied his endless ecclesiastical in-fighting. He emerged from his illness a convinced ritualist who was prepared to fight for his new beliefs. His own adoption of ritual at East Brent, however, was no more than partial. He never used incense or wafer bread or wore vestments. He confined his ritualistic observances to the eastward position at the altar and to using candles and the mixed chalice. But a daily celebration of the

Eucharist was introduced, and the Eucharist itself became the principal service on Sundays. It was not to be supposed that these innovations would pass without protest – especially as they were associated in the minds of some of the parishioners with the sinister influence of Denison's nephew Henry, who had lived at East Brent almost continuously from the age of twelve and was regarded by George and Georgie as the son they never had. Henry was the son of George's brother William, the roving diplomat; and it was when William took up his first governorship in India that young Henry was sent back to be brought up in the more salubrious climate of Somerset. He went to Winchester College for a short while, but was withdrawn after a year to be tutored by George at home – after the pattern of George's own Etonian experience.

Henry was converted at Oxford to full-blooded Tractarianism, making his first confession to Pusey, and was ordained in 1871 to a title at East Brent. His uncle was then still convalescing after his illness, so Henry and the senior curate, C. J. Hawkins, had a comparatively free hand. As Henry put it, 'my uncle trusted me to see that what was done should be done in a normal and right way.' Any changes introduced during the elder Denison's absence from the parish were, says Henry, sanctioned and welcomed by him. Ritualistic innovations multiplied – and complaints soon began to be heard, much of the blame for them being put upon 'Mr. Henry' and his new-fangled High Church ways. The trouble came to a head in the autumn of 1871, when an effigy of the vicar was burnt in an outlying part of the parish.

A complaint was made to the Bishop of Bath and Wells, Lord Arthur Charles Hervey, who had been appointed to the see by Gladstone in 1869 in succession to his fellow-aristocrat, Lord Auckland. Particular exception was taken by the protesters to mission services and to prayers for the dead – which, they claimed, had driven them from the church. There were also complaints about bowings, genuflexions, prostrations and other alleged illegalities. Much correspondence flowed between the palace at Wells and the vicarage at East Brent. The net result was the revocation of the licences of the two curates. By proceeding against them rather than against their superior Lord

Arthur showed prudence or pusillanimity, according to one's point of view. No doubt he considered that the cost and hazards involved in prosecuting an incumbent were too great a risk: curates, however, were much easier prey. He gave no specific reasons to the two men for their dismissal, merely remarking in a letter to Hawkins (25 January 1872): 'My general complaint is that you have used your office as Curate as a means of sowing dissension and division in the Church which you serve; that you have introduced or assisted in carrying out a number of unauthorized practices contrary to, or inconsistent with, the Rubrics of the Prayer Book.'

Anglo-Catholics were outraged at the bishop's behaviour. Their mouthpiece, the *Church Times*, minced no words in castigating him for his interference 'with the good work of a man incomparably his superior in abilities, acquirements, character and influence'. Lord Arthur's conduct, the paper asserted, was both ungentlemanly and unchristian – 'the son of a Marquis has usually access to society where at least a conventional standard of courtesy and mutual deference is maintained.' He apparently regarded the 'supreme duty of a parish priest to be keeping things in a state of quiescence, and never to do any work for God which may displease the Devil'. Working itself into a froth of fury, the paper concluded: 'We cannot refrain from expressing the feeling of indignation and contempt which must be excited in every manly breast by a policy so cowardly as attempting to injure an incumbent whom you dare not sue by oppressing his curates, who are simply without the means of defence.'

Media vilification, however justified, was not in itself going to reverse Lord Arthur's decision. On the advice of Walter Phillimore Henry Denison appealed to Archbishop Tait (who had succeeded Longley in the primacy). The appeal was successful, Tait holding that Hervey ought, before revoking the curates' licences, to have given them the opportunity of complying with his injunctions for the future. But he infuriated Anglo-Catholics by landing Denison junior with the costs of his appeal. In the words of the *Church Times*, 'he has once more committed the scandalous and glaring injustice which has always marked recent ecclesiastical suits – that of invariably condemning Catholics when they lose to pay costs and invariably letting off their persecutors when the defence proves successful.'

Lord Arthur had one more card to play. Although he was forced to renew Henry's licence, he refused to allow him to sit the examination for priest's orders.* Henry, still a deacon, was therefore obliged to take a year's sabbatical at Oxford, where he was priested by Bishop Mackarness and assisted in the parish of St Thomas. He resumed his ministry at East Brent in 1876 and continued for the next twenty years (until his uncle's death) to serve as his curate. The charitable Denison summed up the whole matter in his *Notes* thus: 'The uniform kindness of the Bishop of Bath and Wells has made it easy to put out of sight altogether all the conflict of our difference; the difference itself remaining just where it was.' At least the notoriety which the case had brought to the parish had its silver lining. East Brent became the Anglo-Catholic centre for a large part of Somerset, Easter communions trebling in number and people flocking to the church from far and near. On great festivals, Henry Denison recalled, the street was like a fair with the number of gigs and carts from a distance.

> I have known about forty or fifty people standing outside waiting to get in! I often saw people at the sung Mass on a Gt Feast who had driven from Glastonbury or Wells, fifteen and seventeen miles respectively. . . . It was faith, however imperfectly, manifesting itself in action. . . . What drew people to East Brent was that it manifested the sign of life.

*   *   *

One would have supposed that, after the row over ritualism at East Brent had burnt itself out, the sixty-seven-year-old vicar would have eschewed controversy and lived out his old age in peace. Not a bit of it. He threw himself heart and soul into three more major ecclesiastical battles, defending the Athanasian Creed with the same vigour with which he attacked the allegedly

---

*Hawkins was already a priest, so the same problem never arose in his case. He simply moved to a cure in another diocese.

heretical *Lux Mundi* and the government's attempt to disestablish the Church in Wales.

The dispute over the Athanasian Creed seems bizarre to a generation which has seen its virtual disappearance from the Church of England's liturgical life. But in the 1870s it was still a burning issue – and a meeting in its defence could attract thousands of supporters and rate many hundreds of column inches in the papers. The Book of Common Prayer directed (and still directs!) that it should be recited in public worship thirteen times a year, including all the greater festivals.

Broad Churchmen attacked the Athanasian Creed on three grounds: that it defined the nature of the Trinity and the incarnation of Christ in impossible detail; that its historical credentials were suspect; and that the so-called 'damnatory clauses' contained in it (such as 'Which Faith except one do keep whole and undefiled, without doubt he shall perish everlastingly') were deeply offensive to Christian sentiment. High Churchmen defended the creed on the ground that any attempt to tinker with it would be a concession to rationalism both inside and outside the Church, and that the 'damnatory clauses' were the Prayer Book's clearest condemnation of the current tendency to place morality above faith as the essence of Christianity. They saw themselves as the champions of traditional values, as opposed to people like the Dean of Westminster, A. P. Stanley, who was accused of 'boring holes in the bottom of the Church of England'. The core of Broad Church religion was ethical, based on love for God and neighbour, and its adherents tended to sit lightly to over-precise subtleties of theological definition.

The chance to take a tilt at the offending piece of dogma came in 1870, when the royal commission on the Prayer Book rubrics appointed by Lord Derby's government in 1867 reached the rubric governing the use of the Athanasian Creed. Petitions for and against change rained down on the heads of the commission's members. They considered various alternative courses of action, such as making the use of the creed optional, retranslating it, cutting out the damnatory clauses, adding an explanatory note, or taking it out of the realm of public worship altogether and relegating it to join the Thirty-Nine Articles at the back of the Prayer Book as a simple statement of belief. Eventually the would-be reformers whittled down the possible courses of action to two: adding an explanatory rubric to weaken the damnatory clauses, or introducing legislation to modify the creed's use. Hard-line opponents of change rejected both options, Denison declaring: 'I have always set my face as a flint against the mind of the time.' Following threats by the Tract-arian leaders, Pusey and Liddon, to resign their ministry if the creed was modified in any way, the authorities fell back on the less drastic policy of an explanatory note. But hard-liners like Denison jibbed at even this expedient, on the ground that such a rubric would discourage the use of the creed and be interpreted as a feeble bid to buy off the Broad Church interest. Matters reached a head in April 1872, when the issue was debated in the Lower House of the Convocation of Canterbury. The rival camps were led by Dean Stanley and Archdeacon Denison. At one moment the latter was so incensed at hearing Stanley denounce the damnatory clauses as containing 'falsehood of the most misleading and dangerous kind' that he stalked out of the chamber in dudgeon. But he gave as good as he got, soaring to ever-greater heights of eloquence as he lambasted his opponents. 'I often wonder,' he declared, 'what will be found when the bodies of this generation come to be exhumed. There will be a wonderful amount of cartilege, but very little backbone.' Denison insisted that he wanted neither translation, nor explana-tory note, nor modification of the use of the creed in any way whatever. He was against change of any sort:

> Whatever this House may do, or whatever Parliament may do, whatever any power or authority may do, I shall, so long as I am the minister of a parish church, read that creed exactly as I have always read it, just the same number of times as I have always read it, without one single alteration of language or form. I shall do this, and then leave other people to turn me out of my benefice if they can.

In the end the most that Archbishop Tait could wheedle out of Convocation was an explanatory declaration almost as long as the creed itself. In effect it put the blame for the damnatory

clauses on the Bible, declaring that 'the warnings in this confession of faith are to be understood not otherwise than the like
warnings in Holy Scripture. . . . Moreover, the Church doth not
herein pronounce judgment on any particular person or persons,
God alone being the Judge of all.' But even this modest attempt
at watering down the damnatory clauses was rejected by the
Upper House of the Convocation of York; Parliament was never
asked to approve its inclusion in the Book of Common Prayer;
and Denison continued to recite the Athanasian Creed in its
entirety on the thirteen prescribed occasions each year in his
parish church at East Brent.

*   *   *

The next ecclesiastical controversy into which Denison threw
himself was played out during 1891–2, when he was in his mid-
eighties. It took the form of an onslaught on the 'New Criticism'
– more specifically on an 1889 collection of essays, *Lux Mundi*,
a 'series of studies in the religion of the Incarnation' edited by
Charles Gore. The declared purpose of the essayists – a group
of Oxford Anglican teachers who included Henry Scott
Holland, E. S. Talbot, R. C. Moberly and Gore himself – was
'to put the Catholic faith into its right relation to modern intellectual and moral problems'. To Denison such an intention
smacked of heresy. He described his intervention afterwards as
'the last and most comprehensive of my many battles for the
doctrine of the Church of England'. It even led to his parting
company with the English Church Union because of its failure
to take his own strong line. The publication particularly hurt
Denison and other Anglo-Catholics because Gore, the editor,
was in the High Church tradition and had been appointed the
first Principal of Pusey House, which had been opened in 1884
as a memorial to the great Tractarian leader. To Denison it
seemed the ultimate betrayal that Gore should now, as he saw
it, reveal himself as a modernist snake in the pure Tractarian
grass. In a letter to a friend he lamented that, while men would
fight to the last about ritual, they would do little or nothing
when the basis of that ritual was put aside on the authority of

the latest literary critic. Such reluctance to take action implied an attitude of 'indifference, apathy and *looseness of mind*'.

Denison's first attempt to spike Gore's guns was through a motion in the Lower House of the Convocation of Canterbury. The motion itself was neutral in its wording. It asked merely that 'His Grace the President be respectfully requested to direct the appointment of a Committee of this House to consider and report upon the Preface and Eighth Essay* of the book, *Lux Mundi*, as alleged to contain and involve dangerous error'. Unfortunately Denison added a long *gravamen* (addendum) which prejudged the issue by listing the various errors of which in his view the book was guilty. As a result many who might have voted for the basic motion were frightened off it by the sting in its over-lengthy tail. Denison spoke for nearly two hours, attacking the argument of the book in detail and accusing its editor of heresy. (He subsequently issued the text of his speech as a pamphlet.) His audience heard him out with respect, but were not sufficiently impressed by his arguments to support him with their votes. Instead a procedural motion to adjourn the debate was passed – and his motion therefore fell to the ground. Denison took his defeat philosophically. 'I do not see that there is any more room for a man like me in the House,' he wrote to his wife on the evening of the adjournment debate. The tenor of the opposition speeches, he told her, had been 'mainly a magnifying of Gore personally, and counsels of charitable consideration, amounting to ignoring or overwhelming all considerations of Truth'. Two days later, still in London, he wrote again to Georgiana, remarking sorrowfully: 'I find myself this morning with all the remaining spirit of forty years' Convocation life gone out of me. . . . Both Houses have, in my clear judgment, abandoned their first duty . . . it is thought wiser to live from hand to mouth, and to leave the first principles of the Faith in Christ to take care of themselves.' To his sister, Lady Phillimore, he put it more colourfully: 'My last bit of Convo-

---

*Gore's own essay on 'The Holy Spirit and Inspiration', in which he accepted in principle the new critical views on the Old Testament, thereby breaking with the conservative position of the older Tractarians.

cation candle is burnt out, and I would not give sixpence for another bit, if it was to be had. . . . It is all gone now, candle and wick.'

Denison's Convocation candle might be burnt out (though it was to be re-lit again over Welsh disestablishment), but he had still cards to play in his campaign against the New Criticism. The first was a series of six sermons preached in Wells Cathedral between May 1891 and November 1892. They combined an assault on the rationalism of *Lux Mundi* with a criticism of the indifference and apathy of churchmen generally towards the issues raised by the book. The sermons were published and widely read, but had no noticeable effect on swaying public opinion. Denison was also a signatory to a 'Declaration on the Truth of Holy Scripture' published in *The Times* of 18 December 1891. The declaration was unashamedly fundamentalist in character, and to that extent may have been counterproductive.

The final skirmish in Denison's anti-modernist campaign was conducted through the English Church Union, of which he had long been a prominent member. At a special meeting of the Council of the English Church Union on 11 May 1892 he moved a long resolution which made no specific mention of *Lux Mundi* but began by recalling that the ECU's main object was to 'defend and maintain unimpaired the Doctrine of the Church of England against all attacks from Rationalism from within'. That doctrine had been impaired, the motion continued, by the 'so-called New Criticism', which attacked the integrity and divine authority of the Old Testament and the perfectness of our Lord's knowledge in respect of the Old Testament. The motion ended with a formal protest against 'all denial of the Integrity and Divine Authority of the Scriptures aforesaid; and against all affirmation that the knowledge of our Lord Jesus Christ in respect thereof was a limited knowledge'. But Denison and his allies were in a minority. An amendment was moved to the effect that the President and Council of the ECU 'are of the opinion that the questions which are supposed to be raised by the "New Criticism" are not such as can be discussed under present circumstances with advantage by such a body as the Union'. The amendment was approved by thirty-six votes to fourteen. Denison at once announced his resignation from the ECU. In a letter to one of his sisters a fortnight later he castigated the Union for its blindness in not perceiving that it was 'condemning itself for unfaithfulness and helping to make others unfaithful to themselves – to say nothing of the Church they propose to "Defend and Maintain" '. To have nothing more to do with a body which had exchanged *First Principles* of truth for *Policies* of various kinds', was, Denison assured his sister, 'an immense relief to me'.

In his positively last battle the following year he at least had the satisfaction of finding himself numbered for once among the majority – and a successful majority to boot. The battle was against the Welsh Church Suspensory Bill – the first bid to disestablish the four dioceses of the province of Canterbury which constituted the Church in Wales. Denison joined the protests voiced in the Convocation of Canterbury in May 1893 and in a mass meeting in the Albert Hall later that month. By now he was eighty-seven and crippled by rheumatic gout, but he was still able to argue lucidly against the Bill. In a letter to his niece Lucy he dismissed it as a 'summary disavowal of the constitutional position of the Church of England', the fruit of the anti-Church temper of mind in England and of the refusal of churchmen to hold fast by their Church. The net result, Denison told his niece, was 'the setting up of every man his own religion against the One Faith'. On this occasion his fears were groundless. The Bill was defeated. A later Bill was to be passed, but by then Denison was no longer around to witness the triumph of his opponents.

By now he was becoming less and less mobile. He had to be helped up and down stairs by his stableman-valet, and could only get to church with difficulty – though up to his ninetieth year he was still managing to attend services on three or four days each week. The final high spot of his ministry at East Brent came in July 1895, when he celebrated his golden jubilee in the parish. Over a thousand people crowded into a huge marquee for the official reception. Heading the concourse was the new Bishop of Bath and Wells, George Kennion, who had succeeded

Lord Arthur Hervey the previous year. The jubilee celebrations marked Denison's swan-song. Eight months later, on the eve of Passion Sunday 1896, he died – three months after his ninetieth birthday, and still mentally alert if physically frail. He was buried in the churchyard of the village in which he had ministered for so many years.

*   *   *

What are we to make of a character like Denison a century after his death? On the surface he seems impossibly bigoted – a champion of forlorn causes long-ago abandoned by the present generation. By his contemporaries, however, he was respected, if not revered, as a man who would stick to his principles regardless of possible side-issues. As the *Church Times* remarked in an obituary tribute (27 March 1896), 'Anything like diplomacy was his abhorrence. If in his opinion a thing was wrong, it was wrong, and down went his foot upon it, and he might move that foot who could.' His presence on a committee was seldom an unmixed blessing: he pressed his own case whatever its merits and attempted to ride roughshod over the arguments of his opponents. Admittedly it was easier for him, as a man of independent means, to maintain his independent stance. His comfortable circumstances and professional connections were an undoubted advantage to him in his constant battles with authority. He could speak to high ecclesiastics as a social equal and would never allow himself to be browbeaten by ecclesiastical jacks-in-office. His concern for his parishioners may seem paternalistic or even patronising by present-day standards, but at least it was highly effective – as witness his improvement of the East Brent water supply. As late as 1894, when he was in his ninetieth year, he went through the Local Government Act in order, he told a friend, to be able to inform his people about it. He was larger than life in so many ways, but in none more than in his capacity to turn the other cheek. It must have taken courage, as well as displaying a superhuman quality of forgiveness, to have held out an olive-branch to the vicar of South Brent, the man who had involved him in a bitter four-year struggle in the law-courts, within days of his finally being cleared. By a happy irony, the parishes of East and South Brent have now been united under the Pastoral Measure. One hopes that Denison would have appreciated, if not approved, the paradox.

A.H.M. as seen by 'Ape', Vanity Fair, 31 December 1870

Fr Mackonochie: the famous 'Ape' cartoon

————•◆•————

CHAPTER 3

ST ALBAN'S MARTYRDOM

Alexander Heriot Mackonochie
(1825–1887)

ST ALBAN IS traditionally held to have been the first British martyr. It is sadly appropriate therefore that the church in Holborn, London, which bears his dedication should have been the scene and occasion of a 'martyrdom' endured over a sixteen-year period by that prince of Victorian ritualistic priests, A. H. Mackonochie. Martyrdom is hardly too strong a word, for that is what it must have seemed like to its victim as he underwent prosecution after prosecution at the hands of seemingly relentless antagonists. Each successive prosecution led out of its predecessor, in that Mackonochie never paid more than lip-service to the admonitions of the courts and persisted in continuing (in the words of the Prayer Book) to do those things that he ought not to have done. There was indeed no conformist health in him as he went on erring and straying from the ways thought proper by the Church Association (the Protestant body behind the prosecutions) for a priest of the Church of England. And eventually he died what many regarded as a martyr's death amid the snows of the Scottish highlands, worn out by his stressful ministry in the slums and law-courts of London.

Admittedly there was another side to the coin. Without in any way condoning the actions of his opponents, one can sympathize with the unnamed 'modern historian' quoted by Mackonochie's biographer, Michael Reynolds, to the effect that, 'however much one might admire Father Mackonochie for his integrity, steadfastness of faith, pastoral diligence, courage and holiness of life, one cannot help feeling that these virtues are expressed in a way which makes them admirable rather than likeable, and that there is about him a basic lack of human warmth, and a degree of sheer bloody-mindedness, which makes him an unsympathetic subject for a biography.' Reynolds agrees about the bloody-mindedness. Readers of this chapter must make up their own minds. But, whether heroically stubborn or merely pig-headed, Mackonochie was a remarkable character who deserves to be remembered.

*   *   *

Alexander Heriot Mackonochie was born on 11 August 1825 at Fareham, in Hampshire, where his parents had settled on their return from India. He was the youngest of three sons, of whom the eldest died as a baby. His parents were both Scots. His father, Colonel George Mackonochie, was the illegitimate son of a prominent Edinburgh lawyer and served for almost thirty years in the Bombay army of the East India Company. His mother, Isabella Alison, was the daughter of a naval officer who also came from Edinburgh. The colonel died in 1827, when Alexander was only two, leaving his widow to bring up her two surviving sons on her own. She shared a house at Fareham with her widowed mother and two unmarried sisters, and life for the young Mackonochies was apparently dour and disciplined. Alexander's earliest biographer, Eleanor Towle, remarks that 'in this small household the piety was of a somewhat severe order – a habit and a principle rather than a sentiment . . . even affection [was] kept within the bounds of a systematic self-control.' Such a sober upbringing soon produced its effect. 'Very early there awoke within the youngest boy the desire to devote himself to God in the Ministry of the Church.' His playmates soon began calling him 'the boy-bishop'. Although at this stage he was prepared to yield an 'unhesitating obedience to lawful authority', he was also (prophetically for the future) to concede a 'no less ready submission to the higher dictates of conscience'.

Mackonochie's delicate health precluded the rigours of the normal public-school education awaiting a boy of his class. His mother moved first to Bath and then to Exeter, where he attended private schools. Later she took him to her home town of Edinburgh for a short course at the university. He was confirmed while a schoolboy at Exeter by the celebrated Bishop Phillpotts, who was to feature years later in the affair of the Gorham Judgment. At this period of his life, however, 'the whole temper of the family mind was not only reserved, but averse to the manifestation of religious feeling'. All this was to change. In January 1845 – nine months before Newman seceded to Rome – Mackonochie entered Wadham College, Oxford, as a commoner. The college at that time was a stronghold of Evangelicalism, but he soon became a disciple and intimate friend of Charles Marriott, a leading Tractarian and Pusey's chief lieutenant, whose religious convictions he came gradually to share and on whose spiritual guidance he relied. He became very devout, invariably attending both morning and evening service each day in the college chapel. On one occasion he was extremely annoyed at being delayed in college by the Warden when he was anxious to reach the cathedral in time to hear Pusey preach. He also had a romantic attachment to the House of Stuart and was dubbed by a friend a 'romantic Scottish Jacobite'. But it was not all faith and work. He was a frequent speaker at his college debating society and also shone as an oarsman, being for a time stroke of the Wadham boat. He normally gave no parties, but during training entertained his fellow crew members daily to dinner in his room, acquiring a reputation as a genial host. In June 1848 he went down from the university with a second in classics.

His boyhood vocation for the ministry was still strong, and in Lent 1849 he was ordained deacon by Bishop Denison of Salisbury, brother of the Archdeacon. He served his title at Westbury-under-the-Plain in Wiltshire, a far-flung parish which included the outlying villages of Bratton and Dilton. The vicar was a chronic invalid who left his three curates more or less to their own devices – no doubt on the ground that the resulting opportunities for initiative compensated for the absence of formal training. Certainly Mackonochie had plenty of opportunities to preach during his Westbury curacy. There were three churches to service, and he always had to deliver two addresses on Sundays. In the course of his three and a half years in Wiltshire he reckoned to have preached no fewer than 738 sermons. Not that these were necessarily models of pulpit eloquence. The parishioners thought his manner stiff. And a fellow-curate, Thomas Bowles, judged that his preaching could not be called good in spite of the infinite pains he took:

> He wrote sermons and preached from his paper. He wrote with slowness and considerable difficulty. I have known him write most of Saturday, and, unable to make enough to fill his paper, work on into the night, till he went to bed on Sunday morning rather than Saturday night in despair, and have to fill a few more pages on Sunday morning before the service.

Nevertheless, he improved over the years in this particular department of his ministry. John Keble once heard him preach at Westbury and commented enigmatically: 'Wait awhile, and you will see.'

Mackonochie was painstakingly conscientious in matters of ministerial detail. He described the drudgery of much of his parochial work as 'spade husbandry'. He disdained personal comfort – when, for instance, his landlady put an extra blanket on his bed in cold weather, she would find it the next morning neatly folded and put aside. He usually got up as early as four or five in the morning. His habits of self-discipline extended to his parochial activities. He preferred to devote most of his time to the most desolate and least inviting parts of the parish, being prepared to walk several miles day after day in all weathers to prepare pauper children for confirmation and to minister to the sick and dying in the lowest haunts of the poor and in the Union Workhouse. The then Master of the Union wrote afterwards: 'His life appears to me to have been an unbroken series of acts of self-denial.' He was ordained priest by Bishop Denison in 1850, but became increasingly dissatisfied with conditions at Westbury. The invalid vicar had resigned, but his successor was no real improvement and likewise failed to give the curates any proper training. By this time Bowles had left to take up temporary duty in the parish of Wantage, Berkshire. In 1852 he was about to move on to another post and recommended Mackonochie to apply for the vacancy. All went well at the interview with the vicar, who appointed him to his staff as from Michaelmas.

The vicar whom Mackonochie was now to serve was of a very different stamp from the invalid incumbent of Westbury and his successor. William John Butler (1818–94) – 'Butler of Wantage' – achieved fame as a model parish priest of the High Church school.* Under the 'Wantage system' everything in the parish was planned down to the finest detail. The church was open all day long for private prayer and frequent services, and there was a daily Eucharist, something for which Mackonochie had vainly craved at Westbury. Butler's watchwords were 'faith, prayer and grind'. His curates – who were required to wear cassocks and tall hats in the morning and tail-coats in the afternoon – endeavoured to live up to his ideals.

Mackonochie's special charge was the hamlet of Charlton, where the villagers for long kept his memory green. 'He were a friend to *we*', one of them told Mrs Towle when she was researching for her biography. By this time his sermons had improved from the Westbury days. 'He were a fine preacher,' the old sexton recalled. 'He'd rumple himself up to give it 'em straight and plain till he were red in the face.' H. P. Liddon, the well-known Tractarian divine, who was for a short time a fellow-curate of Mackonochie's at Wantage, told Mrs Towle that he had had an extraordinary knack of expanding a single theme into a whole series of sermons:

> He would, e.g., begin the Prodigal Son or Psalm cxxx on Ash Wednesday, and preach on the same subject all through Lent two or three times a week and without at all exhausting himself or the interest of his subject. The reason was that his real interests were so predominantly practical, and he had always

---

*Among his other achievements Butler founded in 1850 the St Mary's Sisterhood, which later developed into the Community of St Mary the Virgin. In 1864 he was elected Bishop of Natal after the deposition of the heretical Bishop Colenso, but, owing to the disapproval of the Archbishop of Canterbury, Longley, declined the invitation. In 1880 he was appointed a canon of Worcester and in 1885 Dean of Lincoln.

a fund of new experiences or warnings or reflections of this kind ready at hand to illustrate the sacred words.

Mackonochie might be a better preacher at Wantage than at Westbury, but his asceticism continued as before – and even drew a protest from his diocesan, Bishop Samuel Wilberforce of Oxford. 'I am quite sure that with our climate and constitution', the bishop advised him on one occasion, 'such fasting would be absolutely incompatible with work, and for the sake of the parish I feel bound to forbid it.' Wilberforce was again in correspondence with the self-denying curate towards the end of 1856, when Mackonochie was agonizing over whether to accept an invitation to work in the diocese of Newfoundland. His mother was strongly opposed to his going out there, so he wrote to Wilberforce for a ruling. The Bishop at first approved the proposal, but later changed his mind and advised against it. So, for another two years, Mackonochie carried on with the parochial routine of 'faith, prayer and grind' at Wantage.

His next move was to be much nearer home than distant Newfoundland; but it was to have a profound effect on his subsequent ministry, and indeed to point the way to St Alban's, Holborn. The challenge came from the London slum parish of St George's-in-the-East, which included the daunting mission district of Wapping. The parish had been carved out of the parish of Stepney in the reign of Queen Anne and had at first served a semi-rural area. Its character had, however, been changed out of all recognition in the early years of the nineteenth century by the building of the London docks. Their creation had led to a vast influx of sailors of many nationalities, who spent their shore leave and accumulated earnings on the dubious delights that the parish had to offer. These included vast numbers of prostitutes. In the four streets surrounding St George's no fewer than 154 out of 733 dwellings were 'houses of ill fame'. What money the sailors had to spare after their visits to the brothels they were able to squander in the parish's 150 public houses. By the mid–1850s the population had risen to nearly fifty thousand, predominantly working-class. The crowding was horrific, many families being confined to a single room each in one of the hundreds of lodging-houses in which the parish abounded. The resultant combination of squalor and vice presented a formidable challenge to an aspiring mission priest.

This then was the daunting field to which Mackonochie felt himself called. He had first visited the area for a week in November 1857, and had been deeply moved by what he saw. The parish was under the charge of the Rev. Bryan King,* who had been Rector since 1842. But for his first thirteen years he had been assisted by only a single curate (and his curates changed frequently), and he found his time fully occupied in conducting church services and other matters of ecclesiastical routine. His ministry was stigmatized by one of his opponents as 'earnest but ineffectual'. A recent convert from Evangelicalism, he had introduced various mild innovations in the way of ritual (such as wearing a surplice in the pulpit) and attempted to discipline his congregation by, for example, refusing to communicate 'notorious evil-livers'. But he had neither the time nor the temperament to tackle the underlying problems of the area. He was therefore only too eager to accept an offer in 1856 from the Rev. Charles Lowder to set up a mission in his parish which could help tackle the allied problems of poverty and vice. Lowder was to achieve fame as a Victorian slum priest who, by his charismatic powers, was able to infuse the irreligious with his own zeal for Christianity. He was also a ritualist anxious to put his principles into practice, and found Wapping an ideal field for his experiments. His offer to King was made in his capacity as founder and first Master of the Society of the Holy Cross, an organization set up in 1855 to promote a stricter rule of life among the clergy, to establish home missions to the poor, and to publish tracts and pamphlets in aid of Catholic faith and practice. The area of Wapping in which Lowder established his first mission-house was to develop eventually into the parish of St Peter's, London Docks. It had a population of about six

---

*Bryan King (1811–95) had given up a fellowship at Brasenose College, Oxford, to take up his London cure. After his turbulent ministry at St George's-in-the-East, culminating in the riots of 1859–60, his health collapsed and he spent three years recuperating at Bruges in Belgium. He was then appointed to a rural living in the diocese of Salisbury, where he was able to spend his declining years in peace.

thousand, including two thousand Irish Roman Catholics. At first services were held in a room in the mission-house set aside as a chapel, with one missioner officiating and the other holding the door against possible rowdies. But soon a temporary 'iron church' was set up in the garden of the mission-house and dedicated to the Good Shepherd. In 1857 a second mission church, St Saviour's, was opened in Wellclose Square and a second mission-house, with a small school in the loft, established nearby. Lowder was assisted by three other clergymen, but a critical situation soon arose when two of these went over to Rome. Mackonochie's decision to join the staff in the autumn of 1858, a year after his initial visit, must have seemed to Lowder like an answer to prayer. He came originally on three months' trial, but stayed for nearly four years – years which spanned the notorious riots. He proved a pillar of strength during a trying period, and soon became an intimate friend of Lowder's and a close ally in the ritualistic battles that lay ahead. He joined the Society of the Holy Cross, and was later to be its Master for seventeen years.

From the start the mission was unashamedly ritualistic in character. There were frequent celebrations of the Eucharist, and vestments were used in both churches. The benefits of confession were extolled. As far as limited resources would allow, the ceremonial was 'of as solemn and devotional a type as possible, that our people might learn, not only by oral instruction, but by all the outward associations of this solemn service, to worship their Blessed Lord present in His own appointed Sacrament with reverence and devotion'.

The day in the mission-house at Wellclose Square, where Mackonochie was based, began with Prime said in the oratory at seven a.m. This was followed at eight by either Mattins or a celebration of the Eucharist in the church; and Terce in the oratory. Mackonochie then gave Bible lessons in one or other of the schools and thereafter spent the rest of the day in (to quote Mrs Towle) the 'thousand and one occupations which came upon him as a Mission priest in a populous district'. Dinner and Sext were followed by Nones at three p.m. Evensong was sung in church at eight p.m., followed by supper. The liturgical day ended with Compline. The minor offices often had to go by the board in the face of more pressing calls on clerical time. Mackonochie, for instance, would often be busy in church till past ten at night hearing confessions – an increasingly important part of his ministerial work. Although he visited the schools on a daily basis, he was not really good with children. While he was always gentle and kindly, says Mrs Towle, 'there was in him an entire absence of that playfulness which must still linger in the mind and manner of the grown-up man if there is to be sympathetic *rapport* between him and children.' The discipline observed in his class, she adds, was 'Spartan'. He was more at home instructing adults. 'What he said was always carefully read up and prepared beforehand; he never aimed at originality or profundity; but he gave you in clear, simple, well-chosen words the cream of what the best Anglican authorities had said on the subject in hand.'

Mackonochie was a Scot, and possessed his full share of the Scotsman's tendency to be reserved and undemonstrative. But Lowder found him an invaluable aide, who 'by his indefatigable labours, eloquent preaching and unceasing care for souls, set us an example of what mission work really was'. Life in the clergy-house was certainly austere. The beds were apparently a trial to the flesh, and the meals not much better. Lowder, according to a contemporary, 'literally never noticed what he ate. . . . To us poor weaker ones, certain dinners meant sick headaches and agonies untold. Anyone was good enough to be our cook; and – I shudder as I think of all we suffered in this respect.' Mackonochie, himself an ascetic in the Lowder mould, would have suffered less than most.

*   *   *

The clergy at the mission-house soon had graver matters to worry about than uncomfortable beds and unappetizing meals. Six months after Mackonochie's arrival the notorious series of riots began which were to afflict the parish of St George's-in-the-East for the next eighteen months and to give him his baptism of anti-ritualistic fire. It was an irony of history, however, that the fury of the rioters was to be directed not so much against the two mission chapels, where the ceremonial was advanced, as against the parish church itself, which gave less ground for offence. But then the underlying cause of the riots was more social than ecclesiastical, the allegedly ritualistic goings-on at St George's providing a convenient pretext for the rioters. According to J. M. Ludlow, a leading Christian Socialist, the riots were 'largely stimulated by the Jewish sweaters [i.e., exploitative employers] of the East End, whose proceedings Mr. Bryan King's curates, Messrs. Mackonochie and Lowder, had the unheard-of impertinence to denounce and interfere with.' King himself thought the men chiefly responsible were the local publicans and brothel-keepers, whose trade was suffering from the ministrations of the clergy. Certainly some of the rioters were hired for the purpose in a nineteenth-century version of rent-a-mob. A local lad told his teacher: 'It's all a question of beer, sir, and what else they can get. We know them. They're black-guards, like ourselves here. Religion ain't anything more to them than it is to us. They gets paid for what they do, and they does it, like they'd do any other job.'

Ostensibly, however, the riots *were* about ritual. As the priest in charge of the mission, Lowder had been involved in correspondence with the Bishop of London, A. C. Tait, concerning the 'dresses and ceremonies' used in the two chapels. 'I feel deep interest in your efforts to do good,' Tait told Lowder; 'but I am sure that no good will be done by the mimicking of popery.' As a result of his diocesan's strictures Lowder gave up eucharistic vestments in June 1857; but a few weeks before this King himself had begun wearing them as a gesture of support for his missioners. He had already adopted various ceremonial adjuncts, such as a cross, flowers and candles on the altar, intoned prayers and the eastward position. The donning of a chasuble (the gift of some of his parishioners) must have seemed to Protestant-minded members of his congregation the final straw – though King justified his action by invoking the recent Knightsbridge Judgment, which implicitly sanctioned the use of vestments. It was some time, however, before any action was taken. Eventually, towards the end of 1858, Tait summoned King to an interview at London House and urged him to tone down his ceremonial: 'The man must be an utter fool or madman who persists in such tomfooleries, for I can call them by no other name.' King was not amused, and walked out in a huff.

The riots began six months later, the immediate cause being the election of a neighbouring incumbent, the Rev. Hugh Allen, rector of St Jude's, Whitechapel, to the post of lecturer at St George's. Such lectureships in London churches were a survival from medieval times; and, since the lecturers were nominated by the vestry of the parish and elected by the parishioners, they sometimes found themselves at odds with the incumbent. Allen was to prove an outsize thorn in King's flesh. Dubbed by Tait a mixture of Wesleyan Methodist and wild Irishman, he was an ultra-Protestant who could be relied upon to rant from the pulpit against ritualism – and did so. In spite of his misgivings (for Allen had caused trouble at another London church) Tait duly presented him with his licence on 17 May 1859. On the following Sunday Mackonochie noted briefly in his diary: 'Great disturbance at the parish church about W. H. Allen.' Parish lecturers were entitled by Act of Parliament to the use of the pulpit 'from time to time'. Allen made his first appearance at St George's at three-forty p.m. – only twenty minutes before the regular Sunday-afternoon service was due to begin and without having obtained a by-your-leave from the Rector. King happened to be away that day, leaving a curate to conduct the service. Allen flounced into the church with his supporters, entered the pulpit and proceeded to preach. The churchwardens declined to intervene, and the regular service went by the board.

On his return King complained to the bishop in the strongest terms about Allen's behaviour. Tait advised the lecturer to settle his position by, if necessary, recourse to law. On 16 June the Court of Queen's Bench ruled that his intrusion the previous month had been illegal, but that he might be allowed to hold his Sunday-afternoon service before or after the statutory service. Ten days later Allen duly presented himself at the church at the time fixed by King, two-twenty-five p.m., and mounted its pulpit. In the words of the *East London Observer*: 'He found occasion to dwell repeatedly and in a marked manner on disputed doctrine, and pomp and ceremony, troupes of choris-

ters and ritualism, as being opposed to the everlasting Gospel.'
Fired by the preacher's eloquence, the congregation crowded
into the choir-stalls and again prevented the regular afternoon
service from taking place. The pattern was repeated Sunday after
Sunday for many months. It is unnecessary to follow the riots
in detail, but one or two quotations from contemporary
observers will give their flavour. King himself, for instance,
described the scenes in his church on two successive Sundays,
29 January and 5 February 1860, as 'perfectly unparalleled for
their atrocity. The whole service was interrupted by hissing,
whistling and shouting. Several songs were roared out by many
united voices during the reading of the Lessons and the preaching of the sermon; hassocks were thrown down from the galler-
ies; and, after the service, cushions, hassocks and books were
hurled at the altar and its furniture.' And Sabine Baring-Gould,
then working as a lay teacher in Pimlico, wrote:

> Directly the doors were opened, the mob surged into the
> church, scrambling into the pews, some over their backs, and
> into the galleries. . . . There ensued talking, laughing and
> cracking of vulgar jokes before the service began. When the
> choir and clergy entered, there burst forth booing and hooting,
> and during the service unseemly mimicry of the intoning, and
> indecent parodies chanted as responses. When the choir turned
> east at the Creed, the mob turned bodily west.

Eventually some form of police protection was provided – on
one occasion no fewer than 180 constables being on duty inside
the building. But, according to Baring-Gould, the police had
been instructed to take no action unless personal violence was
offered; so their presence did little to restrain the unruliness of
the mob.

The departure of Allen at the beginning of 1860 to take up a
living in Southwark made no difference; by now the riots had
acquired a momentum of their own. Even Tait, whose attitude
in the early days had been ambivalent, later condemned them
in the House of Lords. By this time King had left for a long
holiday abroad, and Mackonochie and Lowder had to rely on
outside help to staff the parish church. Whatever he may have

thought of Mackonochie as a ritualist, Tait had a deep regard and esteem for him as a man. On one occasion he told a priest who was standing in for King at St George's: 'I have not a better man in my diocese than Mr. Mackonochie. . . . I can't say anything against your wishing to help such a man.' Tait's deep regret was that Mackonochie's evangelistic zeal, of which he thoroughly approved, should go hand in hand with ritualism, which he deplored. In later years he was to cross swords with Mackonochie in a big way. At this stage he could extend to him his ready sympathy for the 'peculiarly painful' position in which, as the only licensed clergyman at that moment resident in the parish (Lowder was on holiday), Mackonochie was placed. A little later he wrote: 'I am sure that the manifestation of the kindly Christian spirit of conciliation at the same time that you show your determination not to be intimidated must have its effect.'

The riots certainly proved a sore trial for Mackonochie, then a comparatively young man. But they had their silver lining, as Lowder wrote in his *Twenty-one Years*:

> It proved a good test to the sincerity of our people; threw us back upon the soundness of our own principles; and tended to consolidate and establish our work. . . . The very dregs of the people were taught to think about religion. Many were brought to church through the unhappy notoriety which we had gained; and some who came to scoff remained to worship.

*   *   *

Mackonochie was not to remain long in Wapping. At the end of his first year there he had turned down the offer of St Saviour's, Leeds, by its patron, Dr Pusey, in spite of the urgings of his friends to accept it. Two years later came the offer of another living, much nearer to hand, which eventually he decided to accept. 'My dear Lord', the patron of this living was able to write to Bishop Tait of London on 15 January 1862, 'I have offered the incumbency of the new church of St Alban's [Holborn] to Mr Mackonochie, who has accepted it, and will doubtless before long wait upon your lordship to say so.' The acceptance had not in fact been so automatic as these words might imply: it had been preceded by much haggling over the amount and nature of the ceremonial which would be permitted at the new church.

The church was to serve a district which had previously formed part of the parish of St Andrew, Holborn. With a vast population of 37,000, the parish was ripe for division; and towards the end of the 1850s a means of dividing it came to hand. The benefactor who provided a site for a new church was the second Baron Leigh. According to an article published in the *Church Times* shortly after Mackonochie's death, Leigh wrote to the rector of St Andrew's to say that he had been reading one of Disraeli's novels which contained a graphic description of the people lying about in front of the gates of St Andrew's church; and the thought had struck him that these were *his* people, as he owned a large property in Holborn, and that he was doing nothing for them. Could the rector suggest any means whereby he could benefit these people? The rector both could and did: a site for a new church that was being projected. Leigh wrote back to say that he would give as much land as was required. Meanwhile a second benefactor had turned up to provide the wherewithal to build the church. This was John Gellibrand Hubbard, a London merchant who, it seemed, was anxious to dedicate a portion of his money to the building of a church in the East End. Hubbard, in addition to heading a City firm trading with Russia, was a director of the Bank of England and an MP; he was later ennobled as the first Lord Addington. He was an old-fashioned High Churchman whose Catholicism was limited by the Prayer Book and who had no sympathy for extremes of ceremonial. He therefore seems an unlikely person to have been enamoured of the ritualistic young mission priest of St George's-in-the-East. According to one story, possibly apocryphal, Hubbard wrote to Butler while Mackonochie was still at Wantage, requesting a reference for one of Mackonochie's fellow-curates who, he felt, might be a suitable incumbent for St Alban's – but getting the curate's name wrong. Butler replied that he had no one of that name on his staff, but that another of his curates, Mackonochie, would be just the man for the job. Hubbard was sufficiently impressed by what he saw of Butler's nominee to keep an eye on him when he moved to Wapping. But, while admiring his personal holiness and evangelistic zeal, he was less happy about his ritualistic leanings; and it was his anxiety on this score that caused the negotiations for the transfer of Mackonochie to St Alban's to be so protracted.

Butler, with whom Hubbard corresponded frequently, attempted to reassure him, pointing out that Mackonochie's merits were so great that they would 'counter-balance many things' and that he was quite sensible enough not to offend. Hubbard was unconvinced. He wrote to Butler early in 1861 to say that, if he was to offer Mackonochie the charge of St Alban's, Holborn, he would require assurances on such points as the doctrine of the Real Presence, eucharistic vestments and the use of the sign of the cross before meals. Butler showed Mackonochie the letter; but his answers were considered so unsatisfactory that Hubbard broke off negotiations and offered the living to Liddon instead. Liddon, however, turned it down and pressed the claims of Mackonochie. Hubbard gradually weakened, and Mackonochie made one or two concessions. Eventually Hubbard gave in and offered him the post. Both men apparently thought that they had got what they wanted. Hubbard assured Tait, when telling him of the offer, that Mackonochie 'knows that it is my desire that the work at St. Alban's should be carried out with a hearty allegiance to the Church of England – neglecting none of the means of edification which she supplies either in doctrine or in ritual, but using the large liberty which she allows with loyalty and discretion.' Mackonochie for his part refused to acknowledge any restrictions on his ceremonial activities. In 1875, half-way through the long series of lawsuits, he told the Bishop of London, by now John Jackson, that he had been placed in the church 'much against my own will. . . . I was avowedly a man of extreme views as to ritual, and of deep convictions as to the essential connection of a sound faith and the ritual expression of it. I refused to think of accepting the charge of this parish unless I could do so unconditionally, without any sort of agreement to be guided by the wishes of the founder as to the management of the church or its services, beyond a general desire to consider those wishes so far as my duty to God, to His Church, and to my people would allow.' Mackonochie may have been writing with the benefit of hindsight, but it soon became apparent that he and his patron would seldom see eye to eye. Hubbard had paid the piper (he had spent almost £50,000 on the church, besides giving it a £5000 endowment fund) and considered himself entitled to play the ceremonial tune. In addition to being patron, he was also one of the two churchwardens; and differences of opinion with his nominee were soon to arise.

*   *   *

Mackonochie moved to Holborn immediately after Easter 1862, his replacement being J. L. Lyne, the future Fr Ignatius.* The scene of his labours measured a mere twenty acres in extent, but into this region of dark courts and lofty tenement buildings was crowded a population of eight thousand souls, mainly working-class. The inhabitants were, says Mrs Towle, 'for the most part vendors of fish and vegetables, a few very poor shopkeepers, and many foreigners.' Their earnings were precarious, though when they had any money they tended to spend it recklessly. Drunkenness and vice of all kinds abounded, and the new church was built on the site of a notorious 'thieves' kitchen'. But Mackonochie's reputation soon ensured that the working-class element in his congregation was leavened by a sprinkling of better-class folk which increased over the years.

The new church was not yet completed when Mackonochie began work, and he held his first service on 11 May 1862 in a room over a fish shop in Baldwin's Gardens. In the congregation was the patron's wife, Maria Hubbard (a peer's daughter), who, she informed Mackonochie in advance, 'would like to go with you as one of the people and she will dress herself so as to look

---

*But not for long! Lyne went about dressed as a monk, an enormous rosary hanging from his waist. He was a popular preacher, but left the mission after nine months to found his Benedictine Order.

like your servant-maid.' She turned up disguised in a plain cotton dress but attended by her own maid. Afterwards she wandered about the streets, giving pictures to the children she met. Mackonochie organized the parish into districts, the care of which was assigned individually to himself and his four curates. He found it uphill work to begin with. The small congregation who penetrated the room above the fish-shop were restless and inquisitive, and children used to gather on the pavement and peer through the grating at what was going on within. But gradually the congregations increased in size and reverence, and regular visiting by the clergy produced a good impression on the neighbourhood.

On 3 January 1863 Mackonochie was instituted to his charge by Bishop Tait with the title of Perpetual Curate. (He was normally referred to as the Vicar, though it was not until 1880 that St Alban's officially became a parish of its own.) Seven weeks later, on 21 February, the handsome new church was consecrated. The ceremony was to have taken place on 29 January, but had had to be postponed because of an unfortunate row between Mackonochie and Hubbard – a foretaste of the ecclesiastical in-fighting that was to disfigure the years ahead. The cause of the row appears unbelievably trivial today: Hubbard was upset by reports that the clergy were going round the district in their cassocks or in long cloaks of serge. Mackonochie at once offered to resign, and for the next month the issue hung in the balance. Both Butler and Liddon endeavoured to persuade him to change his mind, but to no avail. Hubbard suggested that he should remain for a time on trial at St Alban's, and that during this probationary period he should give up 'the habitual wearing of cassocks' and 'unsanctioned Ritual practices'. Mackonochie turned down the proposal, but offered to go half-way towards meeting Hubbard's wishes by endeavouring to avoid 'some of the details to which you have objected, so far as I can without the surrender of any fundamental principle'. He cautiously added: 'I feel that it will be quite impossible for me to do my duty here thoroughly unless you kindly trust to my judgment.' Hubbard agreed to accept Mackonochie's compromise proposal, though he asked him to avoid 'unauthorized novelties and doubtful revivals'. Mackonochie thanked Hubbard for his 'great kindness and generosity', and at once agreed to give up wearing his cassock around the parish. The consecration went ahead on 21 February, and all was for the moment sweetness and light. But the writing was on the wall; and the initial brush between patron and incumbent augured ill for the future.

At least the patron meant well. The new church was free of pew-rents; and in an address 'To the Inhabitants of the District of St. Alban's, Holborn' issued on the day of consecration, Hubbard emphasized: 'St. Alban's church is free. It has been built especially for the sake of the poor; but, rich or poor, all alike may enter it without fee or payment, and may find in it a place where they may kneel to pray and stand to praise God, and where they may sit to hear the good tidings of the Gospel.' Later in the address Hubbard remarked hopefully: 'I have the strongest assurance for my confidence that Mr. Mackonochie, as a true and faithful priest of the Church of England, will affectionately teach and discreetly guide the souls committed to his charge.'

In his new cure Mackonochie displayed the same painstaking care for individuals that he had shown in Westbury, Wantage and Wapping. He would endure repeated interruptions with exemplary patience, and never appeared to be in a hurry. This was one of the secrets of his influence. To each of his parochial tasks he would give his undivided attention, even though this meant that his opportunities for leisure were pitiably small. This, according to Mrs Towle, he did not mind, seeing that, 'from the very first, "play" had been left out of his life'. His inability to relax was an obvious flaw in his character, though he apparently enjoyed 'any little distraction which came in his way'.

Mackonochie, though not a handsome man, impressed observers as a striking and impressive figure. A detailed description of his appearance was provided by George Russell, a cousin of Mackonochie's long-time curate, Edward Russell:

> He was tall and spare, though not emaciated, and he bore himself with a singular dignity. . . . His nose was aquiline, his chin prominent, and his mouth was drawn down at the corners

in a rather forbidding fashion. His complexion was clear and bright; his hair a very dark brown; and though the greater part of his face was shaved, it retained on each side a fragment of hair which, in contradiction to the clean shave of Romanism and the luxuriant whiskers of Protestantism, acquired the nickname of 'The Anglican Inch'.

A layman who knew him well described him as:

> tall and broadly built, good-looking without being exactly handsome, having a fine carriage and showing himself every inch a man – a man of character and distinction. He was precisely the sort of person that nobody but a fool would think of taking a liberty with; yet withal so kindly in expression, so ready to give his complete and sympathetic attention, that no one could come within his range and fail to be attracted.

This particular observer added that Mackonochie was so frugal at table that it seemed hardly worth while to cook for him. And one of his curates described the living arrangements in the clergy-house as 'excellent for the soul, not quite this for the body' – and the house itself as 'like an entomological museum *without the pins*'. Mrs Towle remarks that Mackonochie lived as a poor man all his life not only on principle, but because he placed little value on the personal gratifications that money could purchase. His meals consisted mainly of cold meat, potatoes, bread and cheese. His habit was to work in his study till long after the dinner bell had rung. 'When the others were near finishing, he would come in with a radiant and genial face, bolt in three minutes about sufficient bread and cold meat to satisfy half a schoolboy; look at his watch; declare himself already late for an engagement, say in Hackney, and disappear like a lamplighter.' But at one time he did relax so far as to provide his curates with sherry on red-letter saints' days.

Edward Russell described him as a 'precisian' who had brought with him from Butler's Wantage an 'unbounded faith in the organization of that model parish'. Not all his curates, however, shared his admiration for the elaborate machinery imported from Wantage. He never sought recreation for its own sake, and even his reading usually had a practical bearing on his work. But he prided himself on keeping abreast of new ideas and phenomena, such as an unfamiliar school of painting or a fresh discovery in science, even though such periods of study were often a burden to him. He was uninterested in music, art or architecture for their own sake. Where ceremonial in church was concerned, it was its fitness rather than its beauty which appealed to him.

Mackonochie was a competent, though not an outstanding, preacher. According to Edward Russell:

> His voice was harsh and monotonous; his gestures were ungraceful. . . . He had not the slightest eloquence or even rhetoric; but he had quite sufficient fluency, and a complete command of clear, plain, and forcible English. He was wholly free from 'gush'; but his spiritual earnestness, and his strong insistence on practical duty, gave his sermons a peculiar cogency.

Mrs Towle says that he derived no sense of inspiration from a crowded congregation, not did his eloquence kindle into passion in response to the sympathy of the multitude. 'His curious absence of self-consciousness made him too indifferent to be greatly moved by a public verdict; too self-confident to need the support of public approval. . . . He had that element of fanaticism which resolves itself into an unconscious aloofness from other men's minds.' And his very single-mindedness made it difficult for him to see both sides of a question.

According to Edward Russell, Mackonochie had no hobbies or side-interests. 'If he shared such frailties with us, I never discovered them, or observed that he had any real absorbing interests outside his interest in human souls.' After supper in the clergy-house he would hurry away to his room and, 'closing the door with a feeling of intense relief, set himself to make good use of the precious hours of solitude. I know not how late he worked and prayed, but when we fell asleep – and we were not early – his lamp was burning still.'

Russell was one of two curates (the other was Stanton) who spent their entire ministry at St Alban's. A nephew of Lord

John Russell, the Whig Prime Minister, he was a man of intellect and culture whose interests went far beyond the narrowly ecclesiastical. He even sought to augment his priestly training by enrolling as a medical student at St Bartholomew's Hospital, though he left before taking his degree. He was a joint founder of the Guild of St Barnabas for Nurses, serving for almost fifty years as its chaplain and as editor of its monthly magazine. Above all, in the words of Bishop Gore, he was a priest and a saint. 'By a saint I mean a man who puts God first.'

Arthur Stanton – who, with Mackonochie and Russell, constituted the 'famous three' at St Alban's – was content, like Russell, to serve for more than fifty years as a plain assistant curate. By the time of his death in 1913 he was one of the best-loved priests in London, and was known by the locals simply as 'Dad'. The youngest of the twelve children of a wealthy Gloucestershire manufacturer, he decided to take orders rather than enter the family business.* He had early been attracted both to ritualism in general and to Mackonochie in particular, and after a short course at Cuddesdon took up a curacy at St Alban's in 1862. Bishop Tait warned him: 'If you go to Mackonochie of St Alban's you must never expect any Church preferment.' His father kept him well supplied with money, and his salary from St Alban's was a nominal five shillings a year. Both as preacher and as confessor Stanton soon established a formidable reputation for himself. *Punch* might ridicule him as 'Stanton with hyacinthine locks, carrying a portable confession box'; but a contemporary remarked that, as a spiritual guide of men, and of young men in particular, he had no equal. He had an irrepressible sense of humour and on one occasion, when a visitor to St Alban's objected to the smell of incense, remarked: 'There are only two stinks in the next world, incense and brimstone, and you've got to choose between them.' On another occasion, when St Alban's was under fire for its ritualistic excesses, Stanton

---

*Stanton senior raised no objection to his son's plans, and even bought the advowson (right of presentation) of the living of Tetbury in Gloucestershire, so as to secure a potential clerical berth for him. Arthur never thought of taking the living when it fell vacant, however, as he would have felt guilty of simony. The advowson was left to him in his father's will, but he refused the bequest.

pointed out that the only people called 'wise' in the New Testament were the five virgins who were able to carry processional
lights and the Magi from the East who brought incense to the
infant Christ.

In his life of Mackonochie Michael Reynolds describes the
genial life of the clergy-house in its early days.

> One has the impression that the atmosphere was a good deal
> livelier, and less inhibited, than in the average officers' mess.
> Mackonochie, though not himself much given to levity, evi-
> dently enjoyed the jokes of others; his very soberness had the
> effect of bringing out their exuberance. . . . Their corporate
> spirit burned higher and stronger as their leader and their
> church were increasingly beset with troubles. The clergy of St
> Alban's were like a unit of picked assault troops. Their gaiety
> had something of the proud, carefree quality of laughter under
> fire.

Russell, looking back in after years, feels that he and his fellow-curates must have tried their chief's patience sorely at times:

> Some of us . . . flung ourselves with almost boyish eagerness
> headlong into the various enthusiasms of the hour. Startling
> views, religious, political, social and scientific, were broached
> at the dinner-table which must often have been distasteful
> enough to his conservative mind; and I still seem to see the
> look, part-amused, part-amazed, with which he listened to our
> suggestions for the general setting right of the universe. A
> smaller man would have snubbed us. He did not do so – to
> our gain, I think.

The persevering labours of the clergy of St Alban's soon
began to have their reward. The years from 1862 to the first
prosecution in 1867 were years of uninterrupted progress. The
congregations increased to an impressive size. In 1863,
Mackonochie's first full year, 295 baptisms took place, many
being of adults. The Easter communicants in 1864 totalled 291;
by 1865 they had increased to 453. As Mackonochie's fame
grew, he attracted worshippers from other parts of London; but
the congregations were still basically local. The services were

supplemented by a vast amount of social welfare facilities. Mackonochie set up guilds and associations for men, women, boys and girls; parochial schools for 500 children; night schools for both boys and girls; and (among other organizations) a choir-school, a soup-kitchen, a blanket loan fund, a clothing fund, a coal charity, a savings-bank, a clothing-club and a shoe-club. In addition to all these agencies, the church provided food for the destitute and relief for the sick to the value of £500 a year.

Right from the start two fundamental doctrines were taught at St Alban's. The first was the position of the Eucharist as the only divinely-appointed act of worship. The second was the importance of the sacrament of penance. The climax of the Sunday celebrations was the High Mass at eleven a.m., attended by many who had already made their communions at one of the earlier Low Masses. Altar lights, unleavened bread, the mixed chalice and the eastward position were, from the first, features of all the celebrations. Mackonochie first began to wear a chasuble in 1864 and to use incense at Epiphany 1866. The ceremonial began to attract the attention of the 'Ritualistic Reporters' – as the often-ignorant scribes writing in Protestant journals were popularly known in High Church circles. They produced such priceless pearls as 'thurifers swung in procession', 'acolytes suspended from rood-screens' and even 'curates who practised celibacy in the open street'. But it was not only anonymous journalists who let their imaginations run riot. The philanthropic but ultra-Evangelical Earl of Shaftesbury was inspired by a visit to St Alban's in 1866 to claim that, in outward form and ritual, it was 'the worship of Jupiter and Juno':

> Abundance of servitors in Romish apparel . . . such a scene of theatrical gymnastics, of singing, screaming, genuflections . . . as I never saw before even in a Romish Temple. Clouds upon clouds of incense, the censer frequently refreshed by the High Priest, who kissed the spoon as he dug out the sacred powder and swung it about at the end of a silver chain . . . The Communicants went up to the tune of soft music, as though it had

been a melodrama, and one was astounded, at the close, that there was no fall of the curtain.

Others in authority might equally disapprove, but were nevertheless impressed by what they saw. William Connor Magee, the future Bishop of Peterborough and Archbishop of York, visited St Alban's when he was Dean of Cork 'to see what these fellows are doing'. At lunch he was asked what he had seen and replied: 'I have seen something that can never be put down.' A similar comment came from the Broad Church Dean of Westminster, Arthur Stanley, who reported to Bishop Tait after a visit of inspection: 'I saw three men in green, and you will find it difficult to put them down.' Mackonochie himself regarded ceremonial as merely a means to an end. 'You know very well,' he told his parishioners in 1867, 'that the value which we attach to these things is not for their own sakes; it is because of the special character of the service in which they are used. . . . We feel that a gorgeously conducted service ought to mean something. It does mean something – it means that the Holy Eucharist is the Sacrament of Christ's Body and Blood.'

The other twin plank of Mackonochie's teaching was confession, which he urged as a means of grace to which his people had an undoubted right. His straightforward advocacy of its blessings attracted a growing number of regular penitents, not only from within the parish itself but from other parts of London and from further afield. It also attracted the attention of Protestant propagandists, who amused themselves with such lines of doggerel as these appearing in a magazine of April 1868:

> O Confession's rather a charming thing,
> With St. Alban's the proto-martyr;
> Sweet pious gossip the ladies bring,
> Which for soothing words they barter . . .
> Slight penance have they when they go away,
> And there's nothing at all alarming,
> And the beautiful penitents seem to say
> That they think Confession charming.

*   *   *

It was not to be supposed that the ceremonial goings-on at St Alban's would escape the notice of critics whose disapproval would go beyond the ribald words of the versifiers. But why did they single out St Alban's above other ritualistic churches for their hostile attentions? The basic reason is that, by the end of the 1860s, it had come to be regarded as London's most notorious ritualistic church. This was due to its accessibility (it was within easy reach of the West End) and to the size and enthusiasm of its congregation. The latter included by now a good social mix, even the Prince and Princess of Wales joining it occasionally (to the intense annoyance of the Queen).

From the early days, as we have seen, there had been friction between Mackonochie and his patron and churchwarden, Hubbard. Within a few days of the church's consecration in 1863 the latter was writing to Bishop Tait to complain about the use of candles on the altar; and, though that particular bone of contention was smoothed over, Mackonochie continued to cause offence (in Hubbard's eyes) by his ceremonial innovations. These included coloured vestments in 1864 and incense in 1866. On each occasion Hubbard complained to Tait that they had been introduced without the consent of either of the church-wardens. Tait wrote back to suggest that the wardens should submit a formal memorial requesting his intervention. They backed down at this point, though Mackonochie endured several grillings by Tait on the subject of his allegedly unlawful prac-tices. After one of these interviews Tait endeavoured in a letter to bring his erring subordinate to heel: 'I cannot ask you or any man to set aside the dictates of conscience, but I pray your conscience may be guided to see that in the outward ordering of the Church service you are not justified in acting without reference to the Bishop.' To Hubbard's fellow-churchwarden, C. C. Spiller, Tait wrote later in the year: 'It is not the heartiness of the services that any one objects to, but certain peculiarities, the effect of which is to break down the distinction between the reformed service of the Church of England and the unreformed service of the Church of Rome.'

If it had been left to Tait and the churchwardens, matters would no doubt have rambled on in a spirit of uneasy compromise – at the beginning of 1867 Mackonochie was even agreeing to modify the ritual at St Alban's. But there was a more formidable opponent waiting to pounce. This was the Church Association, a body launched in 1865 to fight Ritualism by stirring up litigation, prosecuting unco-operative incumbents and supplying the necessary funds to meet the expenses of going to law – or, in Mackonochie's own words, 'an irresponsible Society formed with the object of forcing upon the Church of England one particular form of opinion not easily reconciled with her own Prayer Book.' The Association launched its initial attack on St Alban's in February 1867. Its object was to obtain a definite legal decision on various disputed points of Church law. The Association needed to find a suitable individual to 'promote' the suit, since an organization was not permitted to do so. The churchwardens, although disapproving of Mackonochie's ritualism, were unwilling to carry their disapproval to the point of a legal prosecution; and there was some difficulty in discovering a suitable alternative agent. The man eventually chosen was a solicitor named John Martin, who lived in Bloomsbury and practised in Lincoln's Inn but whose name stood on the ratebook of St Alban's as the secretary of a school within the parish boundaries.

Martin was a wealthy bachelor keenly interested in ecclesiastical matters, to which he was able to devote a great deal of his time. Although in Anglo-Catholic circles he was denounced as the villain of the piece, he was not quite so bad as his detractors made out – and indeed was no doubt as much motivated by conscience as was Mackonochie himself. According to his own account he agreed to lead the prosecution against his own inclinations: 'The then Bishop of London considered that I was more suited to be Promoter of the suit than the resident parishioner whose name had been submitted to his Lordship on the sudden death of the first Promoter. I personally should not have moved, and was reluctant to give my consent.' Although Martin may have seemed vindictive in continuing to hound Mackonochie over so long a period of time, his better nature showed through on at least two occasions. The first was when he temporarily withdrew from the case on realizing that a successful outcome (for him) might result in Mackonochie's going to gaol. The second was when he was seriously ill and the priest had sent him a message of sympathy. Though he declined the offer of a visit Martin wrote: 'I never entertained any unkind feeling personally towards yourself. I thank you sincerely for your kind sympathy and for your prayers.' His basic quarrel was with the sin of Ritualism rather than with the sinner.

On 28 March 1867 Tait referred the suit of Martin v. Mackonochie to the Court of Arches under the Church Discipline Act of 1840. The hearing formally began on 21 May, though it was not until 4 December that it really got into its stride. This was mainly because the eighty-five-year-old Dean of the Arches, Stephen Lushington, resigned at the end of July and a successor had to be appointed. Lushington, a notorious anti-ritualist, would probably have found Mackonochie guilty on all counts. His successor, Sir Robert Phillimore, who had already appeared as Counsel for Mackonochie in the earlier stages of the trial, would, it was hoped, prove more accommodating. The hopes were to some extent justified. The charges against Mackonochie were: (1) elevation of the paten and chalice to a greater height than was permitted under the Prayer Book rubric; (2) 'excessive kneeling' during the prayer of consecration; (3) using lighted candles on the altar for purposes other than giving light; (4) ceremonial use of incense; (5) mixing water with the wine in the chalice. The case occupied twelve days, the Dean assuring the Court at the start that there was 'no hurry at all'. He pointed out that these cases required an immense amount of documentary evidence. The many authorities cited ranged from Tertullian to Cranmer, from Queen Elizabeth to the Council of Trent. The atmosphere in court is said to have been tranquil and friendly, like that of a 'family party'. The leisurely proceedings (which had been interrupted by a Christmas recess of over a month) finally ended on 18 January 1868; but it was not until 28 March, ten weeks later, that Phillimore delivered his judgment. This covered seventy-six printed pages and took over four hours to deliver. It ruled (with one or two qualifications) against the ceremonial use of incense, the mixed chalice and the excessive elevation of the paten and chalice, but in favour of altar lights and kneeling during the prayer of consecration. No order was made as to costs – which meant that each side would have to pay its own.

Neither side was completely satisfied with the Dean's verdict. The *Church Times* was mystified by the 'complacent satisfaction professed by the ravening Puritans of the Church Association', since, the paper claimed, 'upon only one point [i.e., elevation] have they gained an absolute victory'. In fact the Association was so far from being satisfied that it persuaded Martin to appeal to the Judicial Committee of the Privy Council against the judgment on altar lights, permission to kneel during the prayer of consecration and the disallowance of costs. The case was argued before the Judicial Committee from 17 to 20 November 1868, the court consisting of the Lord Chancellor, Lord Cairns; two former Lord Chancellors; two ex-judges; and Archbishop Thomson of York. It was claimed that Cairns, a member of Disraeli's tottering administration and an anti-ritualist, had had the case moved from the bottom to the top of the list to make sure that he heard it before the Government fell and he lost his job. On 23 December he pronounced the Committee's judgment, which ruled against Mackonochie on all three points – and also required him to pay the costs of the appeal as well as those of the original suit. His supporters were outraged. The *Church Times* thought that the judgment 'merits everything that can be said to the discredit of the learned pundits by whom it was pronounced' and that it involved a 'wilful denial of justice'. The Church Association was naturally elated: 'The principles of the Church of England and Ireland have been vindicated.' But the judgment caused a certain amount of unease among moderate-minded churchpeople. Its veto on altar lights appeared to contradict previous court decisions; its arguments about standing rather than kneeling before the altar unintentionally regularized the controversial eastward position; and its ruling on costs seemed an unnecessarily harsh burden which Mackonochie might well find crippling. Nevertheless, after agonizing on the subject for a month, he told his congregation on 24 January that he would obey the monition (with which he had been served five days earlier) admonishing him to abstain from all the practices which had been held to be unlawful. While disagreeing with the Judicial Committee's claim to either spiritual or constitutional authority, he felt that, having appeared before it, he had no choice but to obey its orders. Round one of Martin v. Mackonochie appeared to have ended in victory for the Protestant faction – on a technical knock-out.

*   *   *

Appearances were deceptive. Round two consisted of successive attempts by the Church Association to compel Mackonochie to abide by the terms of the monition. The first was inconclusive. The second ended with his suspension for three months – a victory for the opposition, you might say, on points.

Mackonochie had announced his intention of obeying the monition. The Church Association, however, was unimpressed. On 2 December 1869, again using Martin as its agent, it lodged a complaint against Mackonochie before the Judicial Committee of the Privy Council. The complaint – which was backed up by the testimony of paid informers – alleged that he had disobeyed the monition by continuing to elevate the chalice and paten excessively, by using lighted candles on the altar, and by kneeling and prostrating himself during the prayer of consecration. Mackonochie conducted his own defence.

It was at this point that he was able to display his Scottish love of logical coherence. To him there was no such thing as a 'distinction without a difference'. In the words of George Russell:

> If he might not elevate the paten above his head, he would elevate it to his chin. If he might not prostrate himself, he would genuflect; if he might not genuflect, he would bow. If he might not have two candles on the Altar, he would have seven lamps above it.

In other words, he based his defence on a literal obedience to the law. On the charge of elevation, he insisted that he was not now elevating the paten or chalice any higher than the Prayer Book rubric permitted. On the charge of altar lights, he claimed that the candles were no longer used at the times prohibited. It was when he came to the charge of kneeling or prostration that he must really have enjoyed himself. In a written affidavit he pointed out that he was accustomed 'reverently to bend one knee at certain parts of the said prayer, and occasionally in so doing my knee momentarily touches the ground, but such touching of the ground is no part of the act of reverence intended by me'. The members of the Judicial Committee were unable to go all the way with Mackonochie's Scots logic. They grudgingly conceded that, in regard to elevation and lights, he had complied literally with the terms of the monition; and they therefore acquitted him on these two charges. But they refused to accept that his defence on the 'kneeling' charge was valid in either the letter or the spirit. It was, to them, a distinction without a difference. On 4 December he was admonished to abstain in future from either kneeling or genuflecting at that point in the service – and was condemned to pay the costs of the suit. Many of the secular papers amused themselves at his expense, the *Daily Telegraph* even breaking into verse on the subject of the 'Merry Manoeuvres of Mr. Mackonochie':

> Mackonochie! Thy words, I trow,
> Will crimson many an English brow,
> And honest cheeks will flush with shame
> At very mention of thy name!
> In such poor wretched, quibbling sense
> Dost thou explain *Obedience*?
> And God's pure worship dare to mix
> With despicable, Jesuit tricks?

One might have supposed that the Church Association would have been satisfied with a judgment which, if not totally con-demnatory of Mackonochie, at least constituted (in the words of *The Times*) a 'severe moral rebuke'. Not so. Its blood was up, and it was determined on obtaining its full pound of flesh. Ten days after the judgment had been delivered it again sent spies to St Alban's and, on the basis of their report, complained to the Privy Council (through Martin) that Mackonochie was again evading the terms of the original monition – this time by getting others to perform acts (e.g., excessive elevation, and kneeling or prostration) which he was forbidden to perform himself. The Committee took its time; and it was not until 16 November 1870 that the new hearing took place. Affidavits had been filed describing allegedly illegal acts carried out by the officiating clergy at St Alban's, and witnessed by the informers, on seven Sundays in December 1869 and January and February 1870; a further affidavit related to an alleged offence by Mackonochie himself on 17 June. Rival affidavits by the defence denied the charges and accused the informers of grave misconduct in church.

Mackonochie was again unrepresented, but was examined orally by Martin's Counsel. He claimed that he had told his curates that he intended to obey the monition, but did not recall instructing *them* to do so; that he had never practised the forbidden elevation since 1866; that he had told his curates that there was henceforth to be no genuflection during the prayer of consecration; and that he himself intended to bow instead of kneeling. In a key sentence which appears to have annoyed the judges he remarked: 'My object was to see how far I could obey the law of the Church without disobeying the law of the State.' In the end the judges preferred the evidence of the informers to that of the clergy. They ruled that Mackonochie had not complied with the terms of the monition in respect of elevation or genuflection; and that the low bow which he had substituted for the latter was a 'humble prostration of the body in reverence' and was therefore unacceptable. They rebuked him for attempting to satisfy his conscience by sheltering himself under the 'narrowest literal obedience to lawful authority'. They ordered not only that he should pay all the costs of the case, but also that he should be suspended from the performance of his clerical duties and offices for a period of three months. The total costs falling on Mackonochie – for the original suit in the Court of Arches, the appeal to the Privy Council and the subsequent proceedings (including payments to the Church Association's spies) – now amounted to £4048, a formidable sum by the values of those days and far beyond the resources of an impecunious parish priest. But, in the eyes of his supporters, the suspension was even worse. On the Sunday following the delivery of the judgment Stanton preached an impassioned sermon in St Alban's based on the text of the Privy Council judgment and ending in a flurry of rhetoric:

> It is the crowning honour of a Priest of Jesus Christ to suffer for his Master's sake. You will not hear the voice of your beloved Vicar for three months, but, as he sits in his stall, his silence will speak more powerfully than the rarest eloquence. . . . We are not only one in faith, but one in suffering also.

Mackonochie summarized his own feelings in an immensely long letter to *The Record*, an Evangelical journal, which it published in its issue of 6 December. He ended by saying that he accepted his suspension as 'purely and simply a legal compulsion', but added: 'I do not for a moment accept it as depriving me of privileges, or releasing me from duties, which God has enjoined upon me as a Priest, and from which He alone can release me.' In spite of the ambiguity underlying these last words (which implied the possibility of his celebrating the Eucharist in private), the period of his suspension passed without incident. The services were conducted by his curates; and, at the end of the three months, Mackonochie took up the reins again and carried on precisely as before.

*   *   *

One must not give the impression that the legal harassment of Mackonochie by the Church Association occupied all his working moments. The actual hours he had to spend in court were comparatively few, though of course the necessary legal preliminaries must have taken up a certain amount of his time, quite apart from the emotional distress they caused him. But, when not organizing his defence against his opponents, he continued to run his parish on the lines he had learned at Wantage and to ensure that St Alban's remained in the forefront of London's ritualistic churches. There were long periods of comparative tranquillity; and the years 1871, 1872 and 1873 were years of more or less uninterrupted peace.

Round three in the battle of Martin v. Mackonochie began in

the early spring of 1874. At the annual meeting of the Church Association on 27 March its chairman announced that a fresh suit was to be instituted against Mackonochie – the 'great offender' among the ritualists. The suit would not only renew all the Association's former complaints, but would also include the question 'whether Mr. Mackonochie is right in erecting in his church a confessional, and giving notice of the times and seasons at which confessions are to be received'. The proceedings were again taken under the Church Discipline Act. The Public Worship Regulation Act, which was to replace it, was not passed until the summer of 1874, and was therefore not yet available to the prosecution.

Up to 1869 confessions at St Alban's had been heard in church at fixed hours, each priest choosing a seat before which the penitent would kneel, screened by curtains from curious onlookers. On the advice of the Bishop of London, John Jackson (who had succeeded Tait in 1868 on the latter's appointment as Archbishop of Canterbury), Mackonochie took a little of the wind from the Church Association's sails by removing all the curtains. As a result, when Martin, on behalf of the Association, applied to Jackson for 'letters of request' with which to launch the planned prosecution, the bishop ruled that there was no longer any ground on which to prosecute Mackonochie for having set up a confessional. However, he accepted all the other points made by Martin as valid grounds for a prosecution – namely, lighted candles during Morning Prayer; undue elevation of the paten and chalice; processions with banners, crucifix and candles; singing the *Agnus Dei*; making the sign of the cross; kissing the Prayer Book; wafer-bread; vestments; and the east-ward position. The case was conducted before Sir Robert Phillimore in the Court of Arches, though the two-day hearing only began on 26 November. Mackonochie appeared under protest but was this time represented, among his Counsel being Walter Phillimore, Sir Robert's only son. The judge was unmoved by his son's eloquence. Indeed most of the offences alleged against Mackonochie had already been declared illegal either by the Dean of the Arches himself or by the Privy Coun-cil, so the result was only too foreseeable. In a reserved judgment

delivered on 7 December 1874 Phillimore senior found
Mackonochie guilty on all but one of the counts (undue elevation)* and suspended him for six weeks. He also ordered him
to pay the costs of the action.

Mackonochie at first gave notice of appeal, but later withdrew
his application when he realized that the appeal would go not
(as he had at first supposed) to a new court consisting entirely
of lay judges but to the Judicial Committee of the Privy Council
as before. In a letter to Tait, his fellow-Scot and ex-diocesan,
explaining the reasons for his change of mind, he ended with an
emotional outburst against the Church authorities:

> With the very rarest exceptions, I have received not one word
> of encouragement from my superiors in the Church. I have
> now been four times dragged before Courts: I have stood in
> Court side by side as a fellow-culprit with a Clerk charged
> with adultery:† I have found in the Highest Court of Appeal
> every door for his escape obsequiously held open, and the one
> door of justice and equity as vigorously barred by the same
> hands against me. I do not, your Grace, complain, but venture
> to state facts.

Tait also had to endure a barrage of complaints from the
parishioners of St Alban's. There was a formal protest sent on
behalf of a committee of church members which attempted to
argue the legal toss with the Archbishop and which remarked,
inter alia, that Martin, the nominal prosecutor of Mackonochie,
had no moral claim to interfere: he had never been a worshipper
at St Alban's or contributed a penny towards its expenses.
Mackonochie, on the other hand, whose blameless character was
undisputed even by his chief opponents and whose pastoral
diligence had won high commendation, had been singled out

---

*He mitigated his judgment on another point by ruling that, though it was unlawful
for the celebrant at Holy Communion to make the sign of the cross in the air, it
was not unlawful for him to cross himself, this being an act of personal rather than
priestly devotion.
†This was a reference to the case of a priest who had been suspended from his living
by the Dean of the Arches for committing adultery with his cook and taking liberties
with his housemaid.

for repeated prosecution for what, at the worst, was 'over-zeal for the beauty and order of divine worship'. Tait was also persuaded to receive a deputation from among the working men of the parish. At the end of the meeting he remarked hopefully: 'Of course this will not be made public.' The secretary of the group replied that they had nothing to fear from publicity and intended to publish a full account. The Archbishop was most put out and complained: 'But this is like coming into a gentleman's house, having a private conversation and then publishing it.' The secretary was unrepentant – and a full report of the meeting duly appeared in the *Church Times*.

Meanwhile the sentence of suspension had taken effect from Sunday, 15 June 1875. To save possible embarrassment Mackonochie had gone off on holiday to Italy, leaving Stanton in charge of the parish. The services continued as before, with undiminished ceremonial, until Jackson summoned Stanton to London House and insisted that he must conduct the services in accordance with the terms of the Purchas Judgment (i.e., no vestment except a surplice; north-end position; ordinary bread). Stanton's reaction was to post an announcement on the doors of the church to the effect that 'There will be no celebration of Holy Communion in this church until further notice.' The following Sunday, 27 June, he mounted the pulpit and, after explaining the situation, invited the congregation to accompany him to the church of St Vedast, Foster Lane, where they were able to take part in a celebration of the Eucharist. There was a great outcry in the press, and Jackson was induced to prohibit the clergy of St Alban's from officiating at any church in his diocese where ritualistic illegalities took place. Stanton thereupon suggested that members of the congregation should attend Holy Communion in St Paul's Cathedral, which many did. Mackonochie, from his Italian retreat, wrote to congratulate his flock on their steadfastness. 'Be sure that you do not lose, wilfully, one Communion or miss hearing Mass on one Sunday without absolute necessity, on account of this sad trouble which has come upon you.'

* * *

The final round of Martin v. Mackonochie was a protracted one, spanning the five-year period 1878–1883. Although there were long intervals of uneasy calm, there must have been throughout this period a feeling of underlying insecurity for the harassed Mackonochie as he wondered what tricks the opposition would get up to next. In the end he seemed to have lost everything – but, in the eyes of many (and not only his close supporters), he had won a moral victory.

The round began with a belated attempt by the Church Association, as usual acting through the accommodating John Martin, to compel Mackonochie to obey the terms of Sir Robert Phillimore's judgment of December 1874. On 23 March 1878 Martin applied to Phillimore's successor, Lord Penzance, to enforce that judgment. Penzance was judge of the new court set up under the Public Worship Regulation Act (see introductory chapter); but, as the application was a continuation of the old suit brought under the Church Discipline Act, he was sitting in his capacity as Dean of the Arches. The prosecution alleged that Mackonochie was continuing to perform ritual acts pronounced illegal by Phillimore; it supported its claim by sworn affidavits. Penzance agreed that Mackonochie was guilty, but felt that it was a bit late in the day for Martin to have mounted this new assault. He therefore declined to pronounce a fresh sentence on the spot, but instead gave the erring cleric an eleventh-hour chance to repent by conforming his practice to the ruling of 1874. But he ordered Mackonochie to pay the costs of an application which he had in effect dismissed.

Mackonochie did nothing; and on 11 May Martin renewed his application, again supporting it with the necessary affidavits. The eleventh hour having passed without any signs of repentance on the part of Mackonochie, Penzance decided that a stiff sentence was needed – and accordingly suspended him from his office and benefice for a period of three years. Mackonochie was stirred into action and, on his lawyer's advice, sought redress from the secular courts by appealing to the Queen's Bench Division against the sentence of suspension. Penzance had based his sentence on the technical ground that the monition appended to Phillimore's 1874 judgment was of the nature of a perpetual injunction, so that any breach of it constituted a continuation of the original offence and could therefore be dealt with under that judgment. Mackonochie's Counsel argued that the suspension represented a punishment for contempt of court – and that no clergyman could be deprived of his freehold, even temporarily, for that offence. By a majority of two to one the judges upheld Mackonochie and granted him a writ of prohibition against the sentence. But his triumph was short-lived. Martin took the case to the Court of Appeal, which, by a majority of three to two, overturned the Queen's Bench verdict. Their judgment was delivered on 28 June 1879; but it was another four and a half months before Penzance again pronounced the three-year period of suspension. This was to take effect on 23 November, exactly one year and eight months after Martin's original application. The grinding of the wheels of law, then as now, was a leisurely business.

At this point a certain air of theatricality, even light-heartedness, enters into the proceedings. Mackonochie was in theory about to be suspended from his living; but neither he nor the ecclesiastical authorities appeared to think that the suspension would be anything but an empty formality. However, the outward ceremonies had to be observed; and Bishop Jackson duly gave notice that his domestic chaplain, W. M. Sinclair (later Archdeacon of London), would present himself at the church on the 23rd (a Sunday), prepared to conduct the services. Mackonochie wrote to a friend: 'The Bishop and I have through his secretary made an amicable arrangement. His chaplain will come down attended by the secretary. He will exhibit the Bishop's licence. I shall read and deliver to him my grounds for not accepting him, and they will go.' So matters fell out. After Mackonochie had read out his prepared statement Sinclair duly announced his discovery that he was not after all to take the service, though perfectly ready to do so. Mackonochie replied, 'Distinctly so'; and the confrontation, 'conducted with courtesy on each side', came to an end. Describing the scene in a letter to a friend, Mackonochie observed: 'The church was crowded. . . . Everything perfectly orderly; two Nonconformist Ministers of eminence quite delighted. A few enemies, but perfect order. One so far forgot himself as to genuflect at the Incarnatus.'

But, if the bishop was content with a mere pretence at attempting to enforce the suspension, others were not so easily satisfied. The Church Association was still determined that the law was not to be flouted in this way and its arch-enemy escape his just deserts. It determined on moving to have him imprisoned (under a statute of George III) for contempt of court. Unfortunately its hitherto obedient instrument, John Martin, turned in its hand. He declined categorically to move in the matter if the net result was to land Mackonochie in gaol. As he later told the Bishop of London: 'It never occurred to me, nor, I suppose, to anyone else, that the judgments of the courts of law could be set at defiance, and that obedience could only be enforced by imprisonment. Had such a result been foreseen, I should not have allowed my name to be used as promoter.' The Association had to think again. Its solution was to institute a new suit against Mackonochie under the Church Discipline Act, with the object of depriving him of his benefice for his continuing disobedience to the law. Martin agreed to co-operate, and a court hearing was fixed for 10 April 1880.

Penzance delivered his reserved judgment on 5 June – and dashed the Church Association's hopes. His reason for dismissing the suit was Martin's failure to enforce the previous sentence of suspension. Mackonochie might have treated a 'solemn decree of this Court' with contempt, but the promoter of the suit had treated it with indifference. The judge therefore declined to pronounce a second sentence of a different kind, deprivation, while his previous sentence, suspension, remained inactive. He granted leave to appeal to the Privy Council; but the Church Association at first concluded that an appeal would be surrounded by so many dangers that there was no reasonable prospect of obtaining a satisfactory result. What caused the Association to change its mind was the result of Mackonochie's own belated decision to appeal to the House of Lords against the judgment of the Court of Appeal of June 1879. He had been reluctantly driven to take this step, first, by the Church Association's insistence that he should pay their entire expenses bill; and, secondly, by the Bishop of London's sequestration of his living for three years. Jackson had in effect done the very thing which Penzance had censured Martin for *not* doing, namely, enforcing the three-year period of suspension pronounced in November 1879. But the effect of the bishop's act was to deprive Mackonochie of his annual stipend of £150, which was 'sequestered' (or impounded) for the benefit of his eventual successor. The *Church Times* castigated Jackson's action as 'thoroughly mean, paltry, and disreputable'.

Mackonochie's appeal – which, with the benefit of hindsight, was ill-advised – came before the Lords in February 1881. In a reserved judgment delivered in April the Appeals Committee dismissed the appeal with costs, reaffirming the three-year sentence of suspension. The news of Mackonochie's reverse put fresh heart into the Church Association; and, scenting final triumph, it decided after all to appeal to the Privy Council against Penzance's judgment of June 1880, which had declined to sentence Mackonochie to deprivation. After the usual time-lag the appeal came in February 1882 before the Judicial Committee, which reversed Penzance's judgment. The case was sent back to him for 'such canonical censure or punishment as to the Court shall seem just'. The unfortunate Mackonochie was summoned to appear before him on 29 July, though, owing to Penzance's difficulty in finding a suitable court in which to sit, the appearance had to be postponed till much later in the year. Before it could take place, the situation had been transformed by the dramatic intervention of Archbishop Tait.

In the autumn of 1882 the Primate lay dying in his sickbed at Addington Palace. Though he had played no small part in making things difficult for the ritualists, he had qualms of conscience at this late stage of his life about the fate of the most illustrious of their number. He realized that, when Mackonochie next appeared before Penzance, he would inevitably be deprived of his living. There was no further avenue of escape, legal or otherwise, down which the vicar of St Alban's could wriggle. This really was the end of the road. Tait felt that, before he died, he must somehow see if he could resolve the impasse. His solution was to mastermind an exchange of livings between the vicar of St Alban's and another ritualist incumbent in the diocese of London, so as to remove Mackonochie from the jurisdiction of the courts which he had defied for so long. It was thought (wrongly, as it turned out) that, if the Church Association wanted to pursue its vendetta against Mackonochie, it would have to start again from scratch by prosecuting him – and would shrink from such a prospect. Officially it was Bishop Jackson who had to give his consent to an exchange of livings, but it was Tait who actually pulled the strings. He pressed Penzance to delay in bringing Mackonochie to book, on the ground that the case was likely to be withdrawn from his jurisdiction; and he did all in his power to hasten an exchange of livings.

At first Mackonochie was reluctant to play ball. It may be that he hesitated to succumb to what might have appeared as a piece of moral blackmail on the part of the Archbishop, who was advertised by his chaplain, Randall Davidson, as being anxious to heal this particular quarrel before he died. Eventually, however, he agreed to meet Tait's wishes. The Archbishop had written originally from Addington on 10 November 1882. 'I need not assure you', he had observed, 'that I do not wish in any way to dictate to you a course of action; but if you feel it possible, consistently with duty, to withdraw voluntarily, by resignation of your benefice, from further conflict with the Courts, I am quite sure you would be acting in the manner best calculated to promote the real power and usefulness of the Church to which we belong.' Mackonochie acknowledged the letter at once, begging for a little time 'for earnest seeking after the guidance of Almighty God', but promising a definite answer 'with as little delay as possible'. However, as day followed day at Addington with no letter from Mackonochie in the Archbishop's post-bag, Davidson grew anxious. He wrote on the 21st to point out that the doctors had by now almost abandoned hope of Tait's recovery, but that, 'among the very few matters concerning the outside world which at present find a recurring place in his [the Archbishop's] thoughts', was the matter of the resignation. By now Mackonochie had been invited to exchange livings with the vicar of St Peter's, London Docks, and his agonizings were almost at an end. On 23 November he wrote to a friend:

The illness of the Archbishop and the tone of his letter as if from his grave has certainly weighed mostly with me; which perhaps is hardly right, as even the most pressing personal considerations have to give way before the public interests of the Church. However, I suppose I have determined to comply with the Archbishop's request. It seems to be God's will. I do believe I am quite indifferent personally . . .

Later that day he wrote to the Archbishop himself:

The conclusion at which I have arrived is to acquiesce in your Grace's wish that I should resign my benefice . . . I accept the line of action which your Grace has indicated, simply in deference to you as supreme representative of Our Lord Jesus Christ in all things spiritual in this land; and not as withdrawing anything which I have said or done in regard to [the State] Courts. This I cannot agree to in any way whatever.

Davidson's relief was profound. He at once wrote to Mackonochie to tell him with 'how strong a feeling of thankfulness to God' the Archbishop had received the news of his agreement to resign. 'It will, I feel sure, be a satisfaction to you to know what pleasure your letter has brought to the Archbishop in these his last days, as it would seem, upon earth.' In a letter Tait himself wrote (or caused to have written) the same day to the Bishop of London he assured Jackson that he had 'in no way committed you by the action I have thought it well to take in the interests of peace' – but of course he had. He added unctuously: 'It seems to me that [Mackonochie] has in this case shown his consideration for the highest interests of the Church by sacrificing his individual feelings in deference to my appeal.' Mackonochie's final letter to Tait, telling him of his formal resignation of St Alban's and of his probable nomination to St Peter's, London Docks, arrived too late for its recipient to take conscious note of it. Only a few hours after its arrival he was dead.

When the news of Mackonochie's resignation broke, the newspapers vied with each other in piling praises on the head of the departed Primate. The *Church Times*, for long the cham-

pion of the former and scourge of the latter, said that the late
Archbishop must have possessed some great qualities 'to have
triumphed so completely over the prejudices and prepossessions
of his whole life'. His death-bed letter, the paper declared, had
been a solemn renunciation of, and apology for, the notions
which he had embodied in the Public Worship Regulation Act.
The long siege of St Alban's by the forces of barbarism had
collapsed thanks to the work of the late Primate and of the
Bishop of London, and the St Alban's lawsuit was as dead and
buried as the Heptarchy. The universal paean of praise for Tait
seems overdone to a more cynical modern generation, as the
element of moral blackmail seems to us only too obvious. A
modern historian, Michael Reynolds, thinks that there was a
touch of 'cool cheek' in Tait's handling of the Mackonochie
affair:

> Here is a man who starts a war, an aggressive war, and carries
> it on – or, at any rate, encourages others to carry it on – with
> the utmost ferocity for a great many years, until in the end he
> becomes frightened and disgusted by the havoc and misery he
> has caused. He then begins to clamour for peace . . . at the
> expense of the other side. He makes no concessions; there is
> no generous peace treaty; the yet undefeated enemy is required
> to lay down his arms in unconditional surrender, and he is
> asked to do so for the sake of peace. Whose peace? The
> Church's, or the Archbishop's? . . .

But Reynolds later softens his strictures on Tait by admitting
that, whatever his motives, he is entitled to a place with
Mackonochie among the peacemakers: 'On reflection, I have to
admit that his appeal to Mackonochie, however cruel in its
personal application, showed a statesmanlike concern for the
general good.' Randall Davidson and William Benham, in their
massive biography of Tait, attempt to put the whole matter in
perspective when they remark that he was always anxious to
relegate the Ritual Controversy 'to the comparatively insignifi-
cant place which he thought to belong to it, in face of the great
problems of faith and morals which were claiming the attention
of the Christian Church'. They add that his priorities through-

out the controversy were, first, the promotion of peace within the Church to enable it the better to face such problems and, secondly, the recognition of the supreme authority of law and order in sacred as well as in secular matters. 'If the latter of these principles was the more obvious throughout his active public years, it was the former which inspired him in the characteristic episode of his last days on earth, the well-known correspondence with Mr Mackonochie.'

*   *   *

What does seem astonishing with the benefit of hindsight is the almost universal belief that the exchange of livings between Mackonochie and the vicar of St Peter's, London Docks, Robert Suckling, really would solve everything. It was widely imagined that for the Church Association to prise Mackonochie from his new cure would require it to institute an entirely new lawsuit – which would be impossible without the consent of the Bishop of London. As the *Church Times* put it:

> There is not the slightest likelihood of its being granted for any such purpose, because not only have the Bishops generally become thoroughly disgusted with the tactics of the litigating Company [i.e., the Church Association], but to permit the revival of the persecution in this particular case would be to defeat the intentions of the late Primate, so definitely expressed in his letter, and to be guilty of a breach of faith towards Mr. Mackonochie himself which it would be difficult to suppose any gentleman, much less any Christian prelate, capable of committing.'

Alas for the paper's pious hopes! The Church Association was made of sterner stuff, and was not to be deterred by such gentlemanly scruples as were likely to animate the 'Christian prelates' seated on the English bench. It was soon advised by its lawyers that there was a good chance of ousting Mackonochie from his new cure *without* having to go back to square one.

Meanwhile the man at the centre of the storm had been instituted at St Peter's – the scene of his former labours under Lowder – on 11 December 1882, four days after Suckling's

institution at St Alban's.* But the year which he was now to
spend in Wapping was to bring him nothing of the satisfaction
which had characterized his earlier tour of duty in the district.
Indeed, according to Mrs Towle, it was 'probably the saddest
year of his life'. This was due to a variety of reasons. He was
twenty years older, and in failing health. He was separated both
from his former parishioners and from his former colleagues,
especially Stanton and Russell, whose companionship he sorely
missed. He was in a strange environment, outwardly similar to
Holborn but unredeemed by the close sense of familiarity he
had experienced in his former parish. He had personally to
attend to a great deal of more or less routine work, such as
accounts and parochial relief, which others at St Alban's had
taken off his shoulders. As Mrs Towle puts it, 'amongst comparative strangers he was again to enter a hand-to-hand struggle
from which no great or cheering results could be confidently
anticipated by a man whose expectations would necessarily be
based upon past experience'. But of course it was the prospect
of a fresh prosecution at the hands of the relentless Church
Association that was to weigh most heavily on him during his
year at St Peter's. The Association was still out for his blood –
and waited only a short while before it pounced.

On 12 April 1883, acting as usual through John Martin, it
applied to the court set up under the Public Worship Regulation
Act for sentence of canonical censure or punishment to be passed
on Mackonochie – in accordance with the directive to Lord
Penzance given by the Judicial Committee of the Privy Council
in February 1882. Penzance, it will be recalled, had never got
round to carrying out that directive: first because of his inability
to find a courtroom in which to sit, and secondly in deference
to the appeal for delay from the dying Archbishop Tait. He
now heard Martin's application in a tiny room at the House of
Lords. The nub of the prosecution's case was that Mackonochie's

---

*Mackonochie spent his Christmas at St Alban's, preaching his farewell sermon at
Evensong on Sunday, 7 January 1883. He began work at St Peter's in mid-January.
His former parishioners raised £1500 towards a testimonial. But, to prevent the
generous Mackonochie giving the money away, they invested it in an annuity
bringing in about £80 a year,

exchange of livings made absolutely no difference to the situation. Martin's counsel pointed out that the original petition against Mackonochie in the 1880 suit had been that he should be deprived not merely of the living of St Alban's but of 'all his ecclesiastical promotions within the Province of Canterbury'. Martin now sought not so much his deprivation (the original plea) as his indefinite inhibition until he gave an undertaking to refrain from his illegal practices. Penzance took the main point, and agreed that the change of benefice made no difference to the situation. Martin's counsel had favoured inhibition rather than deprivation because it sounded less harsh and would give the erring cleric a chance to repent of his disobedience and do as required. Penzance, on the other hand, thought this argument mealy-mouthed. He said that it went against common sense to leave a man in possession of a benefice and yet perpetually to inhibit him from performing the duties that belonged to it. Pronouncing sentence on 21 July 1883, he therefore both deprived Mackonochie of his new benefice of St Peter's and forbade him to officiate in any other church in the Province of Canterbury without a written licence from the bishop of the diocese. The fickle press by and large considered this an inevitable solution. Only the *Church Times* thought otherwise. It suggested that, if Penzance had felt bound to inflict *some* penalty on Mackonochie, he should have made it a nominal one, 'on the ground that the party aggrieved by Mr. Mackonochie's proceedings at Holborn [i.e., Martin] had received complete redress in his surrender of the living'.

Events now moved inexorably towards their sad conclusion. Bishop Jackson issued a writ of sequestration and appointed the churchwardens of St Peter's as receivers of the income of the benefice while it remained vacant. In view of his role as Tait's understudy the previous year in easing Mackonochie out of St Alban's he took this new step with obvious reluctance, and only under extreme pressure from the Church Association. But it was the death-blow as far as Mackonochie was concerned. Although he stayed on till the end of the year, he realized that he would have to go. The loss of the £420-a-year endowment of St Peter's under the sequestration order would soon cripple the parish financially. Moreover, after six months, the patronage of the living would automatically pass to the bishop; and there was no guarantee that either Jackson or his successor would necessarily maintain the church's Catholic tradition. The other bishops might wring their hands at the thought of Tait's dying attempt at peacemaking being thwarted in this way, but there was nothing they could do in the face of Mackonochie's relentless opponents. The ever-diplomatic Davidson was among the first to write a letter of sympathy, this time on behalf of the new Archbishop of Canterbury, E. W. Benson. 'He [the Archbishop] deeply regrets to hear that an endeavour is being made to impugn the action taken with such good intention respecting your resignation of St Alban's a few months ago. He prays that you may be given a right judgment in all things . . .' The right judgment was no doubt aided by Mackonochie's friends, notably Charles Wood, the future Viscount Halifax. 'If you gave up St Peter's *now*', wrote Wood, 'you can save . . . patrons and parish from another conflict which must certainly be disastrous to them, release the 300*l.* a year [*sic*] for the purposes of the parish of which it is now deprived, and, except for the fact that they will have succeeded in persecuting you personally, emphasise the real defeat of the enemy.' Quite *how* Mackonochie's resignation would 'emphasise the real defeat of the enemy' the president of the English Church Union did not explain. But Mackonochie took his advice and that of almost all his other friends and, on 23 December, submitted his resignation to the bishop. He drew attention in his letter to the perseverance with which 'some other persons' had striven to disturb the peacemaking efforts of the late Archbishop Tait. 'It seems that there is little hope of this opposition – now become simply personal against myself – being abandoned by them.' In a letter sent to the daily papers to announce his resignation he said that he had been forced by the logic of facts 'to see that I ought not any longer to impoverish a parish too impoverished already by its own circumstances by keeping from it the income which is due to it from the Ecclesiastical Commissioners'. The announcement of his decision to bow out appeared in the morning papers of New Year's Day, 1884.

*   *   *

The last four years of Mackonochie's life provided a forlorn
postscript to his strenuous ministry of the past. With the good
will of his successor, Suckling, he returned to his old rooms in
the clergy-house at St Alban's and used them as a base for an
itinerant free-lance ministry. On the surface all went well. Suckling
showed not the slightest jealousy of his famous predecessor,
who was content to play an entirely subordinate role in the
affairs of his former parish. But the fire had gone out of him.
Though still under sixty when he had resigned St Peter's, he
was ageing rapidly and his health was not good. In particular,
he showed himself less and less capable of any sustained mental
effort. He found difficulty in putting his ideas into words or in
arranging his thoughts in a connected sequence. In letters to
friends he speaks of being in a mental fog and 'out in the bush
intellectually'. He rarely preached or heard confessions after
1885, and celebrated the Eucharist only on special occasions.
But he was not unhappy and enjoyed the company of his friends.
Notable among these was the Bishop of Argyll and the Isles,
Alexander Chinnery-Haldane, in whose hospitable house at
Ballachulish he was a frequent guest. He also spent much time
with his brother and sister-in-law in their home at Wantage,
where he enjoyed picking up the old threads of his former
curacy. There were still plenty of people around who remembered young Mr Mackonochie and enjoyed meeting him again
after all these years.

The end came suddenly and unexpectedly in December 1887.
On the 10th he arrived at Ballachulish after a three-week stay
in Edinburgh. The bishop was away from home on a round of
pastoral visits, but Mrs Chinnery-Haldane was there to welcome
her guest. He seemed in excellent health and spirits, and anxious
to take some long walks amid the superb Highland scenery. On
Wednesday the 14th he made for the head of Loch Leven, but
did not quite reach his destination; so the next day he set out
to complete the trip. He took a picnic lunch and was
accompanied by the bishop's two dogs, a massive deerhound
and a tiny Skye terrier, who were both devoted to him. When

night fell and he had not yet returned home, concern began to be felt for his safety. The bishop had arrived back from his travels that afternoon and, taking a carriage and pair, scoured the neighbourhood throughout the night without success. On the Friday three parties were organized to search the hills on all sides, but again without result. Two further search parties were now beginning to talk only about finding 'the body'. The parties stumbled about for hours over rocks and ice, and sometimes through deep snow, in a pitch darkness relieved only by the light of their lanterns. Again the search was fruitless. On Saturday morning the bishop set off again with a crowd of men and dogs. They followed the track up into the deer forest of Mamore and searched throughout the day. The light was beginning to fade when a cry was raised that the bishop's dogs had been spotted in the distance. The party hastened on; and there at last the faithful animals were discovered guarding Mackonochie's lifeless body. It was stiff and cold, almost frozen, and the head was half-buried in the snow. On the face, the searchers reported, was a look of peace and joy, without a trace of suffering. But there must have been a distressing struggle among the rocks in the darkness and storm. From the position in which the body was found it was thought that Mackonochie must have been kneeling in prayer before finally losing consciousness. His hat was gone, and also his right boot and stocking. The imagined circumstances of his final moments were put vividly by his old colleague, Arthur Stanton:

> The mystery of his stern, hard, self-devoted life completed itself in the weird circumstances of his death. He seems to have walked round and round the hollow in which he had taken shelter from the mountain storm, trying to keep life in him as long as he could; then, as if he knew his hour had come, deliberately to have uncovered his head to say his last prayers, and then to have laid his head upon his hand and died, sheltered in 'the hollow of the hand' of God, Whom he had served so faithfully; and at His bidding the wild wind from off the moor wreathed his head with snow.

His other old colleague, Edward Russell, who had been summoned by telegram and reached Ballachulish on the Monday night, was deeply moved by the sight of his former chief: 'Though I had watched his face for twenty years', he said afterwards, 'I had never seen it as I saw it then. There was no pallor nor any trace of pain, but only such majesty as I had never known before.'

The rest is soon told. The coffin containing Mackonochie's body, robed in eucharistic vestments, travelled to London by boat and train, arriving on the Thursday morning. As the hearse passed up Gray's Inn Road crowds lined the streets, silent and bareheaded. The coffin was met by the surpliced clergy of St Alban's and borne into the mortuary chapel. At solemn vespers for the dead in the evening the church was filled to overflowing as the coffin was brought in from the chapel; it lay in the chancel, surrounded with lighted candles and almost hidden by flowers. Throughout the night people passed in and out of the church to pay their last respects. For the solemn requiem on the Friday morning the church was again packed to the doors, with hundreds unable to obtain admittance. 'I did not agree with him', one local tradesman remarked, 'but he was a holy man and did more for London than most of us; so I for one shall put my shutters up.' Afterwards a long procession, headed by the choir of St Alban's and fifty surpliced clergy, snaked its way down High Holborn and Chancery Lane and along the Strand to Waterloo Station. Thence the coffin travelled by special train to Woking, and on by hand-bier to the section of the large burial-ground at Brookwood reserved for the parishioners of St Alban's. Stanton read the service, which ended with the singing of 'Lead, kindly light' – with its appropriate reference to 'moor and fen, crag and torrent'. The grave is marked by a cross of Scots granite engraved with a chalice and host and inscribed with the words: 'Jesu Mercy. I.H.S. In Peace. Alexander Heriot Mackonochie, Priest. 15 December 1887.' Another granite cross was erected on the spot in the Forest of Mamore where he had breathed his last.

＊　　＊　　＊

Alexander Heriot Mackonochie was a complex character whose

determination to fight for what he regarded as right seemed at times to develop from dogged insistence into mere pig-headedness. But this was to misunderstand the essential integrity of his motivation. Edward Russell suggested that his most noteworthy achievement was not so much what he did or endured 'in defence of ecclesiastical right', nor any of his numerous works, but rather 'the noble manhood of the man'. Certainly he struck his contemporaries, opponents as well as supporters, as a deeply impressive figure who was prepared to suffer almost anything for his convictions. To a later generation he still seems an awesome, if somewhat forbidding, character. As the then Archbishop of Canterbury, Robert Runcie, put it in a sermon preached in St Alban's at a centenary-year service in October 1987, Mackonochie 'gloried only in his Lord and our Lord . . . This was the source of his holiness, of the urgency of his preaching, and of his unswerving devotion to the Catholic faith as expressed in the life of the Church of England.'

Mackonochie exemplified the vision of the second generation of Tractarians in his urgent desire both to restore Catholic freedoms and traditions to Anglican worship and to bring the gospel, in all its richness and joy, to the poor. On the first issue he was concerned not primarily with such comparatively unimportant matters as his right to wear vestments or to make the sign of the cross, but with the vital need to champion the Church's freedom to order its worship without let or hindrance from the State. On the second issue he fervently believed that a priest's call to holiness involved a readiness to identify himself with the poor. The Bishop of Edinburgh, Richard Holloway, pressed home this point in a sermon preached at Onich, Argyllshire, on 15 December 1987, to mark the centenary of Mackonochie's death. Those great slum priests of the nineteenth-century Catholic Movement, he said, 'their soutanes flapping round their ankles', had gone in search of the incarnate Christ through the bliss and heartache of their great ministry to the poor. 'They didn't use them or recruit them; they *loved* them. They were there before the prim young Fabian social workers descended in their droves.'

This book is about priestly defiance of authority; and

Mackonochie's defiance of authority revolved about his ritualistic activities in church. So this chapter has had necessarily to concentrate on that particular side of his activities at the expense of his devoted labours among his impoverished parishioners. But those labours must never be forgotten.

After Mackonochie's death the clergy of St Alban's carried on in the tradition which he had established – without much serious interference either from the authorities or from the Protestant opposition. Over the years the ceremonial became even more advanced than in Mackonochie's day as more and more Anglicans came to accept without demur practices which had formerly been considered anathema. Of Mackonochie's former colleagues, Stanton soldiered on till 1913 and Russell till 1925. Suckling, his successor as vicar, served for over thirty years before retiring. St Alban's continued to flourish as a notable flagship of the Catholic Revival in London. Then came the blitz of 1941, and the almost complete destruction of the church on the night of Easter Tuesday. The only part to survive, appropriately, was the elaborate chantry chapel added in the early 1890s as a memorial to its first vicar. The Mackonochie Chapel was incorporated in the new St Alban's, designed by Adrian Gilbert Scott, which was consecrated on 17 June 1961. Mackonochie's pioneer work is carried on today in circumstances vastly different from those with which he himself had to contend. He might well raise those formidable eyebrows at some of the more bizarre developments; but, by and large, I think that he would approve of what his successors have built on the foundations which he laid.

Fr Tooth behind bars (from *Vanity Fair*, 10 February 1877)

CHAPTER 4

PRISONER OF CONSCIENCE

Arthur Tooth
(1839–1931)

ARTHUR TOOTH WAS THE FIRST of the Victorian 'reverend rebels' actually to be gaoled for his disobedience – or, as his supporters saw it, to be 'imprisoned for conscience' sake'. He was behind bars for a bare month – far less time than a later 'rebel', Sidney Faithhorn Green, who languished in Lancaster Castle for the better part of two years. Yet Tooth, as the first parish priest to suffer imprisonment under the Public Worship Regulation Act, became headline news throughout the country. His name provided scope for endless journalistic puns; and his determination to forgo his freedom rather than toe the required liturgical line excited the admiration of his supporters and the fury or despair of his opponents. In fact his active ministry as a parish priest ceased as the doors of Horsemonger Lane Gaol closed upon him. Though he remained in nominal charge of St James's, Hatcham, for a year and nine months after his release from prison, he took little part in its affairs. His health had been severely affected by the strain of the events leading up to his incarceration; and, for the last year of his incumbency, the parish was in the full-time charge of a curate whom many assumed would be Tooth's successor as vicar. Once he had formally resigned his Hatcham cure he devoted himself to running a school for orphan boys, a sisterhood and a home for drunkards. He was thirty-nine at the time of his resignation; he was to live for a further fifty-two years, dying at the ripe old age of ninety-one but never again being entrusted with the charge of a parish. After his brief hour of fame he eschewed the limelight, living a blameless but uncontroversial life among his orphans and inebriates. His later career was thus a complete contrast to that of Archdeacon Denison, who lived almost as long but was rarely out of the headlines. Towards the end Tooth seemed more and more a figure from a bygone age, having outlived almost all his contemporaries and having survived to witness the first Anglo-Catholic Congresses of the inter-war years. But, in his prime, he had seemed to many to be a true hero of the faith.

*   *   *

Arthur Tooth was born on 17 June 1839 at Swift's Park, Cranbrook, Kent. He was the eighth son of Robert and Mary Anne Tooth, his father being a wealthy businessman who had made a fortune in Australia from meat-preserving and sugar-baking. Arthur was educated at Tonbridge School and Trinity College, Cambridge, graduating in science in 1861 and then spending a year or so in travelling round the world twice. He was a first-class horseman and a crack shot. On one shooting expedition in the Queensland bush he became separated from the rest of the party and lost his way; he only rediscovered his companions (who had given him up for lost) by following the stars. Material about his early life is scanty, and there are no clues as to why he decided to take orders or when he became attracted to ritualism. But he certainly had leanings towards the ministry while in Australia, and spent some time assisting a priest in an isolated mission station in the outback.

He was ordained deacon in 1863 by Bishop Charles Sumner, to a title at St Mary-the-Less, Lambeth, then in the diocese of Winchester. But he spent only a year there, his vicar, Robert Gregory (the future Dean of St Paul's), apparently finding him too 'advanced' in churchmanship for his tastes. His second curacy was at St Mary's, Folkestone, in the diocese of Canterbury; he was priested by Archbishop Longley in 1864. It was while at Folkestone that he joined forces with his friend Arthur Stanton, of St Alban's, Holborn, in an approach to the

Tractarian leader, Edward Pusey. The two men proposed to Pusey that they should found a brotherhood, with a subordinate sisterhood, at St Saviour's, Leeds, the church founded by Pusey in memory of his daughter. Pusey at first favoured the scheme, but eventually vetoed it in the light of their insistence on retaining control of the sisterhood. So, after a year at Folkestone, Tooth moved on instead to Chiswick, in south-west London, where for three years (1865–68) he was minister of St Mary Magdalene's, a mission in the parish of St Nicholas. Then, after this five-year apprenticeship in three very different parishes, he embarked on his first entirely independent cure as vicar of St. James's, Hatcham, in south-east London, to which he had been appointed by his brother Robert. He was inducted on 18 September 1868, and was to remain there for the ten most eventful years of his ministry.

Hatcham began life as a cluster of orchards and market gardens surrounding a stately home, Hatcham Park House, which occupied the site of the present New Cross railway station. Over the years the rustic pastures fell prey to the speculative builder and, by the middle of the nineteenth century, the mansion had been demolished and the village transmuted into a typical London suburb. The parish of St James was carved out of the over-large parish of St Nicholas, Deptford, in the diocese of Rochester, the church being built and its first vicar installed in the mid–1850s. The population of ten thousand consisted mainly of artisans, though there was a leavening of middle-class folk. The first vicar, Augustus Granville, was of scholarly and artistic tastes, and found a predominantly working-class parish too much for him. In 1863 he bowed out on the grounds of ill-health, leaving a curate in charge. He himself had mildly High Church leanings, though he disapproved of his successor's ritualistic goings-on. The curate was an Evangelical. By the time Tooth arrived in 1868 congregations had shrunk to almost nothing; the fabric of the church had deteriorated and was infested with 'moths, spiders, black beetles and kindred created objects . . . whose time of excommunication had now arrived'; and tramps were in the habit of breaking into the vicarage and dossing down for the night. It was a daunting inheritance. The patronage of the living had gone through a number of hands before passing into those of Robert Tooth. The original patron had been Granville's father-in-law, who passed on the advowson (right of presentation) to Granville, who sold it to a Captain Drake, who in his turn sold it to Tooth – a barrister by profession and, like his brother Arthur, a gentleman of independent means.

On his arrival in the parish Arthur Tooth at once took steps to renew its church life. He began by abolishing the system of pew rents which made it impossible for the poorer parishioners to worship on equal terms with the more affluent: the pews were replaced by chairs. He also refused to charge fees, except for bridegrooms at weddings, and did away with collections at churchings and baptisms. As a result of these measures the poor began attending the church in ever-greater numbers. Tooth was an able preacher, and excelled in the art of giving simple instruction in the faith. The teaching was of course Catholic; and it was reinforced by various ceremonial practices which were still comparative novelties at the time and which were thought by many to be dangerous innovations reeking of Popery. They included lighted candles and the eastward position – innovations which were abominated by Protestants and were (as has been seen) giving rise to protests and prosecutions in other parts of the country. Tooth also installed a continental-style confessional.

His activities were not confined to liturgical renewal. By 1873 he had set up no fewer than fourteen separate organizations, committees and clubs to cater for the needs of the parish and of its poorer parishioners. He founded a boarding-school for twenty-four orphans which received glowing reports from government inspectors. The boys were taught music, and provided choristers and servers for church services. The school was run partly by the Sisters of the Holy Paraclete, a community founded by Tooth. He was himself no mean artist, and painted frescoes in the chancel and on the lower walls of the nave with his own hands – he always insisted on the value of hobbies in keeping a man young and his hands and brain active. In appearance he was tall and slim, with an air of self-possession. At the time of his troubles, when he was in his late thirties, hostile journalists made unflattering remarks about his allegedly squeaky voice and 'unmanly' appearance. The *Irish Times* went so far as to suggest that he had 'stepped out of a pre-Raphaelite painting. . . . If the Christian teacher should look like a Roman Catholic priest, then Mr. Tooth is to be congratulated on his exclusively sacerdotal appearance and manner.' Another critic perhaps got nearer to the truth when he described Tooth as an 'ascetic, devoted, earnest, honest man incapable of seeing two sides of a question . . . endowed less with a great power of will than with an enormous power of won't.' That assessment appeared in the issue of *Vanity Fair* which contained the famous cartoon by 'Spy' depicting Tooth, in long frock-coat and floppy black hat, as a Christian martyr behind bars. But this was in the future; and for his first few years in Hatcham all was comparative sweetness and light.

*   *   *

The first clouds on the horizon appeared in the summer of 1871, when a dissatisfied parishioner complained to the Bishop of Rochester, Thomas Claughton, about certain allegedly Romish practices at St James's. Claughton summoned the vicar to an interview; but Tooth not only declined to go but sent a letter to the papers explaining his reasons for not going. His non-compliance with the bishop's request was fully supported by the parish at large. One of his churchwardens, Edmund Croom, organized two petitions to the bishop, one signed by 166 communicants and the other by 896 parishioners. In a covering letter Croom expressed the hope that Claughton would 'prevent any interference with services that have been the means of great assistance to our spiritual welfare . . . the loss of which would be, I feel convinced, attended with great grief to the members of the congregation'. The letter ended by voicing the further hope that the unity of the congregation would not be broken by 'those who do not care to avail themselves of the many privileges we so greatly appreciate, and who can at another church in the same parish [i.e., the mission church of All Saints, Hatcham Park] obtain the Services they are desirous of forcing upon an unwilling congregation'. Croom subscribed himself 'with profound respect' as His Lordship's 'humble obedient Servant', but the bishop gave him a dusty answer. He pointed out that, while the petitioners asked for protection from 'molestation in worshipping', other petitioners opposed to the present regime at St James's might equally apply to the bishop to protect *them*. He ended unctuously: 'I am, Dear Mr. Churchwarden, with earnest prayer that Grace and Unity may be established and prevail in the Church at Hatcham, your faithful and aff. Chief Pastor, friend and Servant, T.L. Roffen'. In fact he took no action in the matter, nor did the original complainant insist on taking it further. The parish remained at peace for the next four years.

What caused a change for the worse was the passing in 1874 of the Public Worship Regulation Act, and the increased opportunities it gave to Protestant mischief-makers to stir up strife in Catholic-minded parishes. As with Mackonochie at St Alban's, Holborn, the body behind the nominal 'aggrieved parishioners' was the Church Association. Its agents were first spotted at St James's in August 1875, being easily recognizable through their unfamiliarity with the Catholic practices by now firmly established at the church. Three months later Tooth received a letter from the bishop announcing that proceedings were to be taken against him under the Public Worship Regulation Act by three parishioners, Messrs Hudson, Gardner and Gunstone. The congregation, who were solidly behind Tooth, at once moved into action in his defence. Croom and his fellow-churchwarden, Joseph Plimpton, set up a 'Hatcham Defence Committee' under the auspices of the English Church Union, the High Church rival to the Church Association. The committee pledged itself to stand by Tooth; and it master-minded a petition to Claughton asking him to veto the proceedings against their vicar. The specific charges against Tooth were eighteen in number. They included such customary grounds of complaint as vestments, incense, altar lights, the use of the sign of the cross, the *Agnus Dei*, and the celebration of the Eucharist with fewer than three communicants. None of the three 'aggrieved parishioners' was a regular worshipper at St James's. One often attended a Wesleyan chapel; another was churchwarden of All Saints', the Evangelical mission church in the parish; the third had moved away from the parish before the case began. But the three had set the legal (and anti-ritualistic) wheels in motion; and it was now up to Tooth to wriggle out of their clutches.

He began by sending the bishop an immensely long letter, dated 11 March 1876, in which he challenged Claughton to deal with the case himself rather than allow it to come before a secular court which Tooth declined to recognize. Like Denison twenty years earlier, he saw the basic issue as the doctrine of the Real Presence. The State, he declared, was inviting Claughton to 'lend your aid to suppress it by the abolition of those accessories of Divine worship which express it. It is folly to separate ritual from doctrine.' He then threw down the gauntlet to the bishop in no uncertain manner:

> If your lordship can solemnly . . . pronounce me to be a breaker of the church law and a heretic to the faith, for such grievous wrongs I am willing, without a legal process, to take the penalty of deprivation, provided your lordship will take the responsibility of pronouncing it.

Tooth expressed his willingness to concede many points of ritual and to forgo his 'lawful liberty in many matters of detail' where no doctrine was involved. 'But on those which are primitive and Catholic, and which really do involve the expression of doctrine [i.e., the Real Presence], it would be neither just to ourselves nor honest to our opponents to make any concession whatever; we can neither deny the doctrine nor withdraw the ritual.' Tooth ended by putting the onus of responsibility on the bishop: 'The choice is still in your lordship's hands whether you will come forward to administer Church law independently of the State.'

The bishop prudently declined to reply to Tooth's doctrinal arguments, or indeed to take up the challenge to handle the case himself. Instead he passed the buck to the three aggrieved parishioners – who were merely, he pointed out, 'insisting upon their right to have the Services in their parish church conducted in conformity with the Book of Common Prayer, which they allege you to have contravened in some particulars'. 'I must call to your mind', he added, 'that it is the law of the Church and

Realm, to which you have engaged to conform, that I am called upon to administer.' Tooth, in his reply, insisted that he had placed himself 'very unreservedly in your lordship's hands for trial and judgment according to the law and primitive use of the Christian Church . . . your lordship declines to accept the position, and refers me to the Public Worship Regulation Act.' The proceedings against him by 'three chosen champions of ecclesiastical order and Christian verity' had the bishop's consent, said Tooth –

> but it must not be supposed for one moment that their real character is altered in consequence; they are still merely secular proceedings and have not acquired any ecclesiastical force, unless one is to believe that a bishop has super-Parliamentary power, and in passing State law through his hands can alter it and give it something it had not before, a spiritual force, conveying a new character to it.

Meanwhile the two churchwardens had forwarded to the bishop a petition signed by 1454 worshippers at the church of whom 1335 were resident in the parish. They also sent him a second petition signed by themselves and sixty-two other prominent male worshippers – men being more equal than women where petitions (or indeed almost anything else in Victorian times) were concerned. The petitions urged a delay in the proceedings against Tooth until after judgment in the Ridsdale case – a similar lawsuit involving the vicar of St Peter's, Folkestone – had been pronounced. The bishop declined to stay his hand, however, or to interfere with the due processes of the law. The point of no return had now been reached.

Tooth had no lack of champions to back his cause. Archdeacon Denison, who had himself fought and won a long battle in the courts twenty years earlier, sent an open letter to Bishop Claughton, in the course of which he declared: 'In 1856 I refused to surrender the Doctrine of the Real Presence. In 1876 I refuse to compromise the Doctrine by surrendering the Ritual.' Denison accused the bishop of rejecting the Church's power to interpret its own law and of assigning all such power to the secular courts. 'In a word, your position in this matter, as Bishop and Father-in-God, is the Secular position. Mr Tooth's is the Religious position.' Denison's main point was rubbed home in a letter to the bishop from the secretaries of the Hatcham Defence Committee. 'Surrender of the ritual', they wrote, 'would imply a surrender of the true faith in the Real Presence of our ever Blessed Lord in the most Holy Sacrament instituted by Himself. That doctrine we cannot surrender.'

Nor could Tooth. When the case came before Lord Penzance at Lambeth Palace on 13 July 1876 he was not among those present, since he refused to recognize the court's competence to try him. The venue of the trial was unusual. As the judge of a totally new court Penzance had found difficulty in securing a room in which to sit. The Treasury officials were unhelpful; and the judge in charge of the Admiralty Court, to whom he also applied, disapproved of the judicial attempts to suppress Ritualism and likewise turned him down. In the end he was reduced to holding his court in the library of Lambeth Palace, at the invitation of Archbishop Tait. It was a venue which, as we shall see, was to have unforeseen consequences. The eighteen charges brought by the three aggrieved parishioners were solemnly read out in court, and the services held on two Sundays during the previous winter described in detail. The witnesses who gave evidence were all agents of the Church Association. Penzance delivered his judgment a week later. It took the form of a 'monition', or warning, that the practices objected to must cease forthwith, and that 'certain structures' (such as a crucifix and a second altar) for which no faculties had been obtained must be removed. Costs were awarded against Tooth, who ignored the monition and continued in church exactly as before.

Penzance waited another four months and then pounced again. He summoned Tooth to appear before him at Lambeth Palace on 2 December. The library was inadequately heated, and many of those who attended the hearing are reported to have turned blue with cold. The judge himself sat with a rug over his knees. Tooth again declined to appear; and affidavits were produced to show that he had taken no steps to heed the terms of the monition, abandon his ritualistic practices and remove the offending 'structures'. Penzance accordingly inhibited him from conducting services in his church for a period of three months. Under the terms of the Public Worship Regulation Act he would be deprived of his benefice if he continued to defy the court's ruling for three years.

Events now moved rapidly towards a climax. The three-month inhibition had been pronounced on a Saturday. The following day, before his sermon at the main celebration of the Eucharist, Tooth mounted the pulpit to hammer home his determination to defy the court's verdict. He told his congregation that he could not accept the interference of a secular authority in spiritual matters. He called on them not to recognize the ministry of any priest other than himself or one acting under his authority. Ministrations other than his own, he claimed, were 'schismatical and an invasion and a robbery of the rights of the Church of England'. The congregation got the message. A crowded meeting after Evensong on the same day passed a threefold resolution. This expressed 'cordial sympathy' with Tooth in the 'persecution' he was now undergoing; it recognized him as vicar having spiritual charge of the parish, 'notwithstanding the "inhibition" issued by the so-called Court of Arches'; and it refused to acknowledge or support the ministry of any priest 'intruded' into the parish.

Such a public gesture of defiance aroused the wildest excitement not only in the parish but in the Church outside the parish and in the country at large. People and papers took sides on the issue, the Catholic party in the Church being almost solid in Tooth's support. The *Church Times* spoke for many when it declared, in a three-column leader (8 December 1876): 'When a man is willing, for conscience' sake, to suffer serious loss, certainly of goods, perhaps of personal liberty as well, all right-minded Christians will be inclined to sympathize with him in some sense and degree at any rate.' The paper pointed out that this was not a case of an incumbent driving away or disgusting his congregation with ritual novelties, but one in which the vicar, churchwardens and congregation were of one mind in the matter of ritual 'in accordance, as they believe, with the plain directions of the Church of England'. Tooth's positive attitude of resistance, the leader concluded, could not be misunderstood and could 'scarcely fail to exercise a salutary effect upon the public mind. . . . Each instance of firm resistance will drive a very long nail into the coffin of the Public Worship Regulation Act, of Lord Penzance's Court and of the Church Association.'

Tooth had the strong support of two leading Catholic organizations: the English Church Union and the Church of England Working Men's Society (the editor of the *Church Times*, G. J. Palmer, was honorary treasurer of the latter body). A crowded meeting of the ECU passed a resolution in support of Tooth. The resolution was subject to confirmation by a special meeting to be held the following month – and all but led to the resignation of Pusey on the ground that it did not make the legal position sufficiently clear. In the end the Council of the ECU induced Pusey to withdraw his threat to resign by watering down the key sentence of the resolution to read: 'That the English Church Union, while it distinctly and expressly acknowledges the authority of all courts legally constituted in regard to all matters temporal, denies that the secular power has authority in matters purely spiritual.' The Council of the Church of England Working Men's Society also pledged its support of Tooth at a special meeting; and over fifty branches of the society sent him messages of encouragement. Meanwhile newspaper punsters were having a field-day, producing such gems as 'How to remove an incurable Tooth' and 'The Tooth that won't come out'.

Tooth was officially served with the notice of inhibition on 16 December. The next day, the Third Sunday in Advent, the official who had presented it at the vicarage returned to Hatcham to affix a large notice to the church door which spelt out the message to members of the congregation: these included Fr Mackonochie from St Alban's, Holborn. The following Sunday, Christmas Eve, matters took an uglier turn when a nominee of the Bishop of Rochester, Canon Richard Gee, arrived in a hansom cab to conduct the services at St James's in the light of the inhibition forbidding Tooth to do so. Accompanied by the bishop's secretary, he was met at the west door of the church by a reception committee which included Tooth (vested in cassock, surplice and purple stole) and the two churchwardens. Tooth and Gee bowed to each other; and there were then some formal exchanges before Tooth denied his obligation to obey the dictates of a civil court to which he had not sworn canonical obedience. 'I do not wish to show disrespect to a brother priest,' he concluded, 'but I must forbid you to enter this church or to take any services within the boundaries of this parish.' He then asked the two wardens whether they were prepared to assist him in preventing the intrusion into the church of a clergyman 'not recognized by me and acting under the direction of an unauthorized civil court'; and they said that they were. Edmund Croom told Gee that, if he insisted on entering, 'the whole congregation will immediately leave the church and we shall use all means in our power to expel you from the church placed under our guardianship.' Gee realized that he must beat a tactical retreat. 'I retire under protest,' he retorted as he and the bishop's secretary made their way back to the hansom cab and ecclesiastical civilization. Tooth for his part re-entered the church to conduct the morning service. He preached on the text, 'No man can serve two masters', but had to administer communion on his own as his curate, W. H. Browne, had also had his licence withdrawn by the bishop – an exercise of episcopal authority which Tooth *did* recognize. The *Weekly Dispatch* summed up the morning's excitements thus: 'Canon Gee beat a mild and not undignified retreat, and Mr. Tooth celebrated his triumph by indulging in practices of a Romish character more pronounced than ever.'

Tooth had won the first round, but it was to prove a pyrrhic victory. The *Solicitors' Journal* suggested that he might well be committed to prison for contempt of court. More immediately, the Church Association now began to infiltrate agitators into the church to prevent services from being held, or at least to disrupt them to the extent of frightening genuine worshippers away. The first occasion on which these disruptive tactics were employed was the Sunday after Christmas Day, which happened to be New Year's Eve. As the sung Eucharist got under way shouts of 'No Popery' and other offensive slogans were heard, and before long a fight was taking place at the west end of the church. A number of policemen were present; but they took no steps to eject the trouble-makers, who were eventually bundled out of the church by stalwart male members of the congregation. Outside a crowd of over a thousand 'roughs of the lowest class' (as the *Standard* dubbed them) greeted Tooth as he emerged with hisses and groans and his supporters with cries of 'Traitors!' It was a foretaste of what was to come. The Church Association's men hirelings were paid half-a-crown each and the boys a shilling for booing and hooting through the service and fighting members of the congregation.

Among those who had attended the New Year's Eve service was the president of the English Church Union, Charles Wood, the future Viscount Halifax. He described the scene afterwards in a letter to his wife:

> It was a moving sight. I never saw such a congregation; and when, during the hymn 'O come let us adore Him' which was sung at the Offertory, there was a howl at the door, I felt stirred as I have never felt stirred before. Mr Tooth did not begin the Prayer for the Church Militant for about 5 minutes, till the intruders had been ejected – after that all was quiet till the end. . . . I hear they broke some windows at Hatcham last night.

It was soon after his visit to Hatcham that Wood blotted his copybook with the Prince of Wales, in whose household he held the position (as a result of his boyhood friendship with the Prince) of Groom of the Bedchamber. The breach came about through a letter Wood wrote to the *Church Times* in his capacity as president of the ECU. In it he deplored the fact that a layman (i.e., Penzance) had issued a writ in his own name to suspend a priest from the performance of his sacred duties. The nub of the letter pulled no punches:

> Disobedience is sometimes the truest loyalty, and in his appeal to the Bishop of Rochester against what is, to all intents and purposes, the government of the Church by the Privy Council, Mr Tooth has but given expression to the general conviction that the time has come when, whatever the consequences to ourselves individually, an attempt must be made to win back

for the Church of England at least some portion of her former liberties.

The Prince, who had High Church sympathies, objected not so much to the sentiments themselves as to the fact that they had been expressed in public in a letter to a newspaper. His secretary, Francis Knollys, wrote on 3 January to Wood's father, Lord Halifax, to point out his son's indiscretion. 'Charlie . . . apparently supports Mr Tooth in advocating disobedience to the Law, a course which His Royal Highness believes is only recommended by the extreme High Church Party in this case.' Such an attitude, Knollys told Halifax, was regarded by the Prince 'with concern and disapprobation'. After a family conclave Wood wrote to the Prince justifying the view he had expressed as being 'one which is entertained by the whole of those who are called High Churchmen, and which, I will make bold, is the distinct teaching of the Church of England' – but at the same time offering his resignation as a Groom of the Bedchamber. On this occasion the storm blew over and the offer to resign was withdrawn. But four months later, with the threat of further prosecutions in the air, Wood felt that his position in the Royal Household was becoming more and more difficult. So he resigned a post which he judged to be incompatible with his presidency of a militant body like the English Church Union.

If the service at St James's on New Year's Eve had been rowdy, that on the following Sunday, 7 January 1877, was even worse. Both the church's own 'Hatcham Defence Committee' and the anti-ritualist 'Hatcham and Protestant Defence Committee' printed rival sets of tickets to ensure the admittance of their own supporters. Fortunately the Protestant tickets were delivered by the printer in error to the house of the secretary of the genuine Hatcham Defence Committee, so were confiscated. A police superintendent was on duty with a number of constables, who had set up a barricade around the church. The service began quietly enough, but then the Church Association's rowdies – estimated to number between five and eight thousand – swept aside both the barricade and the policemen who guarded it and attempted to batter down the church doors. The doors held, but the size and ugly temper of the mob meant that the congregation had to stay in their seats long after the service ended, in the hope that the mob would disperse. By one o'clock reserves of police had arrived and were able to shield the worshippers as they filed out through the west door amid the shouts and jeers of the assembled onlookers. Tooth, as he emerged under a strong police escort, was greeted with hisses and oaths and cries of 'We'll see you in Newgate.' Mackonochie, who had again come to support Tooth, was chased by the mob all the way back to the station. A parishioner reported that one train was packed with roughs and that, as often as they were sent back by the police, they re-emerged at another point behind their ringleaders – 'The fury of these hired villains was terrible.'

Mob violence had failed to prevent Tooth from conducting his services, at least after a fashion. The Church Association's next move was therefore to invoke the law once more. Acting through the same group of 'aggrieved parishioners', it applied to Penzance to cite Tooth for contempt of court. The complainants were able to invoke a forgotten statute of 1813 which had changed the penalty for contempt of an ecclesiastical court from excommunication to imprisonment. The framers of the Public Worship Regulation Act had assumed that a sentence of inhibition would be obeyed, and had therefore failed to provide for its enforcement. The Church Association and its minions were determined to see it enforced in Tooth's case, however drastic the consequences. Penzance was reluctant to grant their petition, but felt that he had no legal alternative. He therefore returned to Lambeth Palace on Saturday, 13 January, for another session in its chilly library. After hearing fresh affidavits he pronounced Tooth to be 'contumacious and in contempt in not obeying the orders of the court'. He issued an order addressed to the Queen in Chancery. This would be followed by another order committing Tooth to prison.

The following day was Sunday, and Tooth conducted two celebrations of Holy Communion at five and six a.m. Shortly before nine, one of the bishop's officials appeared: he posted a notice on the church door announcing that no further services would be held. The regular congregation then went as a body

contumacy – willful disobedience

to the neighbouring church of St Paul, Walworth, for a Sung Eucharist, while a crowd estimated at eight thousand gathered round St James's. There was much stone-throwing and shouting, but a force of two hundred policemen, many of them mounted, succeeded in keeping order and preventing serious damage. A providential rainstorm diverted many of the rowdies into the pubs nearby. Meanwhile Tooth, the cause of all the uproar, had taken himself off to Tunbridge Wells. His health had been affected by the events of the past few weeks and he badly needed a rest. He knew that he faced imprisonment, but assumed (wrongly) that he would be arrested in Kent and sent to Maidstone Gaol. The Bishop of Peterborough, William Magee, wrote to a friend: 'You will have seen from the papers that the extraction of Tooth goes on. I wish the Church could be chloroformed for the operation. Out he must now come, though what will be the result on the patient is doubtful. . . . The Cabinet Ministers seem rather uneasy about this wretched Tooth-drawing.'

The following Sunday, 21 January, Bishop Claughton made another attempt to infiltrate a priest into St James's to conduct the services on behalf of the absent vicar. It was no more successful than the previous attempt, the reason this time being that Tooth and his churchwardens declined to surrender the keys of the church to the intruder. The bishop's nominee, Richard Chambres, was therefore unable to obtain admission. The bishop in revenge ordered the church to be closed for the day, the order being enforced by the police, who refused admission to a body of would-be worshippers led by the two church-wardens. The anti-ritualist crowd who later turned up to see some more fun were reduced to staring at an empty church.

The climax was now at hand. The next day, Monday, 22 January, Tooth returned to London and went to the house of Thomas Layman, a barrister and a leading member of his congregation. There he was taken into custody by the sheriff's officers and, accompanied by Layman, removed to Horsemonger Lane Gaol, at the southern end of London Bridge. He was housed in the debtors' wing of the prison, the furniture of his cell being minimal (he was allowed to supplement it with items sent in by his friends). His meals were brought in by the nuns attached to his parish; the cell was kept clean by a fellow-prisoner. Tooth was allowed to receive visitors three times a week. They included a fair number of Catholic notables (among them Liddon, Gregory, Mackonochie and Charles Wood), anxious to declare their public sympathy with one who had now acquired the status of a martyr. Wood wrote to his wife after the visit. He told her that Tooth was not being very well treated, but that 'the enemy are in despair at his being there'. And Liddon declared: 'Mr Tooth's sick face in that cage in the court of the gaol quite haunts one.' Many years later Tooth recalled his spell in prison to Desmond Morse-Boycott:

> The gaol was a shocking place for draughts. . . . I didn't mind, and I always was obedient. I expected to be there for years, and I must say they treated me fairly well. The warders didn't know what to make of me. I felt uncomfortable only when I exercised in the yard. There I was seen by the women, who used to wonder what the gay old dog in a clerical collar had been up to. They let me keep my clothes.

Tooth's committal to gaol changed him in a flash, in the eyes of many, from rebel priest to Christian martyr. Even those unsympathetic to his views felt that the penalty was out of all proportion to the offence, and many of the less extreme members of the Church Association resigned in protest. Rumours flew around. The *Church Times* alleged that the Queen herself was insisting on Tooth's liberation and had declared that, if he were not set free by Penzance, she would exercise her royal prerogative on his behalf and set him free at once. 'I suppose these stories really go down with those for whom the *Church Times* writes,' Magee remarked sardonically. Nearer home, a petition in Tooth's favour signed by 1242 parishioners was presented to the Bishop of Rochester; and the *Camberwell and Peckham Times* sighed sympathetically: 'Mr Tooth in gaol with keys in pocket, Bishop Claughton at Danbury with sealing-wax and parchment, and one of the most respectable congregations in South London having to go and cadge sacramentally on other local churches, are sights for gods and men.'

The newspapers were divided on the issue, though those which were hostile to Tooth hedged their bets to some extent. *The Times*, for instance, pointed out that he could emancipate himself at any moment. 'If he is a martyr it is for a mere triviality . . . which he is perfectly at liberty to enjoy under certain conditions.' *John Bull*, which had at one time sat on the fence, now declared: 'For every one that sympathized with Mr Tooth's ritual there will be ten thousand to deplore his imprisonment.' The *Church Times* remained Tooth's staunchest journalistic ally. Its leading article on 2 February appeared under a banner announcement in black capitals: 'THE PRAYERS OF THE CHURCH ARE DESIRED FOR ARTHUR TOOTH, PRIEST, A PRISONER FOR CONSCIENCE' SAKE'. The leader compared Tooth to John Hampden, who had defended the constitutional laws of England against the unjust exercise of arbitrary power. Parliament, it declared, could no more make Lord Penzance a spiritual judge than it could make him a French citizen or a Freemason. Tooth was not merely at liberty to disregard his sentence, 'but could not possibly have obeyed it without unfaithfulness to the Church by acquiescing in, and thereby aiding, such an intolerable encroachment of the secular power as to attempt to take away the exercise of an office which it had never conferred'. Some Protestant leopards, however, could never change their spots. *The Rock* managed a sneer at the stream of visitors to Horsemonger Lane Gaol:

> A well-dressed, well-fed ecclesiastic, holding levées and receiving bouquets of flowers from his lady admirers, and hampers of game from his male friends, is felt to have as little claim to be dubbed *Martyr* as summer excursionists in first-class carriages to Lourdes have to rank as pilgrims.

Meanwhile, back at Hatcham, the church remained closed on the following two Sundays, 28 January and 4 February, being guarded by a strong body of policemen. The regulars were unable to get in because of the police: the bishop's nominee, Chambres, was kept out because he had no key to the church. By then Chambres had had enough and resigned his unenviable position. His successor, Benjamin Dale, was made of sterner stuff and determined to force his way in. This he did on the following Saturday, 10 February, with the aid of two locksmiths from Chubb's, the safemakers, and was able to conduct Mattins the next day, Quinquagesima Sunday. Dale stayed for three months as curate-in-charge. He was an old-fashioned High Churchman who regarded ritual as unimportant but who saw his task as being to keep the peace between the opposing parties. At the start of his ministry, however, he hardly helped matters by immediately removing such adjuncts to worship as candlesticks, flower-vases and figures of angels; he also locked and boarded up the organ and replaced the ornate altar-frontal with a cloth of green baize – referred to by one Catholic observer as a 'dingy bit of green bunting'. But the Protestant faction was also irritated because, on his first appearance in church on Sunday, 11 February, Dale insisted on kneeling before the altar. According to the same observer his sermon was 'tolerably erudite and singularly avoidant of annoyance to anybody'. The next day men from Chubb's arrived to change the locks on all the church doors, so that the old keys were now useless.

If poor Dale thought that his attempt at neutrality would please everyone, or at least offend no one, he was disappointed. By and large, he received a poor press. The *Morning Post*, which to some degree was anti-Tooth, nevertheless referred disparagingly to the 'victory of the truncheon and the crowbar' and dismissed his initial service thus: 'Under the idea that they are doing God service, they go through a miserable show of public worship which, by all accounts, could not be exceeded for baldness and penury, in the presence of a slender congregation drawn mainly by curiosity or the love of opposition.' And the *Church Times* lost no time in castigating the Bishop of Rochester for finding 'a clerk unscrupulous enough to thrust himself into the cure of St James's, Hatcham, and gain possession of the church by means analogous to those employed by burglars. . . . Verily the Bishop of Rochester has little reason to be proud of his work. Throughout the whole of these miserable proceedings he has exhibited neither episcopal dignity, fatherly generosity, nor even the ordinary good feeling to be expected from a Christian gentleman.' But the paper was also cross with those members of the regular congregation who continued to frequent St James's:

> We are extremely sorry to hear that there is a tendency on the part of a few to accept the Irreverend the Intruder. . . . Mr. Tooth's congregation cannot require to be told that to attend their parish church whilst it remains in the hands of Mr. Dale will make themselves accomplices in his acts, will be to commit the grossest schism, and will be cruelly disloyal to their persecuted vicar.

Support for the 'persecuted vicar' was increasing all the time, and protest meetings continued to be held up and down the country. They reached their climax with a meeting of the Church of England Working Men's Society in London attended by over two thousand people. This mass demonstration, coupled with an official warning to the Home Office that 'it would be advisable to release Mr Tooth to avoid serious consequences', stirred the authorities into action. They urged the three original complainants to apply for Tooth's release, on the ground that the law had been vindicated by the successful intrusion of a curate-in-charge into St James's. The three men at first demurred, but then changed their minds and agreed to play ball. On Saturday, 17 February, Penzance returned yet again to the library of Lambeth Palace to hear their application, which he at once granted. Tooth left the prison later in the day. After a brief visit to his parish he left again for Brighton and a period of much-needed rest and recuperation at the house of one of his brothers. With Dale firmly in possession at St James's and the inhibition still in force, there was no way in which he could resume his ministry there except at the cost of a new wave of mob violence. The anti-Tooth faction paradoxically saw his release as a triumph for the law, which in a sense it was. 'Mr Tooth was imprisoned for contempt; he has been released with contempt,' sneered *The Times*. But the *Daily Telegraph* thought that he had got away too lightly: 'Without expressing contrition, without paying the costs, still resolute in taking no notice whatever of Lord Penzance . . . and practically defying the majesty of the law, he is a free man.' The *Nonconformist*, which might have been expected to be hostile to Tooth, likened his case to that of St Paul: ' "Nay, verily, but let them come themselves and fetch us out." ' An article in the same journal by a contributor who had attended the great London protest meeting organized by the Church of England Working Men's Society remarked on the firm hold which the Ritualistic Movement had taken on this section of the community: 'The Ritualistic leaders may not have a large, but they have an earnest and disciplined, following among the lower middle-class – a class over whom archbishops and bishops, deans and canons . . . exercise not the slightest control.'

The season of Lent was an unhappy time at St James's. On the first Sunday after Tooth's release, many members of the 'old' congregation ignored the *Church Times*'s advice not to recognize 'the Irreverend the Intruder' and turned up in force. Representatives of the Protestant faction for their part distributed handbills urging parishioners to 'support them in thanking God for the reopening of the church' and praying that the minister would 'conduct the services with the Protestant simplicity which their fathers have worshipped in since the glorious Reformation'. When the unfortunate Dale emerged from the vestry robed discreetly in surplice, scarf and hood, he faced a congregation split into two hostile camps: about four hundred Catholics to seven hundred Protestants. The result was a disaster – except to newspaper reporters looking for colour. Both sides did their best to be unco-operative. When the Protestants knelt (or 'squatted', as the *Church Times* put it) the Catholics stood up, and *vice versa*. 'We think this course was very undignified,' the *Church Times* reporter remarked with masterly understatement. A member of the 'Hatcham and Peckham Protestant League' turned round the litany-desk so that it faced west rather than east, 'in the hope' (the *Church Times* again) 'that he might thus oblige Mr Dale to offer his supplications to his patrons'; but Dale returned the desk to its original position, describing the gesture of protest as 'petty'. The Catholic contingent left after Mattins: the Protestants remained behind for a service of Holy Communion. The *Church Times* report concluded: 'Mr Dale no doubt gave a sigh of relief when the service was over and well he might, for he had brought things to a pretty pass. If he thinks that this Hatcham case is all over, he is greatly mistaken.'

Things were no better the following Sunday, when the Catholics ostentatiously focused their attention on their own devotional books rather than join in Mattins with the others. The two sides came to blows at one point, when the Protestants attempted to prevent the Catholics from leaving the church after the Litany and before the celebration of Holy Communion. When the latter, led by the two churchwardens, Croom and Plimpton, marched resolutely towards the west door, the Protestants barred the exit. After a struggle half the Catholics forced their way out, Croom being thrown through the door and down the church steps; the door was then locked and the remaining would-be escapers detained inside with Plimpton. Dale mounted the pulpit and rebuked his flock for the unseemly disturbance, as well he might. The service then continued, but there were only seven communicants.

This sort of fracas might please the ungodly, but Tooth and his more sensible supporters saw that it would have to stop. He reminded his old congregation of his Advent Sunday advice to them not to accept the 'schismatic' ministrations of any priest 'intruded' into the parish in his absence. He asked them to stay away from St James's until his return. He then left for the Continent on the grounds of ill-health (having achieved the pinnacle of fame when a wax model of him was put on view at Madame Tussaud's); and, for the most part, his supporters heeded his advice. They went each Sunday to one of several other ritualistic churches within easy reach, and Dale was able to minister without interruption to a dwindling number of Protestant parishioners. As the Catholics saw it, the Church Association had made a desert of St James's and could call it peace. The Bishop of Rochester turned up at the church on Good Friday to conduct Morning Prayer and Ante-Communion, but made no attempt to contact any of Tooth's supporters. His visit inspired a local bard to compose a long 'Lay of Hatcham' after Lewis Carroll, of which a typical verse ran:

'If I should send another friend
   To stay for half a year,
Do you suppose' the Prelate said,
   'That Arthur would keep clear?'
'I doubt it', sighed the Protestant,
   And shed a bitter tear.

On Easter Day there were a mere twenty-two communicants. The Hatcham Catholics were now swelling the congregations of such ritualistic churches as St Peter's, London Docks; St Stephen's, Lewisham; and St Paul's, Walworth. Such a dispersion of the faithful was to prove fatal to the chances of re-establishing a regular tradition of Catholic worship at St James's, Hatcham.

The next major event in the saga was the Easter vestry meeting of parishioners held to elect the two churchwardens for the ensuing year. This would obviously be a trial of strength between the rival parties. The occasion in the past had been a formality – Plimpton and Croom had been re-elected the previous year at a meeting in the vestry at eight a.m. attended by only six parishioners. The election of 3 April, 1877, Easter Tuesday, was a very different affair. In fact it was the post of people's warden that was at issue, the vicar's warden being a nominee of the vicar and therefore much harder to unseat by legal means. The Church Association had distributed handbills throughout the parish in favour of their 'people's' candidate, T. W. Fry. To qualify as an elector, a parishioner had to be a ratepayer – which ruled out all the poorer members (the vast majority) of the old congregation. But the Protestant ratepayers turned up in their scores; and two hundred people in all squeezed into the church vestry for a meeting at ten a.m. which was punctuated by frequent shouts, groans and insults. Fry, for the Protestant faction, was elected by an overwhelming majority of 180 votes to 20, and even the election of the vicar's warden failed to go through on the nod. Tooth's nominee was Robert Webb, who was put forward by Dale on Tooth's behalf. On being shouted down by the opposition, he then proposed Webb on his own nomination amid cries of 'He's a Papist' and 'Go to

Rome'. Dale valiantly stuck to his guns, however, and Webb was formally elected. The new wardens then each nominated two sidesmen of their own ecclesiastical hue – hardly a recipe for future harmony. By this time Dale himself had had enough of the church militant in Hatcham and its warring factions and decided to call it a day. On hearing the news of his impending resignation Webb wrote to the bishop on behalf of the Hatcham Defence Committee, asking him to allow Tooth to nominate his own curate-in-charge during his continued absence. The bishop refused the request, and in the ensuing correspondence made no attempt to disguise his disapproval of Tooth and his determination not to yield an inch in his opposition. Webb gave as good as he got, ending the correspondence with a resounding broadside:

> I deeply regret your inability to consider the claims of the really aggrieved parishioners of St James's, Hatcham, more than one thousand of whom asked your lordship not to sanction the proceedings against Mr Tooth. Had you the same consideration for them as for the *three* parishioners engaged as the instruments of the persecution . . . Catholic Churchmen would not be so strongly convinced as they are that it is the bishops (with some noble exceptions), not the priests of the advanced school of thought in the Church of England, who 'alienate the laity'; and that it is your lordship, not the so-called Church Association, who is responsible for the present distress in this parish.

Dale left Hatcham during the first week in May. As soon as he had gone Fry, the Protestant warden, commissioned a local carpenter to demolish the altar in the side-chapel – the one which Penzance, in his original monition, had ordered to be removed. Tooth had by now returned from the Continent and reappeared on the scene. In a letter to Webb he said that he had come back to London 'first to renew my claim to my position as the lawful and canonically instituted vicar of this parish; secondly, to assert that all services which have been conducted here since my removal from my parish have been schismatical; thirdly, that the various appointments to the cure of souls which have been forced upon my parishioners must, from the nature of the case, be null and void.'

Tooth was not content with mere words. He determined to regain physical possession of his church, at least temporarily. The keys were now in the possession of Fry; so, early on the morning of 13 May, the Sunday after Ascension Day, Tooth's supporters broke a window in the south aisle of the church; Edmund Croom's young son then nipped inside, undid the chain and let in the three hundred would-be worshippers. It was the subsequent ringing of the church bells that alerted Fry that something might be amiss, as no service had been scheduled to take place at that hour. He rushed out of his house, 'completing his toilet on the way', and gathering up two policemen to accompany him. On arrival at the church a scene of sheer farce (graphically described by Joyce Coombs) took place between Fry and his rival churchwarden, Webb. Tooth was just about to pronounce the absolution when he noticed Fry bounding up the nave. 'I give Mr Tooth in charge,' Fry gasped out to the two constables. 'Take that man into custody!' 'You'll do nothing of the sort!' Webb exclaimed. 'What! You won't support me?' said Fry. 'No', replied Webb, 'and you can't do anything without me.' This was true, as neither churchwarden could act without the support of the other. Fry then called on Tooth to 'desist' from his ministrations, but, on receiving no answer, stalked out of the church. He made another formal protest to Tooth in the vestry after the service, but got no joy out of the 'intruding' vicar's monosyllabic replies. But he took his revenge the following Tuesday evening by leading a party of workmen to detach the large wooden crucifix from its supporting rood beam in the nave: in falling to the floor the crucifix was damaged beyond repair. Webb obtained a declaration from the archdeacon that Fry's iconoclastic action was illegal and that he had rendered himself liable to prosecution. But Fry claimed successfully that the original monition had ordered the removal of the crucifix and that, under the terms of the Public Worship Regulation Act, no faculty was therefore necessary. Meanwhile the news that Tooth had returned to celebrate again in his own church 'has caused' (in the words of the *Church Times*) 'a glow of thankfulness in the bosoms of all true-hearted Churchmen'.

*   *   *

The glow was a fitful one, as an unexpected development now occurred: the translation of Bishop Claughton and his temporary replacement by Archbishop Tait. Claughton's departure had been occasioned by the division of the diocese of Rochester and his nomination by Disraeli to be first bishop of the new diocese of St Albans. Tait thus found himself in charge of Claughton's former see until a new diocesan could be nominated. It was an unenviable responsibility as far as Hatcham was concerned, as he soon became the target of petitions and deputations from both sides in the dispute. One deputation was led by Webb and other members of the old congregation, who presented Tait with a pro-Tooth memorial signed by 1200 parishioners. Webb and his colleagues complained about Fry's unauthorized destruction of the second altar and crucifix, and urged the Archbishop to license a curate nominated by Tooth who could take charge of the parish until Tooth's own position could be resolved. They pointed out that some of those leading the opposition to Tooth seldom went near St James's and subscribed not a farthing either to the parochial schools or to the parochial charities. A rival deputation, led by Fry, asked Tait to appoint a curate-in-charge sympathetic to the Protestant point of view, and to grant a faculty for the removal of the remaining articles mentioned by Penzance in his monition – including the continental-style confessional.

Neither delegation got much out of Tait, except a promise to consider the various points they had made. But he was now sufficiently sure of his facts to summon Tooth to an interview at Lambeth. The meeting on 14 June was a private one to which Tait referred very briefly in his diary: 'I have had a long interview with Mr. Tooth, and have pressed on him the duty of conforming to the decisions of Convocation. I fear I shall not find him so amenable to authority as Mr. Ridsdale.' The Convocation resolutions to which the Archbishop referred enjoined that 'no alterations from the long-sanctioned and usual ritual ought to be made in our churches until the sanction of the Bishop of the diocese has been obtained thereto.' Ridsdale was the Folkestone priest in Tait's own diocese of Canterbury who had been the first victim of the Public Worship Regulation Act and who, in the face of an adverse judgment, had meekly given in to the demands of the authorities. Tait's fear that he would not find Tooth as amenable as Ridsdale (who had recently married, and who was therefore reluctant to risk being deprived of his living) was speedily realized. Within a week of the Lambeth interview Tooth was writing to the Archbishop to dispute chapter and verse of the Convocation resolutions to which Tait had drawn his attention – and challenging His Grace to enable him 'to find official and authoritative evidence of the making, enacting and promulging of such canon, constitution, ordinance provincial or other synodical act'. Although he remained 'your Grace's obedient servant', he had set in train a lengthy and tediously repetitive correspondence which continued throughout the rest of the month and well into July. Tooth ended it with a fine flurry of words: 'I must say that I do not care to attempt to defend myself from a charge of wilfulness which cannot be maintained by any authority beyond your Grace's statement.' Tait had got nowhere – and had been reduced in the meantime to keeping the Sunday services at St James's going with a succession of priests who included his son Crawfurd and his chaplain Randall Davidson (the future Archbishop of Canterbury). The entire correspondence was made public, evoking much comment in the press. *The Guardian*, a mildly High Church newspaper, compared the Archbishop's treatment of Tooth to that of a palace cat with a church mouse:

> The little creature dodges here and there, sometimes not without a species of success, in escaping the stroke of its big adversary; but more frequently the claw strikes home, and finally pins the poor animal to the floor. In the case of the mouse, our prevailing feeling is that of indignation at the cruelty of the persecutor, even though the victim may have eaten our cheese. At the human anti-types it is lawful to be simply amused, for Mr Tooth's skin is evidently of such sub-

stance that the point of the Archiepiscopal logic, whatever its force and value, is quite incapable of penetrating to his nerves of sensation.

It was at this point, when the archiepiscopal cat was poised for a fresh attempt to pin the poor mouse to the floor, that the little animal suddenly threatened to evade its tormentor with a master-stroke of cunning. The lawyers of the English Church Union, who were acting for Tooth, suddenly discovered that the original trial might be invalidated because it had been held in the wrong place. The Public Worship Regulation Act laid down that 'the archbishop shall forthwith require the judge to hear the matter of the representation at any place within the diocese or province, or in London or Westminster'. But, whether from oversight in drafting the Primate's requisition to Penzance, or from a discrepancy between the wording of the Act and the rules and orders since drawn up to regulate procedure under it, the word 'province' had been omitted and the judge had been enjoined to hear the Tooth case in London, Westminster or the diocese of Rochester. (Several modern historians have claimed that it was the Act itself that had been carelessly drafted. This was not so. Clause 9 of the Act specifically mentions the word 'province'.) The library at Lambeth Palace was in none of these places, being south of the Thames and in the diocese of Canterbury; therefore, the English Church Union's lawyers argued before the justices of the Queen's Bench Division of the High Court, the entire trial was invalid and its verdict null and void. The justices agreed that there was a case to argue. They allowed the application to go forward and granted a rule *nisi*, which meant that counsel's opinion would be sought. But it was to be another four months before they were in a position to deliver judgment.

By now Disraeli had appointed Claughton's successor as Bishop of Rochester. His nominee, Anthony Thorold, was vicar of St Pancras and a strong Evangelical. Although, a decade later, Thorold was to get on well with Robert Dolling at Landport (see next chapter), he was at this stage thought unlikely to look too kindly on Tooth or any other 'rebel' Catholic in his diocese.

Examining his Protestant antecedents, the *Church Times* cattily remarked that the fact that he owed his canonry to Archbishop Thomson of York and was also his examining chaplain 'amounts very nearly to a formal certificate of professional incompetence'. On 7 August Thorold paid his first visit to St James's and managed in his sermon to offend those Catholic members of the congregation who had flocked back in force to their old church to hear what their new diocesan had to say. They found it not at all to their taste. He began by attacking the former over-ornate services as having hindered rather than helped forward the church's spiritual life. He then stuck his neck out by remarking that, if the Church of England was not a Protestant Reformed Church, 'she is a shameful schism and ought not to have an existence'. This remark was at once taken up by William Grant, a member of the Hatcham Defence Committee, who wrote to the bishop to point out that he had never been required to profess himself a Protestant or to acknowledge himself a member of the Protestant Church: 'My Prayer Book does not contain a single mention of the word "Protestant".' Thorold wrote back to express regret at having pained Grant by the use of the word 'Protestant'; 'but I must honestly tell you that I used it with perfect deliberateness and that I inflexibly abide by it still.' He assured Grant that the Church of England was Protestant in its attitude to the Roman Catholic Church: 'If she does not still protest against the doctrinal errors of that Church, her existence is an inexplicable and gratuitous schism.' Grant remained unconvinced. He sent Thorold a long letter packed with theological arguments so complex as to cause the bishop to cut off the correspondence on the excuse that he had not time to discuss the matter further. Grant retorted by sending copies of the correspondence to the various church newspapers, to Thorold's intense annoyance – and indeed to that of anyone who was looking for a reconciliation between the opposing factions.

All this time, since his return from abroad, Tooth had been a shadowy figure in the background. No church registers for St James's have survived for this period, but, because of the inhibition, it is unlikely that he would have officiated again at the church since his forcible entry in May. He was still in charge of the schools for orphans attached to the parish, however; and, with the future so uncertain, he protected his position on this front by using a providential legacy of £10,000 to purchase a large house and estate at Woodside, on the outskirts of Croydon, to which he determined to transfer the schools. Whatever happened to his position at St James's, they at least would be safe from the enemy.

By now the justices of the Queen's Bench Division had made up their minds. On 6 November they pronounced their verdict, which quashed all the proceedings against Tooth on the technical ground that the trial had been held in none of the three stipulated places: London, Westminster or the diocese of Rochester. The judges were unanimous in their opinion that the discrepancy between the direction and the proceeding voided the whole matter. The joy of Tooth's supporters when they heard the news was unrestrained. The *Church Times* compared the Public Worship Regulation Act to a fish-torpedo, 'which, if unskilfully handled, is just as likely to make havoc with the fleet that uses it as that against which it is directed'. Of more importance, however, than the annulling of the Penzance judgment on a mere technicality, the paper continued, was the blow dealt both to the Archbishop of Canterbury and to Penzance's court:

> It was nothing but the Archbishop's anxiety to make an indecent display of his partizanship by assigning the library at Lambeth as the Court for the person whom he and the Archbishop of York had hired to do their work which vitiated the proceedings; and thus his eagerness to identify himself with the unconstitutional action of the Public Worship Regulation Act has hoisted him with his own petard, and covered him with as much ridicule now as it covered him with disgrace to begin with.

The ritualists were especially delighted with the statement by the Lord Chief Justice that Penzance's court was an entirely new jurisdiction, and nothing to do with the old ecclesiastical Court of Arches. 'The jurisdiction is the creation of the statute [i.e., the Public Worship Regulation Act] . . . it is undoubtedly to my mind an entirely new office, and one with which no former Dean of Arches had anything to do.' This judicial dictum confirmed the ritualists' claim that the new court was purely a creation of Parliament and could claim no kinship with the Court of Arches.

No doubt his supporters imagined that Tooth would celebrate his victory in the courts by resuming his ministry at Hatcham as if nothing had happened. In fact he did what his opponents must all along have hoped that he *would* do – resign his benefice. With the same magnanimity with which he declined to prosecute the original three complainants or the unfortunate Penzance for damages for false imprisonment, so now he wrote to Archbishop Tait on 21 November offering to resign (though without naming a date) in the interest of restoring harmony in the parish. His health had certainly been put under intense strain by the anxieties of the past two years; but his militancy in adversity presents a striking contrast to his meekness in the hour of triumph. Perhaps his spirit really had been broken by his spell of imprisonment, brief though this had been. Whatever the reason behind his change of front, he now told Tait that, 'when it was right that my people should suffer with me', he had not hesitated to throw himself on their patient endurance and to require them to take their part in this matter. His long apologia continued:

> Nothing now remains to be done, and I must relieve them from their difficult position. The patron [i.e., his brother Robert], kindly acting under my advice, will make a new appointment. I resign the care of my parish in the hope that the severance of my personal interest may secure it from future litigation.

He lost no time in bowing out of the parish, having appointed a curate-in-charge, Malcolm MacColl, to take over until his resignation had become effective and a new vicar been nominated by his brother. His final appearance in St James's was on Advent Sunday, 2 December 1877. He celebrated the Eucharist at eight a.m., assisted by MacColl, in the presence of over 250 of his parishioners. He left the church immediately after the service and took a train to Croydon, where his schools were to be re-established. He spent the next eight months on a long tour abroad, from which he only returned in August 1878. With or without chloroform, the Tooth had finally been extracted.

*   *   *

There is no space to deal at length with the subsequent history of St James's, Hatcham; but no account of Tooth's ministry there would be complete without at least a brief reference to the fate that befell his two immediate successors. Joyce Coombs, in her *Judgment on Hatcham*, has delved deep into this sad chapter in the history of the parish; and her detailed narrative of the ministries of Malcolm MacColl and Henry Aston Walker makes full if depressing use of the available source material.

MacColl must not be confused with the Canon MacColl who excited the wrath of Queen Victoria about this time because of his denunciation of the Bulgarian atrocities. The Hatcham MacColl was a moderate Catholic who had been ordained in Scotland and, before coming to St James's, had been priest-in-charge of St Augustine's, Bermondsey. It was widely assumed in the parish that he would be Tooth's successor as vicar. This assumption was at first encouraged by Tooth himself, who let MacColl move into the now empty vicarage. What apparently caused Tooth to change his mind was the fact that MacColl had got badly into debt when trying to raise funds for building a permanent church in Bermondsey. The builder had now served a summons on him, which obviously raised doubts about his suitability for a permanent post at St James's. Tooth put off naming a date for his own resignation. Meanwhile MacColl had been doing his best to reconcile the conflicting interests at the church by toning down the ceremonial – though not sufficiently so to satisfy the Protestants. Attempts continued to be made to disrupt services, matters reaching a head with the Easter vestry of 1878 and the election of a people's churchwarden. Once again the meeting was packed with the supporters of Fry, the outgoing warden, who proposed one of his cronies, William Henry Sanders, to succeed him. Sanders, he assured the meeting, would promise to put down Ritualism and uphold Protestantism. Sanders was duly elected by 120 votes to 20. He at once proceeded to make life as difficult as possible for poor MacColl, even going so far as to stand at the foot of the pulpit steps to demand of visiting preachers of whom he disapproved that they should produce their 'letters of orders' authorizing them to officiate. For their part the Catholics failed to give MacColl much support, regarding him as a renegade who had abandoned many of the practices for which Tooth had fought. So, by endeavouring to please both parties, MacColl succeeded in satisfying neither.

Tooth, who had been travelling in the Far East during the first half of 1878, now returned home to an enthusiastic reception by his supporters. But he kept away from his old church, reportedly because of differences of opinion with MacColl. Rumours flew around, including one that the living was to be offered to Arthur Stanton, Mackonochie's curate at St Alban's, Holborn. A petition in favour of MacColl, signed by over a thousand parishioners and communicants, was dispatched to Bishop Thorold. In the event it was not Stanton who succeeded Tooth as vicar but another curate of St Alban's, Henry Aston Walker. Tooth finally resigned on 21 November, but Walker was not instituted until early January 1879. There were no services on Christmas Day, MacColl having already left (with profound thankfulness, no doubt) to take up a curacy at St Mary Magdalene's, Paddington. His subsequent ministry took him to Kensington, Jersey and Clydebank; he died in 1914.

Walker's time at Hatcham was no happier than MacColl's – and lasted a great deal longer. He can have had no illusions that all would be a bed of roses, but presumably thought that he could somehow succeed, where MacColl had failed, in uniting the opposing factions in the parish. He was speedily disillusioned. MacColl had been a happily married man with a family to support him. Walker, like Tooth, was a bachelor, but, unlike Tooth, could not count on the support of a united congregation. The result was a lonely six-year martyrdom. Walker, like MacColl, was constantly struggling to mollify the Protestant members of the congregation without mortally offending the Catholics. The lengths to which some of the former went were extreme even by nineteenth-century standards. Even the bishop was shocked. On one occasion he accused the new people's warden, A. J. Thorman, of encouraging 'intolerable and offensive espionage' on members of the congregation so as to frighten them into not making their communion (in order to reduce the total number of communicants to less than the required Prayer Book minimum). On another occasion Thorman applied for a summons against a Catholic stalwart for 'illegally' acting as server in the administration of Holy Communion; the magistrate refused to grant it.

In the summer of 1884 Walker's health at last broke down under the continued strain and he suffered a severe mental breakdown. Although he eventually recovered he realized that he would have to resign a cure which had now become intolerable. He put off his resignation for a while, however, when he learned that the patronage of the living had passed from Robert Tooth, Arthur's brother, into less friendly hands. The reason for the sale of the advowson (or right of presentation to the living) was a simple one. Robert Tooth had been declared bankrupt; and the advowson, as one of his assets, had had to be sold. It realized £800 – £200 more than Arthur Tooth was prepared (or could afford) to offer. Why the matter was kept a secret from the congregation remains a mystery, as the wealthier members could surely have clubbed together to buy the advowson. As it was, the original purchaser made a quick profit by reselling it for £1400 to the Church Patronage Society, an Evangelical body. The writing was now truly on the wall. Walker eventually resigned after the Easter vestry of April 1885, but he can have had no illusions as to the fate of the parish after his departure. His fears were soon realized. The new patrons appointed as his successor a staunch Protestant, Sydney Augustus Selwyn, vicar of Sheerness, Kent, whose five-year reign saw the total abandonment of the parish's Catholic tradition.

Walker left the parish in June; Selwyn was appointed in August, but was not instituted until 7 February 1886. He lost no time in removing all traces of the former regime. Altarfrontals, vestments, candlesticks and crosses vanished into oblivion – as did the old choir, whose members declined to turn up for evening communion services. They were replaced by more amenable choristers. More significantly, in a backward move, Selwyn reinstated the pews which Tooth had removed in favour of chairs. The revived pew-rents brought him in £450 a year, treble the amount of his annual stipend, and effectively discouraged his poorer parishioners from attending church. Under Selwyn St James's went up-market, developing into one of countless churches of its type catering for middle-class suburbia. As such it flourished exceedingly – as did Selwyn, who ended his ministry as vicar of the plum living of Sherborne, Dorset. Poor Walker's ministry also had a happy ending. He recovered his health and went on to be the much-loved vicar of Chattisham, Suffolk. He died in 1906.

*   *   *

And what of Arthur Tooth himself? On his return in the summer of 1878 from his long convalescence abroad he could legitimately, if he had wished, have resumed his reign at Hatcham. But by then many of his old congregation had abandoned St James's for other churches, and the remainder were at sixes and sevens with their Protestant neighbours, so this option might well have provided him with cold comfort. He would have felt that his martyrdom had already lasted long enough. Or he could have forsaken the Church of England for the Church of Rome, like a number of Tractarians before him. But he was a totally committed Anglican and would have regarded such an act of apostasy as a betrayal of all he had stood for. So he fell back on the third alternative of throwing himself heart and soul into the caring ministry of running his schools, sisterhood and home for alcoholics. Such tasks had formed an important part of his ministry at Hatcham, but only a subsidiary part. Now they became his full-time occupation, to which he was to devote the next fifty-odd years of his life. Although, by the time of his death in 1931, all the Catholic practices for which he had fought had become commonplace throughout the Church of England, Tooth himself never returned to the parochial ministry. This was not because he was reluctant to take charge of another parish, but simply because he was never offered one.

'The Church of England has been everything to me,' he wrote

to a friend in his old age, 'but there is a long record that I am
nothing to it. No one can accuse me of self-seeking. I ask for
nothing and I make no complaint. With a rebuff now and then
from the authorities, I have unwillingly lived as an outsider; but
this is no fault of mine, and so most likely it will be to the end.'
He used to advertise in the *Church Times* as being free to take
duty, but never obtained anything permanent. Joyce Coombs
suggests that his reason for resigning St James's was almost
certainly the desire to enlarge the orphanage and to continue
unimpeded the type of religious instruction which in Hatcham
it was increasingly difficult to support. But, according to Donald
Cormack, there was no specifically religious instruction given
during school hours at the orphanage, nor did Tooth seek to
impinge his own views on the boys committed to his charge.
At all events he regarded his half-century of pastoral care first at
Woodside and afterwards in Kent as a totally fulfilling ministry.

The Woodside estate outside Croydon into which Tooth
moved after his departure from St James's was spacious enough
to house all the three institutions which he had founded while
at Hatcham: St Michael's School for Orphan Boys; St Gabriel's
School for Orphan Girls; and St Raphael's Convent, to which
was attached a small home for alcoholics. The estate included
farmland, parkland and a small lake, together with a large mansion, outbuildings and stables. The house had been built in 1788
to a classical porticoed design by Valentine Wright. It had been
occupied from 1869 to 1878 by a racing entrepreneur, Henry
Dorling, the inventor of the popular 'Correct Card' for race-
goers. Tooth stocked the house with many of the native artefacts
he had collected while on his foreign travels. He added an
extension which housed the nuns and which, when the estate
was sold, became the Ashburton Library. The estate was self-
supporting, the 'farm' being more of a market garden, though
pigs were kept. By the time of the First World War the grounds,
tended by sixteen gardeners, housed over four thousand fruit-
trees. Tooth was landlord of a highly desirable property. Concerts and sales of work were held regularly, and the school was
even featured in *Cook's Guide to London*. There was an open
day for visitors once a week.

Central to the whole undertaking was the small community of Sisters – the Order of the Holy Paraclete – who looked after both the orphans and the inebriates. They were responsible for all the cooking (including baking bread) and for settling the accounts. They also did such odd jobs as chopping wood and going round London begging for clothes for their charges. The alcoholics received advanced treatment in the form of auto-suggestion through hypnosis. Tooth was fascinated by hypnosis, and would make use of it for the painless extraction of teeth! The girls' school did not survive for long because of the shortage of Sisters and the development of the work among women alcoholics; and Tooth concentrated on the educational side of his work at St Michael's, the school for boys. This was techni-cally an 'orphanage for the sons of gentlemen', though to qualify for admittance it was only necessary to have one parent deceased. On its move to Woodside it began as a public elemen-tary school, receiving a grant from the Board of Education and regular visits from government inspectors. But in 1915 Tooth decided to forgo the grant and manage St Michael's as an inde-pendent school. The ages of the boys ran from five to fourteen and the numbers fluctuated between thirty and seventy. Teach-ing at the school throughout the Croydon period was formal. There was very little practical work, the question-and-answer method being preferred. The curriculum was bookish, and during World War One there were evening classes in French and shorthand. Although Tooth was a science graduate and maintained a fully-equipped laboratory at Woodside, he appears not to have shared its secrets with his pupils. The bookish atmosphere inside the school, however, was balanced by a healthy diet of outdoor activities. In addition to the normal games routine of football and cricket the boys were expected to help the gardeners with such tasks as sawing logs for the fires, tending the fruit-trees and collecting and storing the fruit. Tooth, himself a good horseman and shot, also encouraged his pupils to ride, shoot and swim – and to learn about farming and camping with a view to possible emigration.

Strangely, for an institution founded under church auspices, no specifically religious education took place within school hours, though St Michael's was recognized as a Church of England school. Each morning, however, the boys attended a celebration of the Eucharist in the chapel conducted by Tooth, and there were three celebrations on Sundays. Croydon was then a detached enclave in the diocese of Canterbury, so for his first four years at Woodside Tooth had Archbishop Tait as his diocesan. It is not recorded that Tait ever visited the school – though the chapel was inspected on his behalf by the vicar of Croydon, who voiced his uneasiness about a 'movable crucifix on a ledge at the back of the Holy Table'. No doubt Tait shrank from the prospect of another lengthy correspondence with his old antagonist, so the crucifix was allowed to remain.

Though he had little direct responsibility for their education, Tooth was a firm favourite with the boys – and not only because he was in the habit of regaling the older ones with titbits from the special fare provided by the Sisters for his evening meal (he would eat little or nothing himself). One old pupil recalled: 'The boys were one and all attached to Father Tooth. His appearance in the grounds was the signal for a rush in his direction, and it was considered an honour to be first to arrive and take his arm.' He provided firm guidance in moral principles, but never forced his advanced religious views on the boys. Though he was a man of fixed ideas who would suffer no compromise or doubt, he never looked back in anger, only in laughter – and there were no tears of regret for what might have been. As for the boys, he loved them as a father, and endeavoured to give them as near a family life as was possible in an institution.

After forty-five years the school found itself having to move. By the 1920s Woodside stood out as a rural enclave in Croydon's growing suburban sprawl. The property was compulsorily purchased in 1924 by the Borough Council for £20,000. The house was demolished, and the convent extension converted into a public library. Tooth decided to move the school to Kent and, with the proceeds of the Woodside sale, purchased a property at Otford, two miles from Sevenoaks, where the school continues to this day. Attached to the house were ninety acres of pasture and woodland, so that the school's rustic amenities were not lost through the move. By this time, however, Tooth was well into his eighties and no more than a figurehead in the running of the school. But he had also, with the process of time, developed into one of the Grand Old Men of the Catholic Movement and was wheeled out on appropriate occasions.

Although he was growing old when the motor-car first appeared on the streets, he took up the new invention with enthusiasm, and at the age of seventy drove his own car to Land's End and back. He was always alert and interested in current questions of the day, showing a penetrating wisdom in his remarks and an outlook which made him seem much younger than he really was.

There was a great gathering held in February 1927 to celebrate the golden jubilee of his release from prison. On the platform beside him sat Lord Halifax, ten days older than Tooth and still president of the English Church Union, who had been among the visitors to the Horsemonger Lane Gaol all those years ago. A jubilee booklet produced in honour of the occasion included quotations from an article about Tooth that had appeared the previous year in a Kentish newspaper. 'Father Tooth is in his eighty-ninth year,' the writer of the article remarked, 'but his is a wonderful nature; he refuses to grow old, and still looks out on life with the keenness and romance of youth. He is passionately devoted to boys, and his life-long service to them now takes the form of a school in his quiet country mansion, which is also their home – spiritually and temporally . . . he has spent himself almost entirely in their service.'

Tooth's final appearance in public took place three and a half years later. Desmond Morse-Boycott (who used to take his choirboys year by year to visit Tooth at Otford) recalls the occasion in his book, *They Shine Like Stars*:

> No more dramatic event has occurred in the history of the [Catholic] Movement than when he walked out, bent with age, to take part in the High Mass on Stamford Bridge Football Ground during the Anglo-Catholic Congress of 1930. The shout of welcome was one of the great authentic shouts of Church history . . . massed choirs . . . a vast company of

priests in robes; ranks of servers in scarlet and fine linen . . .
and thousands of lay-folk . . . looking down upon the arena,
upon the sacred ministers in golden vestments, the bishops in
copes and mitres – all combined to make such a scene as
Arthur Tooth could never have imagined on the desolate day
when he left the prison . . .

Eight months later, on 5 March 1931, Tooth died peacefully
while sitting in his chair at Otford Court. He was buried in the
Crystal Palace District Cemetery next to his old friend Thomas
Layman. The funeral sermon was preached by Fr Frederick
Croom, son of his one-time churchwarden. He left his money
– £38,000 – to the only two remaining Sisters of the Community
of the Paraclete to survive his death. He had offered £10,000
towards the re-establishment of the shrine of Thomas Becket
(to whose memory he was devoted) in Canterbury Cathedral,
but the Chapter rejected the design by Sir Ninian Comper and
nothing came of the idea.

By the time of his death Tooth was a largely forgotten figure.
At the turn of the century the mere mention of his name would
have been sufficient to arouse passionate concern, but now the
news of his death was received with no more than polite interest.
As the *Church Times* remarked at the start of its long obituary
notice: 'He figured in the history of the Church of a past
generation, now almost forgotten by his successors, who are yet
too close to the immediate past to realize the part he played in
it.' Everything Tooth had fought for in the cause of Anglo-
Catholicism had now been won. But, unlike other stalwarts of
the Catholic Movement, he was content to bow out once the
immediate crisis was over and, being of independent means, was
able to devote himself to the care of his boys without having to
worry about where the next penny was coming from.

The central conundrum still remains: why did he suddenly
abandon his militancy when he did? Although, as the years
progressed, he might have found it increasingly hard to secure
the offer of a parochial cure, in the immediate aftermath of the
Hatcham years Catholic patrons would surely have been only
too anxious to secure his services for their parishes. The answer

must be that the months of stress leading up to his imprisonment really had taken their toll. His friends and supporters might shout at him from the sidelines to stand firm and return to the centre of the fray, but *they* were not required to leave the sidelines. He had already suffered what many regarded as months of martyrdom – and had then been set free on a technicality without having truly vindicated his cause. Had he resumed the reins at St James's after his conviction had been quashed in the High Court, he would have been an optimist to suppose that he had seen the last of his troubles. His opponents would have been sure to renew their attack on a different front, and he would have had to face fresh worries with his health still under severe strain. (The history of St James's under his successors, MacColl and Walker, shows what might have been in store for him.) It was a prospect before which a strong man might well have blanched. Who can blame Arthur Tooth for deciding that discretion in his case would be the better part of valour, and for retiring once for all from the ecclesiastical fray?

R Radclyffe Dolling

Fr Dolling in his Portsmouth prime

CHAPTER 5

---◆◆◆---

SAINT OF THE SLUMS

Robert William Radclyffe Dolling
(1851–1902)

'WITH DOLLING ONE HAS TO accept perpetually the prospect of a crisis.' The *cri-de-coeur* came from the Headmaster of Winchester, William Fearon, in the course of a letter he wrote to the new Bishop of Winchester, Randall Davidson, during the early days of what was to prove the final Dolling crisis at St Agatha's, Landport, Portsmouth. The issue which had brought on this particular crisis was a doctrinal one – Masses for the dead. It ended with Dolling's dramatic decision to resign immediately. He regarded Davidson's rules to restrain as fetters to bind him. Although he had intended to retire anyway from St Agatha's a few months later, he seized on Davidson's attempt to impose conditions on his conduct of worship as an excuse to leave prematurely in a blaze of publicity. He seemed in fact to crave a martyr's crown.

Dolling had been at Portsmouth for ten years, in charge of the Winchester College Mission at St Agatha's. There he had made a name for himself as a slum priest of charismatic powers and enormous organizing ability. He packed the people into the pews by the power of his oratory. He kept open house in his parsonage. He launched an ambitious programme to cater for the social side of parish life. He took on the slum landlords, the brewers and the brothel-keepers – with a fair measure of success. His sacrificial efforts transformed one of Portsmouth's worst slums and brought hundreds of souls to Christianity. But his evangelistic zeal and social crusading went hand in hand with advanced ritualistic teaching – and it was this course which brought about successive clashes with the Church authorities, culminating in the showdown with Davidson. With the two previous Bishops of Winchester, Harold Browne and Anthony Thorold, Dolling had established a *modus vivendi*; and, though the volcano smoked visibly from time to time, it never erupted. How and why things finally came to a head within weeks of Davidson's arrival in the diocese will be described in due course. It was, however, Dolling's earlier ministry which formed the training-ground for his Portsmouth decade.

*   *   *

Robert William Radclyffe Dolling was of Anglo-Irish descent. He was born at the Old Rectory, Magheralin, County Down, on 10 February 1851, the sixth child and eldest son in a family of nine. Paradoxically for a fervent Anglo-Catholic, his forebears on both sides had been Protestant in their sympathies. On his father's side he was descended from a French Huguenot refugee who had fled to England in 1580. On his mother's side he was descended from Scottish settlers in Ulster. Dolling's grandfather migrated to Ireland, becoming incumbent of Magheralin (a nearby village, Dollingstown, was named after him). His father, also named Robert, was a land-agent by profession; for many years he managed the estates of the Mercers' Company in the North of Ireland, residing at Kilrea, County Derry. Dolling's parents were both deeply religious. His father, a warm-hearted, genial man, was a Protestant Evangelical who disliked both Roman Catholics and Tractarian Anglicans. When his son began seriously to think of ordination he said at first that he could not bear to see him a ritualistic priest. He later changed tack, however, and told his eldest daughter: 'I am sure dear Bob is all right. He has such firm faith in our Lord Jesus Christ.' Dolling's mother, a great-niece of the first Earl of Caledon, was described by a friend of the family as 'the truest Christian gentlewoman I ever met . . . simple, generous, unselfish . . . a high-bred lady in the highest and noblest sense of the word'. The young Robert imbibed his parents' piety from an early age. In the words of one of his seven sisters, 'he was the child of many prayers'.

His religion from the first had a practically benevolent streak. On his fourth birthday he was seriously ill and confined to bed. When his birthday cake was brought to his bedside he remarked piously: 'Cut a piece for everyone in this house – *and for those in the kitchen.*' Throughout his life he never forgot those in the kitchen. His strong religious instincts were apparent from an early age. He used to make his sisters sit on chairs in the nursery while, vested in an improvised surplice, he conducted impromptu services. His theology showed a practical turn. At the age of four he remarked to a guest at dinner who had expressed puzzlement over the doctrine of the Trinity: 'I've got meat and potatoes and gravy on my plate. That's three things. But it's only one dinner. That's like the Trinity.' In spite of his Evangelical upbringing, his humour, urbanity and sympathies tended to be more characteristic of the Catholic South of Ireland than of the Protestant North.

Dolling was sent to England for his education. He went first to a preparatory school in Hertfordshire, The Grange at Stevenage, and from there in 1864 to Harrow. Among his fellow-Harrovians was one Randall Davidson, two years his senior, though there is no evidence that the two had any close dealings with one another while at school. In 1868 Dolling went on to Trinity College, Cambridge, but he left after a year without taking his degree: ill-health, and particularly ophthalmia, made study difficult. It was for health reasons that he spent the next year abroad, mainly in Florence. He returned to Ireland after his mother's death in January 1870 and assisted his father in his land-agency work. Unlike most Irish land-agents he was a favourite of the tenants, whether Protestant or Catholic, and was so trusted that he had no need to carry the customary revolver when collecting rents. T. P. O'Connor remarked of him that, though North of Ireland in blood and upbringing, he was South of Ireland in the tenderness of his heart and the readiness of his sympathy.

After his father's death in 1878 Dolling continued for a while as a land-agent, but spent much time in London. He attached himself to St Alban's, Holborn, to which he had been attracted by the warmth and personality of Arthur Stanton. His growing sympathy with Anglo-Catholicism led him to admire the combination of sacramental teaching with vigorous social work which he found at St Alban's. He threw himself into the latter, choosing as his particular sphere of work the St Martin's Postmen's League, which had been founded by the clergy of St Alban's as a system of free clubs for the use of postmen between letter-deliveries. Dolling became warden of the League's Southwark branch in 1879. He was so popular among the postmen that they soon christened him 'Brother Bob' – and so well-known that letters directed simply to 'Brother Bob, London' would always find him.

It was towards the end of 1881 that he decided in favour of ordination; and early in 1882 he entered Salisbury Theological College. But here he proved a fish out of water, in that he was interested not so much in theology, exegesis or Church history as in practical Christianity. The Principal, E. B. Ottley, wrote afterwards: 'It must be confessed that as a student he was not in all respects successful. He was not adapted to student life, and he came to college too old, after too long a spell of active mission work in London, to settle down to strenuous reading. . . . It was almost impossible to induce him to read.' The unacademic Dolling lived largely apart from his fellow-students, who christened him 'the Land-Agent'. He rarely bothered to attend lectures and but thinly disguised his contempt for formal study. He found the choral services in the cathedral a great trial and used to read a book during the anthems. He spent as much time as possible in the mission parish of St Martin: preaching constantly, penetrating the hidden byways of the parish and gaining an impressive influence among its young people, many of whom visited him in his rooms at college. He can be said to have revolutionized the missionary work of the parish.

He was ordained deacon in Salisbury Cathedral by Bishop Moberly on 20 May 1883; and it was in the diocese of Salisbury that he served his title as curate of Corscombe, in west Dorset. But the arrangement was a nominal one, its purpose being

merely to provide Dolling with a stipend while he carried on
his main work as a missioner in the East End of London. In
fact he spent very little time in Dorset, though the lads and
lasses of Corscombe used to gather wild flowers to send to
Brother Bob's East-enders. His main field of activity was as a
missionary deacon in the parish of Holy Trinity, Stepney. He
was nominally connected to the parish church, but in practice
confined almost all his attention to the district of which he had
charge. There he achieved the same reputation as he had won
while a lay missioner among the postmen. The services in the
mission chapel were dignified but homely. Their spirit was
summed up by a local Nonconformist: 'I don't care whether
he's a Ritualist or a Roman Catholic; he preaches Christianity
in a way I have never heard before, and hardly ever expect to
hear again.'

Dolling was ordained priest in St Paul's Cathedral on Trinity
Sunday, 1885. But his priesting was to coincide with his first
brush with ecclesiastical authority. The offending prelate on this
occasion was the newly-appointed Bishop of London, Frederick
Temple. Hitherto Dolling's superior had been the Suffragan
Bishop of Bedford, Walsham How, who had treated him sympathetically in recognition of his special gifts. Temple, however,
insisted on regarding him as an ordinary curate rather than as a
special missioner licensed to Bishop How. Dolling declined to
accept a licence as curate to the vicar of Holy Trinity, Stepney,
and resigned on 1 July 1885. 'It was on the altar of red tape that
his work was sacrificed,' his curate and biographer, Charles
Osborne, observes of the summary termination of his East End
ministry.

*   *   *

Dolling now had sufficient experience to accept an independent
charge of his own; and an offer was not long in coming. The
Winchester College Mission had been established in 1882 in one
of the most run-down areas of Portsmouth. At first it had no
place of worship of its own, but in 1884 the mission church of
St Agatha was opened to serve its needs. The first missioner was
the Rev. Robert Linklater, a moderately ritualistic priest, but

after three years he had had enough, and Dolling was chosen to succeed him. Winchester College, with which the appointment lay, would have been well aware that Dolling, like Linklater before him, was a ritualist; but any qualms the college may have had on that score were outweighed by the new missioner's reputation as an outstanding evangelist and tireless worker among the poor. Bishop How had sung his praises to the college authorities, who were speedily won over by the charm of his forceful personality.

In his memoir, *Ten Years in a Portsmouth Slum*, Dolling has left a vivid account of his initial interviews with the headmaster, William Fearon, and with the Bishop of Winchester, Harold Browne, in whose diocese Portsmouth then lay. His meeting with Fearon proved a happy augury of the good relations he was to enjoy with the college during 'ten years of the happiest life that I can imagine possible for anyone'. Fearon was to prove a staunch friend to Dolling in the various clashes with authority that marked his Portsmouth years. The interview with the bishop also went off well, though, says Dolling, 'I think at first he was more nervous than I was.' This would have been because Browne, though no rabid Protestant, was a middle-of-the-road Anglican nervous about extremism in churchmanship; and he expressed the hope that the new missioner would 'not do anything foolish'. Dolling recalls that it was too late for him to return to London that night, so after the interview he had to pawn his watch in order to pay for a bed. He also visited his predecessor, Linklater, who explained to him his ideals for making St Agatha's into a 'centre of Catholic devotion' in which dignified services would be supplemented by social work of all kinds and descriptions. Dolling was fully prepared to base his own activities on those ideals.

He began work in Landport on Michaelmas Day, 1885. He found the two prevailing notes of the area to be 'poverty and sin'. Men drank because their stomachs were empty and the pub was the only cheerful place of entertainment. Girls became prostitutes because their mothers had done so before them, regarding it as a necessary circumstance of life if they were to survive. On his first Sunday afternoon Dolling saw two young sailors dancing with two girls in the street. One couple, the worse for drink, toppled over, and Dolling stepped forward to help them up. 'My endeavour was evidently looked upon from a hostile point of view, for the parish voice was translated into a shower of stones until the unfallen sailor cried out, "Don't touch the Holy Joe. He doesn't look such a bad sort." ' On another occasion, at a children's service in St Agatha's, two boys calmly lit their pipes and began to smoke. Dolling comments in his book: 'One remedy alone seemed possible – to seize them by the back of the neck and run them out of church, knocking their heads together as hard as I could.' Low wages led to constant poverty. One week's sickness for the breadwinner of a family meant a fortnight's living on the proceeds of pawning clothes and furniture.

Such was the milieu in which Dolling was to toil unremittingly for the next ten years. It was a mass of small and overcrowded dwellings – in the words of Charles Osborne, 'a sort of municipal Cinderella sitting in rags amid its better cared-for sisters of the borough'. The staircases were so narrow that Dolling, a tubby figure of a man, sometimes stuck half-way and had to be pushed up or pulled down from below. Although the population of the district was only five thousand, it boasted over fifty pubs and as many brothels, while its slaughter-houses were notorious. The secret of Dolling's success in such a setting was that the man suited the environment. Its vices afforded a perpetual challenge to his fighting instincts. 'He preferred making history', says Osborne 'to studying its pages with the aid of midnight oil.'

Dolling was assisted by a staff of curates and lay workers who were responsible for most of the district visiting. He himself had necessarily to be at the centre of things, holding the reins and making sure that everything ran as smoothly as possible. Lord Northcliffe, the newspaper tycoon, who was associated with him in the management of a camp for poor boys at Broadstairs, Kent, described him as among the very best men of business he had ever met. 'He appealed to me, primarily, by reasons of his great power of organization. He not only knew how things ought to be done, but he was able to make the most unlikely people do them. He knew how to make weak people self-reliant, how to check the zeal of the exuberant.' Osborne calls Dolling an ecclesiastical Cecil Rhodes, planning ever fresh developments. His study was more like the office of a company chairman or departmental head than that of a humble parochial clergyman.

In his *Ten Years* Dolling describes the gruelling timetable of his typical day. He got up at five-thirty and roused the boys in the parsonage who were going to work or the sailors who had to board their ships by half past six. After perhaps half an hour of reading or sermon-preparation Dolling would be in church by seven to say his first Mass. This was followed by Mattins and a second Mass. Breakfast at eight-thirty was attended by a shorthand clerk who would take down most of Dolling's correspondence while the meal was in progress. The morning was spent in continuous meetings with people – 'parish people, inquisitive people, people with real troubles, people with imaginary ones; but the door was always open, and everybody came upstairs as they liked'. After one o'clock dinner Dolling might take an hour or two's rest, perhaps walking to Portsdown Hill or the sea. Tea was at five-thirty and another service in the church at half past seven. 'Then clubs, gymnasium, etc., till 10 p.m.; supper and prayers and everybody in their room at 10.15 p.m. At 10.30 the door was locked, and anyone coming in had to ring the bell.'

Dolling shared two convictions with his helpers which underlay his ministry. One was to popularize the Catholic faith in order to make the Church a lively body rather than one bound up in books. Ritual was valuable, in his view, as a visual aid. The second conviction was that the Church should cater for the social as well as for the spiritual needs of its people. Politically Dolling was much more radical than his predecessor, Linklater. And in the parish itself his Christianity was invariably of a practical kind. He had no use for pious types who volunteered to assist for airy-fairy reasons. Once, when a youth fell on his knees before him and expressed a wish for a monastic habit, Dolling pointed to the crowded and disordered shelves of his library and exclaimed: 'If you want to do something useful, get up and dust and arrange those books.' The would-be monk soon wearied of his task.

In Linklater's day the church itself had catered for social functions as well as for worship. Dolling felt, however, that a church should not be used for non-religious purposes, even when the chancel was screened off from the nave. He therefore acquired a redundant Baptist chapel near the church which he turned into a gymnasium. It became the focal point for his social work in the district. Its proximity to the parsonage helped to accustom its patrons to associate recreation with religion. The rules were simple: no gambling, no bad language, no losing of temper, no annoying anybody else.

One of Dolling's special gifts was his ability to surmount barriers of class in his dealings with his parishioners. He not only mixed well himself with all sorts and conditions of folk, but he enabled others to feel similarly at ease. He was merciless, however, to those who showed signs of class-consciousness. Once, when a clergyman's wife made some disparaging remark about Dolling's girls' club ending with a reference to her own daughters, 'My girls are ladies', Dolling retorted sharply: 'My girls are ladies too.' Much of his work at Landport consisted in helping lame dogs over stiles. He was always ready to give a bed at the parsonage and food to a man going through a difficult time, in order to help him get on his legs again. But he was too sharp to be taken in by impostors. He combined compassion with shrewdness, and could soon spot a fraudulent cadger. One friend remarked: 'I never knew any man who could "size" a fellow up so quickly as Dolling could.' He was good with children and had a particularly soft spot for working-class mothers. In a telling phrase he once remarked: 'They have no baize doors between the nursery and the bedroom.' But sometimes the mothers would answer back, and on one occasion Dolling was rebuked for his insistence on outward reverence: 'I shan't let my boys go to your school any longer, because kneeling wears out the knees of their trousers.' The fruits of Dolling's labours may be summed up in a report he made to his well-wishers about halfway through his time at Landport:

We have put into the army 39 young men, into the navy 57 young men. We have emigrated to Australia, America, and elsewhere 63. We have started in life over 100 young men who lived with us. We have reformed 25 thieves just out of gaol. We have sent into service and into shops about 100 girls. . . . We have turned many drunkards into self-respecting, church-going people. We have rescued 144 fallen women, and got them into Homes. We have maintained, and are maintaining, in preventive Homes 124 children, snatched from the brink of ruin. We have shut up in the district over 50 brothels. . . . We house 6 old couples free of rent. . . . We feed for a halfpenny a meal 180 children. . . . We teach over 500 children in our Sunday-schools, and 600 in our Day-schools. . . . We have a nigger-troupe, an acrobatic troupe, dancing-class, and glee club; a sewing-class; a large temperance society, and Band of Hope; a lending library, and three penny savings banks.

*   *   *

Winchester College, as patrons of the mission, paid Dolling his stipend; and he regarded it as an important part of his ministry to cement close and friendly relations with the staff and pupils of the college. W. A. Fearon, who served as headmaster throughout Dolling's years at Landport, called his association with the college 'pure, unbroken sunshine'. In a chapter which he contributed to Osborne's 'life' (and in which allowance must be made for a natural bias in favour of the missioner) Fearon claims that Dolling succeeded in making the school feel a personal pride and vital share in the work of the mission – 'not as an alien interest, but as an essential part of the daily life of the school'. As for the ebullient missioner himself, says Fearon, 'there can be no doubt that many a Wykehamist has been helped by Dolling's influence and Dolling's example to form a higher resolve for life; to recognize the obligation, in whatever profession he might adopt, to do something for the bettering of his fellow-men – to find his ideal in serving rather than in enjoying.'

Dolling appears to have remained a boy to the end of his life, in the sense that he could always forget his own preoccupations and throw himself into the fun and games of those around him.

As an Old Harrovian he understood the public-school ethos, and seems never to have been troubled by the fashionable doubts of later times as to whether a public-school education might be élitist in encouraging class divisions. He was able to identify entirely with the Wykehamists. 'We have two great blessings at Winchester,' he remarks in *Ten Years*. 'We are a small school – only four hundred – and none of our men [i.e, boys] are very rich.' He was certainly a patriotic, if honorary, Wykehamist. At football and cricket matches, says Fearon, he was a prominent figure on the ground, 'more angry than most if our side lost, jubilant in victory'. In the words of a pupil who came to know him well, 'Here was a man who was obviously one of us.'

There was a two-way link between the school and the mission. Twice a year, in January and September, Dolling paid an official visit to the school, preaching in the chapel on the Sunday afternoon. He also paid regular but less formal visits to the separate school houses, spending an afternoon and evening with the boys and taking his evening meal with them. It was through these visits that he really got to know the boys (or 'men', as he always insisted on calling them) and to exercise a lasting influence on many of them.* 'An unbroken chain of upright English gentlemen', he calls them in *Ten Years*; 'not perhaps the most brilliant, but certainly among the most dependable men of their time'. In return for his visits to them, many of the young English gentlemen – two seniors at a time – paid weekend visits to Landport to see something of the work of the mission.

From time to time, in addition, a party from St Agatha's would visit Winchester. On the first occasion (in 1886) the hosts were a little taken aback by the unorthodox behaviour of the guests. 'They broke into the Warden's garden and stole his fruit,' Dolling recalls. 'They climbed over the wall of the bathing-place and laughed at the men who were learning to swim; they tried to kiss the ladies who waited on them; they most of them got drunk before we went home.' As the visitors became accustomed to the

---

*Including Edward Talbot, a future Superior of the Community of the Resurrection. Talbot was so moved by one of Dolling's sermons that he put a pound in the collection – a whole term's pocket-money.

school and its ways, so their initial rowdiness gave way to less rumbustious behaviour. By the mid–1890s the numbers of visitors had to be restricted to 160, most of whom paid their own fare. 'One whole day's perfect enjoyment', says Dolling; 'everyone sober, not a rude or rough word, and yet some of us were the identical people who had gone ten years before, and all of the same class, all the mission's children.' But, if the visitors' behaviour was now impeccable, their appetites were unrestrained:

> Great was the bustle, carving and filling of plates and glasses. Great was the heat, for it was high midsummer. Every guest had four or five helpings – one is recorded to have had seven – so that the waiters and waitresses were busily employed. Not only the College servants were there, but masters with their wives and daughters.

This particular commentator recalls that even the headmaster handed round potatoes as if to the manner born.

*   *   *

Dolling calculated that he spent the equivalent of one day a week on what he called 'begging' – raising money both locally and further afield for the work of the mission. During his ten years at Landport he raised a total of almost £51,000, an enormous sum of money for those days. Of this, £11,000 came direct from Winchester College, though he reckoned that a further £15,000 had come privately from individual Wykehamists. St Agatha's was a poor district, but Dolling persuaded no fewer than 286 of his parishioners to contribute regularly to church funds. The local money came mostly in coppers, threepenny-bits and sixpences – shillings and half-crowns being rare and gold unknown. Sunday collections averaged over £4.

During the ten years Dolling spent over £1300 on postage and travelling. A lot of this went on his 'money-grubbing'. Every quarter he sent out to all his regular subscribers an account of the quarter's work, drawing in further donations. But most of his begging was by word of mouth. He spoke in private drawing-rooms, in public halls, at concerts and in schools; these efforts brought in over £3000. Sometimes he came home two or three times a week from London by the midnight train, so that at last he found it cheaper to take a season ticket. Even his journeyings had their perils. He suffered much from the cold when travelling at night, so one of his sisters bought him a fur coat. A woman in one of his audiences commented: 'If I had known he had a coat like that, I should not have put five shillings in the collection!'

Dolling was down-to-earth in his attitude to giving. He quotes with approval an account of a meeting held to sympathize with a poor woman who had just lost her husband. 'Two gentlemen delivered very eloquent speeches, which drew tears from the eyes of those who heard them. The third speaker said, "I have no eloquence, but I sympathize £10", which he put down upon the table.' Dolling himself was fund-raising to the last. The ornate new church which replaced the old St Agatha's (and indirectly caused his resignation) cost over £11,000 to build. When Dolling left he still owed the builder £3000. By herculean efforts after his departure he succeeded in paying off the debt.

* * *

But of course it was far from being sunshine all the way. Dolling was constantly in hot water for one reason or another, and was never slow to take up the sword on behalf of what he regarded as a righteous cause. In his own account of his Portsmouth years he distinguishes between his 'battles civil' and his 'battles ecclesiastical'. In the former he took on the various vested interests which were responsible to a greater or lesser extent for the sorry state of so many of his parishioners. For those who were officially responsible for the welfare of the less affluent members of society he had a profound contempt. Of a particular Board of Guardians he remarked dismissively: 'Some were rather the guardians of the rates than the guardians of the poor.' In his battles with big business he allied himself to temperance workers, labour leaders and trade unionists. He fought the land-lords of Portsmouth over slum dwellings. He fought the shop-keepers over sweated labour and the excessive hours worked by shop-assistants. He fought the brewers over ill-conducted public houses. In his 'battles civil' he often found himself on the same platform as those who disagreed with his ecclesiastical stance. Thus, in his fight to secure relief for the overworked shop-assistants (the 'better shops' remained open till seven-thirty from Monday to Thursday, till ten on Friday and till midnight on Saturday, while the little shops 'never seem to close at all day or night'), his chief ally was a leading Baptist minister who also supported him on the drink question.

It was as a temperance reformer that Dolling made his main mark (and the most enemies). He was himself for most of his life a total abstainer (though an inveterate smoker), so that in this field he practised what he preached. Portsmouth at that time was notorious for its drink problem, much of it due to the large numbers of soldiers and sailors in the town. With a population of 160,000 it had 1040 places licensed for drink – or, deducting 25 per cent for children and abstainers, one licence for every 115 inhabitants, far above the national average.

Fifty-one of these public houses were in Dolling's own mission district; and, as he remarked in his quarterly letter of September 1888, you had to presuppose fifty-one landlords of immaculate virtue 'if for a moment you would imagine that they would not use every method, legitimate and otherwise, to attract customers'. Many of these pubs were in fact of highly questionable repute. The landlords, besides adulterating the drink, would often allow gambling and betting on their premises and encourage the singing of bawdy songs to make the men who roared the choruses all the thirstier. Many of the 'fallen women' of the district had fallen as a result of frequenting the pubs, and Dolling's efforts were directed equally at tackling the problem of prostitution. During his ten years in Landport he was instrumental in closing at least fifty brothels. On one occasion he revealed the name of the owner of the property and was threatened with legal proceedings. Dolling was unabashed and said that he would welcome the opportunity of exposing the miscreant. The result was that the landlord in question improved the 'moral condition' of his property rather than take his critic to court.

Dolling was not the only Portsmouth citizen to tackle this particular form of vice. Others of the clergy were concerned, together with Nonconformist ministers, doctors and trade-union leaders. A 'Portsmouth Social Purity Organization' was formed in 1893 under the presidency of Canon Edgar Jacob, vicar of Portsea and later Bishop of Newcastle and of St Albans. It was Jacob who, in his capacity of Rural Dean of Landport, was to cross swords with Dolling two years later by revealing to Bishop Davidson the extent of his ritualistic practices. But on this occasion the two men saw eye to eye, and Dolling took a key part in the fight for 'social purity'. The Organization set up a twenty-member committee to investigate the whole question of intoxication and breaches of the licensing laws within the borough, the manner of conducting the public houses and the moral condition of the streets. The committee presented its report in February 1894, revealing a deplorable state of affairs.

The mayor of Portsmouth was not amused. Only ten days before the publication of the report he had been much offended by a sermon Dolling had preached in London on behalf of the Christian Social Union. The subject of the address was 'Soldiers and Sailors'; and in the course of it the preacher alleged that most garrison towns, Portsmouth among them, were 'sinks of iniquity'. He backed up his claim with a mass of statistics relating to the number of public houses in the borough and to its generally unwholesome condition. The national papers reported the sermon at length, provoking a storm of patriotic indignation on the part of Portsmouth's publicans, shop-owners and lodging-house-keepers, who all feared the possible effect on their trade. The mayor rushed to the defence of his fellow-citizens with a furious indictment of Dolling as a mischievous scaremonger. 'The stigma which he has cast upon the town is not true,' he thundered – and sought to prove his assertion by an account of a visit which he had paid the previous evening with a local police inspector to fifty pubs between the hours of nine-forty and eleven p.m. and during which he had detected not a single drunken man on licensed premises.

Then, a few days later, came the damaging report by the Social Purity committee, and the mayor was in a quandary. He might attempt to dismiss Dolling as an ill-informed fanatic, but he could hardly laugh off a body of citizens headed by the influential Canon Jacob. Nor was his position made any easier when, in August of the same year, Jacob's organization published an open letter to the magistrates who were about to sit for the granting of licences to publicans. The letter was circulated throughout Portsmouth, and its mass of statistics was hard to refute. Nor did it seek to minimize the connection between drink and prostitution: 'Our evidence goes to show that in some parts of the town licensed houses are used as recruiting grounds for this unholy calling.' Between them the report of the committee and the open letter had their effect. The magistrates were in future not quite so ready as before to grant a licence to anyone who applied for it. The strength of Dolling's example was even recognized by one of Portsmouth's leading brewers, who wrote to him shortly before he left in 1896: 'While perhaps there are many who have not agreed with all your methods in carrying out the very difficult task you undertook amongst us, yet on all hands it is granted that you have done a great and noble work while in charge of your mission, and have courageously faced difficulties before which many an earnest, good man would have quailed, and have overcome them.'

*   *   *

It was, however, Dolling's 'battles ecclesiastical' which were to end in his leaving St Agatha's under a cloud of either glory or notoriety, according to one's point of view.

Dolling was a ritualist, but he never carried his ritualism to extremes. To him it always took second place to what he regarded as more essential features of worship. He had no patience with ceremonial minutiae – and once boxed the ears of a precious youth who had accused him of holding his hands 'incorrectly' at the altar. Nor did he have any time for the endless letters in Anglo-Catholic newspapers regarding trivial points of ritual. To him, it was the Mass itself that mattered, not the particular ceremonial observances surrounding it. 'What we have got to do in the Church of England', he would constantly reiterate, 'is to put the Mass into its proper place.' He certainly did that at St Agatha's. There were several celebrations on Sundays, and at least one celebration every weekday. Nor did he believe in half-measures. He once remarked: 'Some, in teaching Catholic principles, are like a bathing woman who coaxes the child in by gradual stages: in this Church we are like one who plunges the child in at once from head to foot.' The patient either 'took' the prescription, or else left in disgust. But there was method in what might have seemed his madness. A Roman Catholic friend said of him after his death:

> He was, in spite of his easy adoption of nearly the whole system of Catholic dogma and practice, an Evangelical to the backbone; that is to say, his whole interest was in the saving of those individual souls – and they were thousands – with whom he came in contact, and not in any ecclesiastical system for its own sake. He cared as little for theology and scholarship as did S. Francis or John Wesley, and it was because he discovered by intuition and experiment that Catholic beliefs and practices were efficacious for the sole end he cared about that he adopted them fearlessly without much deference to Bishops or Articles.

A significant part of the trouble that arose from time to time was Dolling's cavalier attitude to the Book of Common Prayer. He was above all an evangelist, and he felt that the Prayer Book, though suitable for instructed churchpeople, was inadequate as a missionary means of introducing the faith to ill-informed Christians. He was convinced that its language was unintelligible to such people, and that to evangelize them effectively required a more flexible form of worship than the Prayer Book could provide. So the gospel preaching at St Agatha's went hand in glove with special mission services and much extempore prayer – though the ritualistic side of the coin was apparent in the use of incense, servers in scarlet cassocks and frequent celebrations of the Eucharist.

Most of Dolling's non-liturgical services took place during the week. On Monday evening there was a prayer-meeting – 'our Dissenting service', as he called it. During the service intercessions of a simple character were offered for, among others, soldiers, sailors, emigrants and the sick, 'our dear dead' being remembered at the end. On Tuesday and Wednesday evenings the Prayer Book service was used: and on Thursdays 'Vespers of the Blessed Sacrament', consisting of psalms, a short lesson, a

hymn, the *Magnificat* and collects. The Tuesday, Wednesday
and Thursday devotions were followed by a short address or
instruction from one of the clergy. The Friday evening service
took the form of Stations of the Cross, each feature of the Passion
forming a subject of special devotion as the priests moved from
one picture on the walls to the next; Dolling usually conducted
this service himself. On Saturday nights Compline was said.
Dolling summed up his own attitude to his services in *Ten Years*:

> I believe you want two kinds of worship – one very dignified
> and ornate, which enables them to realize that they are making
> an offering to the Lord of Heaven and Earth; the other very
> simple and familiar, that they are talking to a loving Father who
> knows all their needs and wants to help them. If you had the
> ornate worship alone, there would be a danger of mere ritual-
> ism. If you had the familiar worship alone, there might be a
> danger of what some people seem to be so unnaturally afraid of
> – too much familiarity. At any rate, saying Evensong every
> night, you would certainly have neither of the dangers, but, on
> the other hand, you would have none of the educational or
> heart-touching power.

It was his use of non-liturgical services that first got Dolling into
trouble with the ecclesiastical authorities. The row was
occasioned by a meeting in Portsmouth's 'Protestant Hall'
attended mainly by Orangemen and Nonconformists and consisting of diatribes against Dolling. A 'gentleman from London'
ended a violent speech with the words: 'If we had a clergyman
like Mr. Dolling in our neighbourhood, we would soon take him
by the back of the neck and kick him out of the parish.' A voice
from the gallery retorted: 'He weighs fifteen stone, and you might
find it difficult!' The meeting forwarded a petition of protest to
the Bishop of Winchester, Harold Browne,* who, it will be

---

*Browne was an able and popular prelate who had succeeded Samuel Wilberforce at
Winchester after nine years as Bishop of Ely. He was twice thought of as a possible
Archbishop of Canterbury; once in 1868 in succession to Longley, and again in 1882
in succession to Tait. On the second occasion his claims to the primacy were strongly
pressed by Queen Victoria, and only his advanced age (he was then seventy-one) ruled
him out.

recalled, when interviewing Dolling at the time of his appointment, had expressed the hope that he 'would not do anything
foolish'.

Those attending the meeting had been mainly residents from
other parts of Portsmouth, which led Browne to observe of them:
'I do not think that the persons appealing to me have any *locus
standi*.' Nevertheless, he felt that he could not ignore them
entirely, since Dolling was technically in the wrong. He asked
him to confine his services and mode of worship within the
confessedly legal ritual of the Church of England – 'I am told that
your own people generally, though attached to you, would prefer
a less pronounced ritual.' Dolling wrote back that he was perfectly willing, if ordered, to confine his services to the Prayer
Book, but that such a change would mean a great diminution in
the congregations – especially on weekdays, when the services
complained of were used. The bishop retorted that the missioner
'should be satisfied with what is purely Anglican as sufficient for
all purposes of devotion, and not liable to create suspicion or to
stir up strife. Stations of the Cross, acolytes in crimson cassocks,
incensing the *Magnificat*, and the like, certainly excite bitter animosity in an eminently Protestant town like Portsmouth.'
Browne admitted that no complaints had come to him from
anyone resident in the district of St Agatha itself, but suggested
that other Portsea priests who were doing great work in formerly
neglected regions 'feel that the scare produced by advanced ritual
is seriously detrimental to them'. He prudently, however, made
no attempt to define the precise limits within which Dolling
should confine his services in future. Indeed, according to
Dolling, the bishop admitted that Vespers of the Blessed Sacrament, one of the rites to which exception had been taken and of
which he had previously been ignorant, was one of the most
beautiful and scriptural services he had ever read.

Things went on at St Agatha's much as before. But Browne
evidently kept a wary eye on the church; for, a year later, he
instructed his suffragan, Bishop Sumner of Guildford, to request
Dolling to give up various extra-liturgical observances in order
to meet the diocesan's objections. The 'excrescences' which the
missioner was urged to expunge were (1) incense; (2) Compline,

in which 'the choir practically absolve the priest'; (3) extempore prayer; (4) Vespers of the Blessed Sacrament in cope; (5) Vespers for the Dead. Dolling noted the request, but carried on much as before. He had an affectionate regard for Browne, whose character and piety he respected, and, according to Osborne, 'was always ready to resign should episcopal remonstrances with which he disagreed become episcopal demands which he could not conscientiously obey'. Luckily Browne, like many of his fellow-diocesans a peace-at-any-price man, was content to let this particular sleeping dog lie – though he could never bring himself to conduct confirmations at St Agatha's himself, but allowed Dolling to choose an episcopal deputy.

The number of confirmations during Dolling's ten years at Landport totalled 580. He gives a detailed breakdown of this figure in his *Ten Years*. Forty-six of those confirmed, he says, joined the army or navy; 38 emigrated; 171 left the district or else moved too far away to remain communicants; 40 died. Of the remaining 285, 46 lapsed altogether from communion; 37 were irregular in their attendance; 202 were members of the Communicants' League, communicating at least once a month. When Dolling arrived in 1885 there were a mere dozen names on the roll of regular communicants; when he left at the beginning of 1896 the roll contained the names of no fewer than 441 people. From a purely statistical point of view, if from no other, his methods certainly brought results.

The next major controversy in which he became involved was, however, political rather than ecclesiastical in its nature. It was sparked off by a Lenten lecture delivered at St Agatha's in 1890 by the Rev. Stewart Headlam, Warden of the Guild of St Matthew. The Guild was much more radical in its views than its contemporary, the Christian Social Union; and Dolling felt that a series of addresses given to the men of his district by its members would help to counter the secularist philosophy preached in the radical working men's clubs of Portsmouth. Unfortunately Headlam himself was a controversial figure who had incurred the displeasure of the Bishop of London, Frederick Temple, for, among other things, advocating the ballet (considered immoral by many churchpeople) as a graceful form of theatrical performance. In advance of his visit the local papers were filled with letters denouncing him as a propagandist for the ballet. As a result of the free publicity curiosity grew; and, on the afternoon of the lecture, the church was packed with men from end to end.

Headlam's address was on 'The Social Question'; and, in its broad outlines, it made many of the same points that Dolling and his curates were constantly making in their own sermons. It began by stressing in general terms that Christianity must address itself to society as well as to the individual, but went on to consider particular ways by which fairer social conditions might be achieved, such as higher taxes and free education. By modern standards the proposals were mild enough, but to the gentry and middle classes of Victorian England they appeared revolutionary. The lecture was widely reported in the press, and repercussions were not slow in coming.

Bishop Browne was first off the mark with a letter to Dolling expressing outrage at Headlam's 'highly inflammatory political address, calculated to set class against class'. He claimed that the lecturer had been disciplined by his own bishop 'for teaching on the very subject on which you advertise him as a preacher'. The 'so-called Christian Socialism' exhibited not only in Headlam's address but in the writings of Count Leo Tolstoi and others appeared to the bishop to strike at the roots of all Christianity: 'I must consider whether the good of our Mission is not more than neutralized by the evil of those whom you associate with you; and whether I can suffer it to go on under my authority.' This was strong stuff by episcopal standards; but worse was to come. G. B. Lee, Warden of Winchester and titular head of the college (which was responsible for paying Dolling's stipend), wrote to express his displeasure. 'With your ultra High-Church proclivities on the one hand, and your Socialist teaching on the other, no sober-minded and loyal citizen can be expected to support the mission, my connection with which must now be severed so long as you continue to be the head of it.' Canon Jacob, the rural dean, threatened to cancel his guinea-a-year subscription to the mission.

Dolling was unabashed. He yielded to the bishop so far as to arrange for the remaining lectures in the series to be delivered in the gymnasium rather than in the church, but protested at the tone of Browne's remarks about the lecturer – he had himself, he said, preached in favour of almost all that Headlam advocated. He was more concerned, however, with the letter from the Warden of Winchester, on the ground that it must surely represent the mind of the school authorities. These had the legal power to cancel his licence, since, as a mere missioner, he did not enjoy the customary parson's freehold. In spite of attempts at mediation by the head-master, Dolling announced his resignation in the course of a sermon preached in St Agatha's on Sunday, 9 March, 1890.

As soon as the news broke, the citizens of Portsmouth rallied to his support. Many who objected to his political or ecclesiastical views revered him as a man and were dismayed at the thought of his being, in effect, drummed out of the town. A crowded public meeting was held in Landport under the chairmanship of General Harward, a member of the ultra-Tory Primrose League. A mem-orial was handed in, signed by two thousand of Dolling's par-ishioners. Tributes to him were voiced on every side. A leading Nonconformist, A. J. Owen, declared that Dolling had carried out in his district work which no other man had ever attempted before. He had devoted his life to the poor, who were never tired of talking of his goodness towards them.

Meanwhile, on the day the meeting took place, Dolling had gone to Winchester at the headmaster's invitation to try to resolve the matter of the warden's letter – which had been the main ingredient behind his decision to resign. Fearon was now able to assure Dolling that Lee had acted only in his capacity of a private subscriber to the funds of the mission, and that his letter need not therefore be construed as a vote of censure on behalf of the college. Dolling insisted on the warden's making this fact public; and Lee agreed to write a brief letter to the Portsmouth papers of which the key sentence read: 'I am not, and never have been (as is commonly supposed), the head of the Winchester College Mis-sion. I have never been even a member of the committee.' As soon as the letter appeared, Dolling wrote to the headmaster and to the bishop agreeing to withdraw his resignation; and the storm in this particular ecclesiastical teacup soon subsided. The whole incident, trivial as it may appear in retrospect, brought to a head a question which had for some time been threatening the peaceful development of the school and college mission movement – namely, the proper amount of control which should be exercised by the subscribers to a particular mission over the priest in charge of it. Dolling's views, both ecclesiastical and political, must have been well known to the Winchester College authorities at the time of his appointment; and they would therefore have been to blame if, having put him in charge of the mission, they now refused to give him reasonable liberty of action in carrying out his duties.

*   *   *

In 1891 the death of Bishop Harold Browne brought to Winchester as his successor a man who leaned over backwards to accommodate Dolling: Anthony Thorold, formerly Bishop of Rochester. Thorold, an Evangelical, found himself out of sympathy with many of Dolling's ritualistic practices. But he approved of him on two particular grounds: his zeal for evangelism and his championship of the poor. Thorold's manner might appear stiff and precise, but he soon achieved a *rapport* with the more outwardly emotional Dolling which was to last throughout his Winchester episcopate. He was shrewd enough to see that Dolling's ritualism was no series of formalized observances, but was motivated by his belief that it was only in this way that he could win souls to Christ; and Thorold could forgive almost any alleged sin committed by one who was so obviously devoted to the service of the poor. As his biographer puts it:

> This [St Agatha's] mission was destined to cause the Bishop grave anxiety. But its origin, the character of its chief, the daring and successful assault which its clergy and lay-workers had made upon vice and sin in the wickedest quarter of the great town of Portsmouth, called out all his impulsive enthusiasm. He might differ widely in opinion from many of its ritual practices, but how could he dare not to encourage a work so zealously done for Christ?

Nevertheless, he soon found that he could not entirely ignore Dolling's ecclesiastical critics. Though he repeated over and over again that he would never throw him to the Protestant lions, he had at least to acknowledge the lions' existence. Matters came to a head in November 1892, when an observer from the Protestant Alliance, armed with a notebook and a pair of opera-glasses, was present at a 'children's Mass' in St Agatha's. The result of his observations was an inflammatory report which included such titbits as: 'Last came Father Dolling, a biretta perched on his most disloyal head.' On the basis of this report and a copy of one of the children's service-books, the Alliance urged Thorold to withdraw the licences of the clergy of St Agatha's or else to compel them to act as 'ministers of the Protestant Reformed Religion of this country'. Thorold found himself having to defuse what threatened to become an awkward situation.

The argument centred mainly on whether *The St Agatha's Sunday Scholar's Book* was or was not compatible with the eucharistic teaching of the Church of England. The bishop felt that it was not, and wrote to Dolling on 16 December asking him to consider quietly discontinuing its use 'when you can do so without loss of self-respect or feeling of giving way to ignorant clamour'. Dolling wrote back agreeing to withdraw the book and to substitute another in its place, though he insisted on its essential Anglican orthodoxy. Meanwhile, however, Thorold had written to the secretary of the Protestant Alliance in defence of Dolling. He conceded that the general substance of the book was 'quite irreconcilable with the Eucharistic teaching of the Church of England' and that, moreover, Dolling's work at St Agatha's was 'disfigured by errors and eccentricities which I sincerely deprecate'. Nevertheless, that work was of a kind which very few other men were capable of accomplishing and reached a class of society too frequently left to itself out of sheer helplessness and despair. 'In my opinion, the substantial good he is enabled to effect by his self-denying and Christian activities far outweighs by its usefulness any distress that may be caused to those who are gravely alarmed by doctrines and practices which they consider to be quite inconsistent with the standards of the Reformed Church.'

When he came to the actual subject of the complaint made by the Alliance the bishop was studiously vague – beyond saying that he was in correspondence with Dolling. He took refuge in some woolly generalities about his belief in the missioner's readiness to accept his 'fatherly direction when responsibly and kindly offered'. So he was not best pleased when, without his consent, the Alliance sent copies of the letter to the Portsmouth and London papers and the controversy received nationwide publicity. He summoned Dolling to Farnham Castle to discuss the situation. Dolling insisted that the book represented the legitimate Anglican teaching of the Church of England on the subject. However, to pacify the critics, he agreed to tone down those parts of it (principally the preface) to which objection had been taken by substituting statements taken exclusively from Anglican authorities. The bishop was not entirely satisfied with the revised version; but at least Dolling had met him half-way. They now resumed their normal friendly relations.

*   *   *

Dolling had now reached the final scene in the Landport drama: his showdown with Bishop Randall Davidson in the autumn of 1895, resulting in his dramatic departure early the following year. The *casus belli* was a question of ritual connected with the new permanent church of St Agatha built to replace the old mission church, which could no longer cater for a growing congregation. The foundation-stone of the new church, which represented the crown of his labours, was laid on 27 October 1894. The plans had been approved by Bishop Thorold; but Thorold died the following summer, and his successor, Davidson, was enthroned in Winchester Cathedral less than a fortnight before the date fixed for the official opening of the new church. Like Thorold, Davidson had been translated from Rochester; but, unlike Thorold, he was not so prone to take Dolling on trust. In their altercations Dolling found the future Archbishop of Canterbury a far less pliable antagonist than his more tolerant predecessor in the see.

The drama began in a small way over the seemingly mundane question of a licence for the new church. Dolling wrote to Davidson on 28 September to tell him that the building was due to be opened on 27 October. He claimed that Bishop Thorold had told him that no new licence would be needed, as the new church was 'practically joined by the vestries' to the old one. Davidson seems to have doubted whether his predecessor had said any such thing; and he consulted the rural dean, Canon Jacob, who took the view that the old licence could not possibly cover both churches and that a new licence would therefore be required. Davidson thereupon instructed Jacob to visit the new church and satisfy himself that everything was in order. The visit duly took place; and the rural dean reported to Davidson that all was in order save for one feature, namely, a proposal to place an altar in the south aisle which was apparently to be used exclusively for 'Masses for the dead'. There were two other altars in the church; and it was the question of this third altar that was to precipitate the final crisis.

The traditional practice of offering prayers on behalf of the dead is closely connected with the doctrine of Purgatory. The justification for the practice is the belief that those in Purgatory are still part of the Church who can be helped on their way to Heaven by the intercessions of the living. Before long the Protestant reformers began to denounce the custom, partly on the ground that it was unscriptural, partly through their rejection of the doctrine of Purgatory (coupled as it was with the much-abused sale of indulgences). In the Church of England's Prayer Book prayers for the dead had been absent since 1552, on the ground that it was purposeless to intercede for souls who were already in either Heaven or Hell. Since the middle of the nineteenth century, however, the practice had been increasingly adopted by Catholics in the Church of England – and nowadays it is common among all churchpeople apart from ultra-Evangelicals.

Requiem Masses at that time, however, were of doubtful legality in the Church of England, and Davidson felt that he could not possibly sanction off his own bat a third altar specifically associated with prayers for the dead. He therefore declined to grant a licence for the new church unless either the legality of the third altar was sanctioned by the church authorities or the altar itself was removed.

Dolling – to whom requiem Masses were a vital article of

faith – went to Farnham on 25 October, two days before the opening ceremony, to see Davidson. The bishop warned him that this was no red-tape question of the number of altars, but concerned the services said at those altars. In spite of their opposed viewpoints, however, the two men got on reasonably well. Dolling assented to a memorandum in which the bishop put the two possible courses of action: either the site of the proposed third altar could be screened off pending the bishop's final decision, and the opening service go ahead as arranged; or else the plan for the altar could be scrapped, in which case Davidson would at once grant a licence for the new church. In the course of the interview Dolling, according to the bishop, disclaimed any intention to hold his resignation over Davidson as a threat. He pointed out that in any case he proposed to leave St Agatha's in a few months' time – around Eastertide – now that it had developed from an experimental mission into a fully-fledged parish. If therefore Davidson should rule against the third altar and Dolling feel obliged to resign on the issue, it would mean merely that his immediate withdrawal would 'expedite a little what was already arranged'. When he arrived back in Landport, however, Dolling presented the recent interview in more dramatic form. He told his congregation that a crisis had arrived for St Agatha's. If the bishop found himself unable to license the third altar (and so, in effect, expressed his disapproval of prayers for the dead), 'I am at once to resign so that a successor may be appointed who will remove the altar.'

The new church was opened on 27 October by Bishop Ridding of Southwell, a former Headmaster of Winchester and founder of the mission, amid outward rejoicing but inward qualms. The site for the third altar was screened off in accordance with the first of the agreed alternatives in Davidson's memorandum. On the day of the opening the present headmaster, Fearon, wrote a letter of commiseration to Davidson. With Dolling, he said, 'one has to accept perpetually the prospect of a crisis', though they had managed to survive similar crises in the past. 'One can only pray that now the vast good he has done may not be undone by want of self-control in the last act.' Fearon drew attention to the unfortunate personal element in the present controversy deriving from the necessary involvement of Dolling's old enemy, Canon Jacob. 'Jacob is like a "red rag" to Dolling. There have been faults on both sides; but the fact is the 2 men's temperaments are such that they can hardly help being in antagonism.' Fearon expressed his deep regret that 'even indirectly we should be the cause of bringing you anxiety and trouble in such early days of your Episcopate among us'.

Davidson could certainly have been spared this particular trouble, but there was no getting away from it. On 15 November a second and rather less harmonious interview took place at Farnham Castle between the bishop and his unco-operative missioner. Dolling was suffering from a bad attack of influenza, which made things no easier. The interview took the form of an intensive grilling by the bishop, in which Dolling had to answer a long string of questions not only about prayers for the dead but about other related liturgical matters such as non-communicating attendance at the Eucharist.* On the surface the meeting was friendly enough, but Dolling, in his own account of it, compares Davidson's attitude unfavourably with that of his predecessor:

> My intercourse with Dr Thorold had been so very different. There had been perfect freedom in all conversations between us . . . A hundred times the memory of him flashed across my mind, and his many words of prayer came back again and again to my remembrance. I was sitting in the same study, but now I was accused; and I was conscious that my own and my people's happiness, nay, perhaps the safety of weak, timid souls, was hanging in the balance. I pray that none of my readers may ever have such an hour and a half as I passed at Farnham.

Davidson, for his part, was anxious in his pragmatic way simply to ascertain the precise benefits which Dolling believed that

---

*This referred to a celebration of the Eucharist with fewer than the three communicants specified by the Prayer Book as the necessary minimum (in addition to the celebrant). Dolling felt that to give way on this point would mean either the surrender of the weekday Masses or an artificial roster of communicants to form a quorum at each celebration.

special prayers, and the offering of the Eucharistic Sacrifice on their behalf, would bring to the faithful departed. But the 'flu-ridden Dolling was no theologian at the best of times, and obviously the interview went badly for him. Davidson took three weeks to reach his decision, which went against Dolling. The nub of the bishop's immensely long letter was that he had come to the conclusion that 'I should act wrongly were I, on my personal authority, now to sanction the erection and use of the proposed third Altar in the situation and for the purpose you have described to me.' Davidson professed no wish to dictate to Dolling, or to dogmatize about prayer for the dead – 'a term obviously capable of a great variety of meaning'. But, whatever liberty of private opinion and individual devotion might be permissible,

> I have no hesitation in saying that I should depart both from the spirit and the letter of our Church's formularies were I definitely to sanction the addition of a third Altar to St Agatha's with the knowledge that one main purpose of its erection is that it should be a centre for services and teaching of the character above described. I myself believe your teaching on this subject to be contrarient to some of the distinctive principles of the Church of England.

The day after receiving this blockbuster of a letter Dolling sent in his resignation to the Headmaster of Winchester – and wrote to inform Davidson that he had done so. The one practical question, he said, was that he felt he must continue to conduct the services as he had for the last ten years – and this by implication the bishop was forbidding him to do. The two men were still poles apart, though they continued to exchange letters. Davidson insisted that there was no need for Dolling to resign if he would only give way over the third altar. Dolling insisted that he had no other course but to resign because of the bishop's demand. 'I believed directly I read it that the judgment forbade us to say our Mass for the Dead, or to have Celebrations without Communicants. The surrender of these two points I felt it impossible to make.' His successor would say Mass for the dead every Friday – but in the words of the Book of Common Prayer.

Dolling adds bitterly in his *Ten Years*: 'I am an excrescence; ergo, when an opportunity arises, it is wise to lop me off. But, if mine is intended as an object-lesson, I fear it will hardly be so accepted by the other excrescences. They are all well sheltered by their freeholds [*which Dolling was not*], and few bishops to-day would like to undertake the odium of a ritual prosecution, far less the expense it entails.'

A modern historian, Nigel Yates, pours scorn on the wide-spread Anglo-Catholic belief that Dolling's resignation from St Agatha's was an act of persecution on Davidson's part. Such a claim, he says, is a clear misreading of the evidence. Dolling was intending to leave anyway, and Davidson's interference provided him with an excuse to leave in a dramatic way on his own terms. He gave Davidson little time to make concessions. 'There is plenty of indication from his subsequent episcopal career that Dolling might have been as capable of calling Davidson's bluff as he was Browne's or Thorold's when they raised similar objec-tions to his ritualism. If Dolling was a martyr for ritualism, his martyrdom was entirely self-inflicted.' But there is no doubt that, at the time, Dolling appeared to many as a popular hero sacrificed on the altar of episcopal red-tape. And, for all Davidson's care and conscientiousness in the matter, his clash with Dolling provided an unfortunate introduction to his Winchester episcopate.

The Anglo-Catholic *Church Times*, commenting on Dolling's resignation, pointed out that a charismatic individual of this type was often incapable of treading the beaten path. 'Rules which to others are safeguards are to him fetters, and the society he serves will be wise in recognizing this fact.' It was to the credit of the rulers of the Roman Church, said the paper, that they had known how to utilize, without discouraging, the genius of such men as Francis of Assisi, Dominic and Ignatius Loyola. 'It will be the wisdom of the rulers of the English Church to choose for the arduous but honourable work of pioneers men who have the power from God to turn men from darkness to light, and when they have chosen them to trust them with large discretionary powers. The battle with the forces of evil cannot be fought in kid gloves.'

The news of Dolling's resignation produced a wave of sympathy both from the people of Portsmouth and from far beyond. Many of the sympathizers, while not on his ecclesiastical wavelength, yet admired the heroic nature of his philanthropic activities. In the words of the *Saturday Review*, 'his life and work shrivelled to miserable ashes the ritual controversies that burned around him.' While Dolling's Evangelical opponents rejoiced and even held meetings of thanksgiving to mark his departure, Nonconformists as well as High Church Anglicans offered prayers that he might stay. Efforts at mediation were in fact made to try and induce him to change his mind. John Pares, a leading Portsmouth layman and personal friend of Dolling, took up with the bishop Dolling's own suggestion of conducting his usual services at one of the other two altars in the new church. Davidson was unhelpful. 'Nothing', he told Pares, 'would give me greater satisfaction than to learn that Mr. Dolling is willing to remain at St. Agatha's and to bring his services into general harmony with the due order of the Church of England. He says not a word to lead me to think that he would feel such a course would be possible.'

The news of Dolling's departure was received with mixed feelings at Winchester College. The boys were almost all on his side, but the headmaster could not but appreciate the bishop's dilemma. He sympathized with Dolling, but wrote to point out that the College had already strained its position in order to give him a reasonable liberty of action: 'I hoped you would make the return to our affection of being willing to withdraw quietly, and to do your utmost to allay an agitation which is already doing us much harm.' The Warden of Winchester, Godfrey Lee, he who had objected six years before to the lecture by Stewart Headlam and who had then had to eat humble pie, was delighted at Dolling's discomfiture. He told Davidson that he had withdrawn his own support from the mission 'owing to Mr. Dolling's papistical doctrines and practices'. Episcopal advice in the past, said the warden, had always been thrown away on Dolling – 'and I should be very glad to hear that he had left Portsea.'

Lee was soon to have his wish granted. Dolling conducted

his final service at St Agatha's – Solemn Vespers – on the evening
of 9 January 1896. He and his sisters Elise and Geraldine, who
had been his most devoted helpers at the mission, left
Portsmouth the following morning. But, if his Protestant critics
had supposed that the churchmanship of St Agatha's was to be
lowered with his departure, they were in for a grave disappoint-
ment. Temporary charge of the mission was entrusted to a monk
of the Community of the Resurrection, Fr Paul Bull, with the
consent of the bishop and headmaster. Dolling's permanent
successor was the Rev. G. H. Tremenheere, curate of Holy
Redeemer, Clerkenwell, who took charge of St Agatha's on 21
February 1896. Two years later, when the new church was
formally consecrated and St Agatha's became a fully-fledged
parish of its own, he was instituted as its first vicar. Tremenheere
was appointed by the College, but thereafter the patronage of
the living lapsed to the bishop. Where Catholic teaching and
ceremonial were concerned Tremenheere carried on in the
Dolling tradition, deferring to authority only in the matter of a
greater conformity to the Book of Common Prayer. The Protestant interest therefore gained little as the result of Dolling's
resignation, though the bishop was satisfied that the services at
St Agatha's had by now been brought into 'general harmony
with the due order of the Church of England'.

                    *   *   *

The remainder of Dolling's ministry proved a sad anti-climax.
It was over two years before he received another parish. The
intervening period he occupied partly in the composition of his
autobiographical *Ten Years in a Portsmouth Slum*, partly in an
extended tour of North America. As far as the Church of
England went, however, he was considered by many of the
bishops as an *enfant terrible* who must be discouraged from
ministering in their dioceses. The most notorious case of such
an episcopal inhibition was when the Bishop of Durham, B. F.
Westcott, asked the vicar of St Mary's, Tyne Dock, to withdraw
an invitation to Dolling to conduct a parochial mission there –
purely on the ground of the imbroglio at Landport. This was
grossly unfair to Dolling, since he had been guilty of no ecclesi-

astical offence. He had resigned his charge because of his inability to accept conditions laid down by his diocesan; and Westcott's action cast an undeserved slur on Dolling's character and was bitterly resented by his supporters. Westcott attempted to make amends in a letter he wrote to Dolling a year later to explain that he had taken the line he had 'with great pain and sorrow' – and went on to lecture Dolling on the duty of surrendering 'our own will and judgment to our responsible rulers'; but by then the damage had been done. Another bishop, J. J. S. Perowne of Worcester, forbade Dolling to preach a course of Lenten sermons in Evesham parish church; the churchwardens sent a strong remonstrance to Perowne. But by no means all the bishops took such a legalistic line; and Dolling was able to accept numerous invitations to preach without any episcopal veto. He gave frequent addresses in many of London's West End churches during his jobless period, and even occupied the pulpit of St Paul's Cathedral. He also visited the north of England and Scotland, preaching to large and enthusiastic congregations.

Ten Years in a Portsmouth Slum was written during the early months of 1896 at the house of his sister Josephine in Earl's Court, London. It is a substantial publication, Dolling's only full-length book, and gives a detailed, frank and graphic account of his ministry at St Agatha's. He treats the various controversies in which he became involved from a necessarily subjective point of view – though, in the case of his final dispute with Davidson, an appendix gives the full text of the many letters which passed between the two men, so that it is possible to check Dolling's version of events against the actual correspondence. The book was published in May 1896, and within two years had gone into a fifth edition. It had a wide sale among churchpeople of all schools of thought. The *Methodist Recorder* was typical of many when it said of the book: 'We shall cherish the memory of a life wholly devoted to lifting up the destitute and outcast.'

During his period in the wilderness Dolling received several offers of work, but nothing came of any of them. The Dean and Chapter of St Paul's considered appointing him to St Mary's, Somers Town, but then discovered that a necessary condition of the post was that its occupant should have already ministered for six years as a priest in London – which of course ruled out Dolling. He was also invited to take on the incumbency of St Raphael's, Bristol, but this was more a chaplaincy to a sisterhood than a normal parish and was therefore unsuitable. While he was in America he was offered the charge of a mission district in the parish of St Paul, Middlesbrough; but this offer too fell through, as the rector could not meet Dolling's stipulation that the district must first be made into a legal parish of its own – Dolling was determined not to run the risk of a repeat of his experience at Landport. An effort was also made to secure for him the living of St Nicholas, Deptford, in Kent, a working-class parish which would have suited Dolling's peculiar talents; but nothing came of it. He even received an invitation from the Bishop of Mashonaland to take up a post in Bulawayo, Rhodesia, involving a ministry to young men. Dolling was grateful for the offer, but felt that he was too old to grapple with the problems of colonial work.

As the months passed he began to think that he would never succeed in finding another suitable post within the Church of England. So, when he was invited by a priest in Philadelphia to conduct a mission in his parish, he decided to make it the basis for a North American tour and accepted with alacrity. He spent over a year in the United States, landing in New York on 26 May 1897 and not returning to England until July of the following year. His programme was a hectic one. In his first ten months he delivered over four hundred sermons and addresses in eighty different churches, besides conducting several parochial missions. He came armed with letters of commendation from dignitaries, including one from Davidson which paid tribute to his 'irreproachable moral character and remarkable earnestness, devotion and capacity', while remaining discreetly silent about their recent difference of opinion.

Dolling's main engagements took place in New England, New York and the Mid-West. He spent Holy Week and Easter in Chicago, preaching and hearing confessions in many of the city parishes. It was while he was in Chicago that he at last received the offer of an English parish that he was able to accept: St

Saviour's, Poplar, in London's East End. Paradoxically, within hours of cabling his acceptance, he received from the Bishop of Chicago an invitation to take charge of the cathedral as its dean. In the bishop's words, 'his reply was that, if the invitation had reached him twenty-four hours sooner, he would have returned an immediate and grateful acceptance; but that, on the evening before, he had received from England an appointment to a field in East London in which he discerned a call from his Master and which, for that reason, had a paramount claim upon him.' During his last few weeks in the States Dolling relaxed to some extent, visiting Montana, Utah and California and enjoying an interview with the celebrated Mrs Baker Eddy, founder of the Christian Science Movement. He sailed for England in July, and was instituted at St Saviour's on the 22nd of that month.

*   *   *

'This dullest, greyest parish in East London' was how Dolling described his new cure. Into its forty-four acres were crowded at least ten thousand people, mainly working-class. Although there was a surface similarity between St Saviour's and St Agatha's, in that both served slum districts, the East End parish lacked the colour and bustle that had characterized the scene of Dolling's former labours. He found Poplar a dull place after Landport and, in a magazine article written two years after his arrival, explained the reason why:

> There, every street differed from every other street. . . . Here, every street, every house, is identically the same. There we lived a rollicking, jovial, if sinful, life; here we manage to exist much less viciously, because we are as a whole bloodless and anaemic. There one's chief duty was to repress; here it is to incite. A Saturday night at Landport was a joyous experience, even if one sorrowed over the sin; a Saturday night here is as dull as ditch-water.

Admittedly there were no gangs of thieves in Poplar and no streets 'wholly given over to sin', and the pubs were less sordid. But Dolling obviously hankered after his old haunts and found Poplar a sad contrast.

In spite of its shortcomings, however, he did his best. And he was able to use his energies in tackling the social problems of the area, in particular the East London water famine of 1898, the overcrowding and the smallpox epidemic of 1901. He chaired a meeting of male parishioners in the church to protest against the meanness of the East London Water Company in restricting the supply of water to six hours a day at the height of summer. The meeting had its effect on the company, though it also produced an anonymous letter making a different sort of protest:

> Will Mr. Dolling permit one who was a Catholic member of the English Church before Mr. Dolling was born to recommend to him the use of the collect for rain as much more likely to attain the desired end than holding meetings for the abuse of laymen at least as honourable as Mr. Dolling? The withholding of rain from a district is God's punishment, and to ninety-nine Catholics in a hundred the present visitation upon the East End of London is consequent upon the appointment of Mr. Dolling to S. Saviour's whilst he has not done penance for his misdoings at S. Agatha's.

In the smallpox epidemic Dolling came into collision with the Poplar Board of Guardians, many of whose members were opposed to vaccination. He provided free vaccination at the dispensary attached to the mission-house in order to supplement the half-hearted efforts of the local authorities.

He never enjoyed the same success locally in Poplar that he had had at Landport. His Sunday congregations rarely exceeded two hundred out of a total population of ten thousand. But, if his services were poorly attended, he was preaching to crowded congregations in other parts of London – and was a welcome visitor to the pulpit of St Paul's Cathedral. Towards the end of his life, however, he was able to do less and less pastoral visiting, owing to the pressure on his time of fund-raising and other administrative chores.

In March 1901 his health began to fail. He was advised by his doctors to go abroad, and he spent April travelling in Spain. It was to no avail. His health continued to deteriorate, and in September he was dispatched to take the waters at Aix-la-Chapelle.

After six weeks there he spent a fortnight in Belgium before returning home. He continued to go downhill physically over the next few months. He celebrated his fifty-first birthday on 10 February 1902, but, following an injury to one of his feet, got through his long list of Lenten engagements only with difficulty. The last Sunday at which he could still manage to conduct services at St Saviour's was Easter Day. Shortly afterwards, following a successful operation on his foot, he moved to the house of his sister Josephine in South Kensington to convalesce. He had been invited to preach a course of post-Easter sermons at the Berkeley Chapel in Mayfair, but could manage only two of them. He grew steadily weaker, though he still seemed to think that he would recover from his illness. It was not to be, and the end came on the afternoon of 15 May.

His death was mourned as if he had been a reigning monarch or national hero. References to his life and ministry featured in the sermons preached in many churches on the Sunday following his death – Whit Sunday. A solemn requiem Mass was celebrated on Tuesday morning in St Cuthbert's, Philbeach Gardens, and his body was then borne in procession across London to its penultimate resting-place in St Saviour's, Poplar. The church was crowded that evening for Vespers of the Dead, and all through the night a solemn vigil was kept by clergy, relatives, friends and parishioners. From four a.m. onwards crowds of working men visited the church to pay their final respects. From four-thirty to nine a.m., masses were said every half-hour, the celebrant in each case being one of Dolling's former colleagues.

The hierarchy of the Church of England may have been wary of him during his lifetime, but they made amends in the hour of his final departure. Leading the mourners at the solemn requiem Mass in St Saviour's were the Bishop of London, A. F. Winnington-Ingram, and the Bishop of Stepney, Cosmo Lang, vested in black copes. It was the former who delivered the funeral address and who summed up his tribute with the words: 'When everybody else had given a man up it was always said, "Dolling will take him." ' After the service the body was carried in procession a second time through streets lined with sorrowing spectators to Waterloo station, whence a special train took it to

Brookwood for interment in the cemetery there. Bishop Lang read the last part of the burial service and gave a simple address. Dolling was buried, appropriately, in a grave next to that of Alexander Heriot Mackonochie. At the head of the grave a Celtic cross bears the short inscription: 'ROBERT RADCLYFFE DOLLING, PRIEST. MAY 15, 1902. R.I.P.'

*   *   *

So much has been written about Dolling that it is not difficult to imagine what manner of man he was. But, for those whose imaginations need prodding, there is a lifelike and sympathetic portrait of him in an early novel by Sir Compton Mackenzie, *The Altar Steps*. The novel is the first in a trilogy about a priest who (unlike Dolling) eventually finds his way to Rome. Sir Compton was a personal friend of Dolling, who appears under the fictional (and physically appropriate) name of Father Rowley. Dolling's tubby figure often came as a surprise to those who were expecting the spare, ascetic-looking type of individual associated in the popular imagination with Anglo-Catholicism. A *Daily Mail* pen-portrait written towards the end of his life describes him as 'sturdy, broad-shouldered, thick-set, with smiling, clean-shaven face, and with all the best traditions of the English public school about him'. An American newspaper description of about the same date begins: 'The reverend gentleman is very like a "Mediaeval monk"; we suppose it is because he is stout that he always sits when he preaches, and he moves himself from side to side in his armchair in movements anything but elegant.'

In his approach to problems Dolling was pragmatic rather than introspective. The same trend was apparent in his literary tastes: he preferred novels to more abstract works. He was no intellectual, and took little interest in speculative philosophical questions. Nor did he claim to be much of a theologian. On more than one occasion he remarked: 'It does not matter whether there be one Isaiah, or two, or forty, provided the book so called contains a message from God.' He was more concerned with such practical issues as the failure of the Church of England to develop vocations to the ministry among men of all classes.

He had little respect for the Church Establishment as such. He castigated the 'heresy' of regarding the parson simply as the resident gentleman in every parish whose influence was based mainly on his social position – and preferred the Roman Catholic concept by which, in theory at any rate, a peasant might rise to become a prince of the Church. Above all he despised the Church of England's genius for destroying enthusiasm (which it had certainly tried to do in his own case). In a magazine article published three months before his death he poured scorn on the notion of the Anglican ministry as an easy profession in which a man could live comfortably like his brother the squire (but on a poorer scale). The bishops, he wrote, had but one opportunist canon of conduct: 'Be commonplace, be respectable, after the sober manner of the Church of England.'

In spite of his reputation as a ritualist, Dolling was by no means in the mainstream of Tractarianism, nor was he a direct product of its influence. Though he had absorbed the sacramentalism of the Oxford Movement (and was deeply spiritual in his own devotional life), he had no use for its more austere side and complained that the Movement had been 'made up out of books'. His Catholicism was essentially warm-hearted and humane. As a preacher he impressed by the passion and power of his oratory. At Winchester his talks to the boys had never been mere pi-jaws; on his visits to the school he had never played the priest but had behaved as one of the boys. He always refused to allow himself to be blinded by polite and conventional phrases or to take things for granted because it was pleasant to believe them. After his death *The Times* referred disapprovingly to his 'injudicious rashness', though it admitted that he had 'elevated injudiciousness into a fine art'.

The Nonconformist *British Weekly*, in a fulsome obituary, represented him as one of the nineteenth century's great religious figures, on a par with St Francis or John Wesley. Later in its obituary the paper remarked that 'he had the dust without the palm'. (In this he was the exact opposite of his contemporary Lord Rosebery, the Liberal Prime Minister, of whom his Eton tutor remarked that he 'sought the palm without the dust'.) A naval officer who had first known Dolling at Portsmouth summed him up as 'the nearest approach to a great man with whom I have ever come into personal contact'. But the last word must surely lie with the obituarist in the magazine *Truth*, who considered that, 'so far as one can judge from report, he deserved the title of Saint as truly as any subject of Papal canonisation.' Even in an age like our own, in which the demythologizers like nothing better than to topple the heroes of yesterday from their pedestals, that verdict would surely still stand.

*   *   *

And what of St Agatha's, the district which had made Dolling a household name to his contemporaries? Under his successor, G. H. Tremenheere, it gradually settled down into the worthy but unexciting routine of a well-run but run-of-the-mill Anglo-Catholic parish. The glory was indeed departed, for Tremenheere was no Dolling and his name is virtually unknown today. He stayed for fifteen years, taking over from Dolling in 1896 and overseeing the transition of the former mission district into a parish of its own. His successor, C. W. Coles, arrived in 1911 – and was still there at the time of the German blitz on Portsmouth thirty years later. The church was spared, but the parish was virtually depopulated by the bombs. Coles lived in the vestry until his resignation in 1953 following a breakdown in his health; he had been vicar for forty-two years.

The twilight of his ministry coincided with the twilight of St Agatha's as a living church. The year after his retirement it was taken over by the Admiralty for use as a storehouse. It lost its Lady chapel in 1964, and has since been under threat from road proposals and a projected dockyard extension on adjoining land. But it is a fine building, designed in the Italianate Romanesque style, and has been championed by such bodies as the Victorian Society and the Friends of Friendless Churches. An application for consent to demolish was refused by an inspector after a public enquiry, but allowed in 1973 by the Secretary of State for the Environment. The temporary abandonment of both road and dockyard proposals as a result of a squeeze on government spending, however, led to a reprieve for the church, though its future remains uncertain. Hampshire County Council has been restoring it in recent years, and it is possible that it may become a concert-hall.

How would Dolling have regarded such a fate? Maybe with equanimity, in the face of the parish's changed circumstances. He was essentially a practical man who was concerned with souls more than with bricks and mortar. After all, he would have said, a church is not so much a building as a body of believers; and at least his beloved St Agatha's would have been saved from the bulldozers – and continue to give pleasure of a different sort to the faithful.

Fr Ignatius: a photograph taken during his North American
tour in 1890–91

CHAPTER 6

MONASTIC PIONEER

Fr Ignatius (Joseph Leycester Lyne),
(1837–1908)

IGNATIUS IS THE ODD MAN out in this Victorian portrait-gallery. He was regarded by most people in his own lifetime as an eccentric, if not a madman, and he presents a sharp contrast to my other four 'reverend rebels'. He was certainly a rebel; but the cause for which he fought was not so much to establish Catholic practices in parishes hitherto denied them as to reintroduce the monastic life within the Church of England itself. He failed in his endeavour, his failure being either heroic or pathetic according to one's point of view. But he paved the way for other pioneers; and, paradoxically, his memory is outwardly more revered today than is that of his staider if more successful contemporaries. Neither Richard Meux Benson, founder of the Cowley Fathers, nor Charles Gore, founder of the Community of the Resurrection, enjoys an annual commemoration on the scale of the gathering each August at Ignatius's tomb at Llanthony, in the Black Mountains of South Wales. He may have appeared a charlatan to many of his contemporaries, but his memory lives on – and grows ever greener as time softens the edges of his eccentricities and his supporters recall the more attractive features of his personality. They can forget the fact that he had to wait thirty-eight years after his ordination to the diaconate to receive the priesthood (from highly suspect episcopal hands); or that few of the novices he attracted to Llanthony ever stayed there long; or that the various 'miracles' associated with his name are hard to substantiate. They can concentrate instead on his personal piety, on his extraordinary appeal to the man in the street and on his phenomenal power as a preacher – which could draw crowds of football-match proportions to listen to his oratory. Three full-length biographies have been written of this astonishing man; but none of them can fully explain the paradoxes of his character. He was, in the strict sense of that term, unique.

*   *   *

Joseph Leycester Lyne was born in London on 23 November 1837, five months after the accession of Queen Victoria. He was the second son, in a family of four boys and three girls, of Francis Lyne and Louise Genevieve Leycester, his father being a member of an old Welsh family settled in Cornwall and his paternal grandmother an Italian. His father traded as a merchant – but only fitfully, as he was living in hopes of a legacy from a wealthy kinsman which was slow in coming and, when it eventually came, turned out to be much less than expected. Lack of capital soured the life of Francis Lyne and, to some extent, handicapped his second son in his bid to revive monasticism within the Church of England.

Joseph – or 'Leycester', as he was often called in deference to his mother's wishes – exhibited an interest in religion from an early age. When he was only four he would 'preach' to his brothers and sisters, robed in a nightgown and insisting that it was more than a mere game. This infant precocity was reinforced by a fear of hell-fire which dominated his life until his 'conversion' in the Isle of Wight when he was nearly thirty. 'I became a monk in the first instance as a means of saving my soul from hell,' he wrote in his miniature autobiography. 'This was *before* my conversion. *After* it I remained a monk as an act of gratitude to the Lord Jesus for revealing Himself to me as my personal Saviour.' The Lyne parents belonged to different religious camps. Francis was an Evangelical who frequently disapproved of his son's High Church goings-on. His wife had Tractarian sympathies and became a disciple of Pusey. Leycester had the greatest regard for her, describing her as 'the saintliest, sweetest

woman that ever lived, my friend always'. But, though he sometimes quarrelled with his father, he could also express gratitude
to him for having 'as a gentleman, a man and a Christian sent
us from him forewarned and forearmed to face the foes'.

When he was seven Leycester went as a boarder to Manor
House, Holloway, a prep school for boys. Three years later he
was nominated to a place at St Paul's School by one of the
governors, whose wife had been impressed by the charm of the
boy's youthful oratory at a dinner party given by his father at
which Leycester had been deputed to propose a toast to 'the
Ladies'. His piety at St Paul's earned him the nickname of
'Saintly Lyne' from his schoolfellows – and a glowing tribute
from the High Master, Dr Kynaston:

> My recollections of Joseph Leycester Lyne are among the
> freshest and most pleasing reminiscences of well-nigh the third
> of a century's superintendence of St Paul's School . . . he was
> most unlike all boys that I ever knew, with none of their
> pardonable short-comings, and more true holiness and spiritu-
> ality of mind and character than usually falls to the lot of
> Christians . . .

Leycester left St Paul's after only four years, and after what
his biographer, Donald Attwater, coyly describes as 'a misunder-
standing between his parents and an usher'. Actually the 'misun-
derstanding' arose over a beating he had received from one
of the under-masters who had found him absorbed in some
engravings of the Temple at Jerusalem when he should have been
studying Latin and Greek. According to his earliest biographer,
Baroness de Bertouch, the master not only confiscated the pictures but 'condemned their owner to receive forty-two strokes
of the cane upon the hands – two strokes for each picture'. The
baroness, describing the alleged punishment as an 'inhuman
torture', claims that young Leycester 'fell unconscious' and that
for a time his life was almost despaired of. 'The governors
expelled the perpetrator of this act of barbarity.' This version
of the incident appeared in print before Ignatius's death and was
published with his approval. It was challenged after his death,
however, by an Old Pauline who claimed that the beating had

in fact consisted of 'a few sharp cuts that most other boys would have grinned at but which injuriously affected Lyne, weak and hysterical as he seems to have been', and that it was quite untrue that the master responsible had had to resign. Discussing the incident at some length in his own biography, published nearly sixty years after the baroness's, Arthur Calder-Marshall suggests that the truth lies somewhere between these two versions. 'I think that there was a cold savagery in the master's punishment of Leycester Lyne. Saintly Lyne was too good by half, and there was a sadistic satisfaction in finding him wrong. On the other hand, I am sure that he did not give forty-two strokes – though he may have said that he was going to.'

Whatever the truth of the affair, it undoubtedly produced a nervous breakdown in the boy's health. 'The caning', says Calder-Marshall, 'accentuated the conflict between Leycester's life of piety and the discipline of learning lessons.' The doctors prescribed 'repose of mind and body for at least a year'; and Francis Lyne transferred his son first to a farm at Harrow Weald and then to the care of a Lincolnshire clergyman, George Wright, who catered for the needs of boys considered unsuited to public-school life. Leycester spent four years under Wright's tuition, first at Spalding and then at Worcester. He seems to have been much too good for his fellow-pupils. As Wright wrote afterwards:

> In his relations to his school fellows and to myself, his life was exemplary. He did not join in those athletic sports that his companions adopted. He, even at his age, seemed to take a more exalted view of our duties and his own. His dormitory was his domestic chapel. The cathedral of our city witnessed his uniform and pious attention to that duty which was suggested by the Scriptures, to remember his Creator in the days of his youth. . . . He left me accompanied by the prayers of his youthful friends, who felt themselves unable to follow his laudable example.

He was prepared for confirmation by the rector of St George's, Bloomsbury, Montagu Villiers (afterwards Bishop of Carlisle and of Durham), with whom the pious Leycester failed to see eye-to-eye. 'He asked me if I loved the Lord Jesus and was willing to renounce the world for His sake, which I was only too glad to answer in the affirmative. But I had no knowledge of faith in Christ's finished and present salvation. The examiner missed the point of my difficulty' – which was that Leycester was compelled to God more by fear of hell than by love of Jesus. In spite of his doubts, however, he was duly confirmed and made his first communion. But he soon found himself at odds with his Low Church father, who both frowned on his communicating fasting and forbade him to make his communion oftener than once every two months.

Francis Lyne's opposition to his son's religious leanings went further. Leycester wanted to train for the ministry. Francis flatly refused to help him financially – 'Not one one penny piece will I give to his college expenses' – so he went to his mother instead. She contacted a relative in Scotland, Robert Eden, Bishop of Moray, Ross and Caithness, who assured Mrs Lyne that, in the sight of God, young Leycester was 'not called upon to yield religious conviction to unreasonable parental prejudice'. He promised him a place in Trinity College, Glenalmond, an Episcopalian seminary in Perthshire which had been opened in 1847 thanks partly to the efforts of W. E. Gladstone. There still remained the problem of the penny pieces; but these were forthcoming via Louisa Loscombe, a maiden lady of Worcester who had been Leycester's confidant for the last year or two and who firmly believed in the genuineness of his vocation. He enrolled at Glenalmond in the autumn of 1856.

＊   ＊   ＊

He appears to have lived a blameless life at college. The warden, Dr Hannah, recalled him in after years as a 'person of good moral character, much religious earnestness, attractive manners and commendable attention to his studies'. Ignatius himself, with the benefit of hindsight, conceded that he had been well taught as far as 'head knowledge' was concerned, but that he had left college 'as ignorant of Jesus as my personal Saviour as when I entered it'. His theological tutor, William Bright, who was later to become a professor at Oxford, likewise commended him for his piety and earnestness and added: 'I never had a student who knew his Bible so well.' But the young Lyne did not shine equally in every subject. 'Theology was always a delightful and easy study to me, and I had no trouble in learning my Bible and Prayer Book backwards; but oh dear! those problems and metaphysical monkey-puzzles, they were too much for me altogether.' He left Glenalmond after two years – and after a second nervous breakdown. This was apparently brought about by anxiety over his looming examinations and led him to believe at one moment that he was at death's door. He recovered, however, in time to pass his examinations and to leave the college with flying colours – but also with two years to fill in before he was old enough to be made deacon, the qualifying age being twenty-three. Through the good offices of Bishop Eden he was appointed catechist of a mission church outside Inverness; but he soon antagonized the parish schoolmistress by preaching what she considered 'popery' to her pupils. Leycester (influenced by the Tractarian atmosphere of Glenalmond) insisted that the doctrines he was putting across were in perfect conformity with the Book of Common Prayer, but the schoolmistress and other locals declined to be convinced. A formal complaint was made to the bishop, with the result that Lyne soon found himself without a job. He had had his first major brush with authority – and was launched on his career as a reverend rebel.

His next port of call was Glen Urquhart, deep in the Highlands, whither he had gone at the invitation of a new friend, Mrs Cameron, whom he had christened 'Granny'. She it was who suggested that he should move to her estate in the glen, which housed an Episcopalian church at present without a minister. Lyne jumped at the opportunity, and before long had begun a Sunday school, trained a church choir and instituted a system of cottage visiting. In spite of his Tractarian teaching his zeal was such that he was soon attracting Presbyterians to his church in large numbers – to the fury of the local elders. It was one thing to cater for the needs of 'Granny' Cameron's mainly English guests during the shooting season; it was quite another to lure away members of their flock and preach popish doctrines to them under the nominal banner of Episcopalianism. The Scarlet Woman must not be allowed entry into the glen – and once again complaint was made to Bishop Eden. Lyne was told to pack his bags and remove his over-zealous presence from the neighbourhood. This second rebuff was too much for him, and he suffered another breakdown. His mother had to be summoned to Scotland to nurse him; before long she took him back to London with her. He spent most of 1860 recuperating from the effects of his Scottish misadventures.

In November he celebrated his twenty-third birthday and was therefore of an age to qualify for ordination. Henry Phillpotts, the High Church Bishop of Exeter, was sympathetic: for him the black marks which young Lyne had acquired in Scotland were not quite so black as they would have appeared to an Evangelical diocesan. Lyne was ordained deacon on 23 December 1860; but, because he lacked a university degree, two conditions were imposed: he must stay a deacon for three years before his priesting, and he must not preach in the diocese of Exeter until he had been priested. At the time of his ordination he made another significant resolution. As he recounts in his autobiography, 'I took a mental vow to live a celibate life for Christ's sake and His work.' He accepted the offer of an unpaid curacy under George Rundle Prynne, vicar of St Peter's, Plymouth, and a noted Tractarian sympathizer. At first all went well, and the young deacon threw himself into his work with enthusiasm. In a subsequent tribute to his erstwhile helper Prynne remarked that he had been 'animated with a very true spirit of devotion and zeal in carrying out such work as was assigned to him. His earnest and loving character largely won the affections of those among whom he ministered.' This was no doubt true enough, but leaves much unsaid. For instance, his main duty was to visit the poor and sick; and, in the course of his visitations, he made no secret of the fact that his primary interest was in the souls of those visited, not their bodies. He was therefore unsympathetic to their material needs unless they happened to be churchgoers.

This facet of his ministry led indirectly to the first of his so-called 'miracles'. The incident was sparked off by a rebuff he had experienced in one of the houses he was visiting, that of Mrs Egg or Hatch (Baroness de Bertouch, who tells the story, is not sure of the name). The lady, preoccupied with the cares of bringing up a large family, had aroused the curate's wrath by resolutely refusing to have any of her children baptized. 'We don't want you or yer religion neither,' she is alleged to have shouted, 'so just clear out.' Lyne retorted by pronouncing a solemn curse against the family for turning him out of the house; and the next moment the eldest child, a girl of fourteen, was, says the baroness, 'stricken with abject idiocy, and her whole body broke out from head to foot in the most loathsome sores'. The doctors were said to be baffled, but luckily the wretched mother realized that this was an 'awful judgment called down from Heaven' and sent a district visitor to beg Lyne to revoke his curse. 'He breathed a prayer. Instantaneously the idiotic teenager was restored to lucidity and the disfigured flesh regained its childish purity.' Contemporary newspapers, however, contain not a mention of the alleged miracle; and Arthur Calder-Marshall, weighing up its truth or falsehood, concludes:

> The Egg or Hatch incident clearly had some basis in fact. The sending of the young curate packing sounds authentic. One of the children may very well have been ill at the time or fallen ill soon after. But the rest is a thaumaturgic fantasy, produced perhaps by the realization, deep down, that the harassed mother had at least a superficial justification for her words.

More important than Mrs Egg (or Hatch) to the ministry of Joseph Leycester Lyne in Plymouth was a very different sort of woman, Priscilla Lydia Sellon, who was the first to encourage him in his vocation to revive the monastic life for men within the Church of England. Mother Lydia was herself pioneering the revival of the monastic life for women. The daughter of an admiral and a forceful woman of independent means, she had founded the Society of the Most Holy Trinity at Devonport and was its first Superior. She was at this time in her late thirties and took an immediate liking to the young curate fifteen years her junior. He, for his part, hailed her as his spiritual mother. By this time he was already calling himself Brother Joseph, founder and self-styled Superior of a guild for men and boys entitled the Society of the Love of Jesus. With the support of Dr Pusey, her own spiritual director, Mother Lydia made over to the fledgling community a house nearby belonging to the SHT which they could use as a monastery. 'Brother Joseph' took up residence with two companions, but the experiment lasted only forty-eight hours. He was then seized with an acute attack of typhoid fever. Congestion of the brain followed, he lost all power of speech and hearing, and for a time his life was in danger. But he was encouraged by a message from Pusey: 'Do you think that our Lord would have allowed you to love and serve Him so long if He had intended to let you perish?'

When he was sufficiently recovered he went with his parents to Belgium to convalesce. It was there that, in his own words, his monastic vocation was 'deepened by all I saw and heard. I longed to be to our beloved Church of England what Père Lacordaire and other religious men were to the Churches of France and Belgium.' As a first step he decided to dress as a monk. Mother Lydia's sister Caroline made him a habit. Actually she made two, as the parcel containing the first one was opened by Francis Lyne, who, disapproving of his son's 'monastic fiddlesticks', hid the contents. A replacement – a rough serge cassock and hood – was sent to Leycester in Brussels, where he wore it openly, to his father's annoyance.

It was while he was in Belgium that he first met Charles Lowder, who, as we saw in the chapter on Mackonochie, was running the mission attached to St George's-in-the East. Lowder needed a successor to Mackonochie on the latter's appointment to St Alban's, Holborn, and persuaded Lyne to take on the post. His nine-month spell in the East End began well, as he could fill the mission church by the power of his preaching. In a guarded tribute Lowder later testified to his 'usefulness and energy' and to his success in evangelism. 'He made his influence very widely felt in the conversion of many souls to God, some of whom I still know to be living as good and sincere Christians.' Lyne had no hesitation in visiting every household in the district, however unsavoury – and even, on one occasion, strolled into a particularly disreputable dancing-hall and announced in a loud voice: 'We must all appear before the judgment-seat of Christ.' Wapping also witnessed two more 'miracles' performed by him (for which the sole authority is the ever-credulous Baroness de Bertouch). On the first occasion he prayed by the bedside of a dying girl who turned up next day at the early Mass *perfectly cured*. On the second occasion another girl, Lizzie Meek, who was critically ill with typhoid, was actually dead by the time the young curate appeared on the scene and he was only able to restore her to life with the aid of a 'relic of the True Cross'. In the neighbourhood, says the baroness, the resurrection of Miss Meek was a 'fiery nine-days wonder' – unrecorded, however, in the local press. But the incident had an unhappy sequel. Lizzie, restored to life, was urged by Lyne, in gratitude for her 'resurrection', to enter Mother Lydia's branch house at Ascot as a postulant. But, being engaged to be married (to a 'coloured' man), she declined to play ball. Lyne at this point took on the mantle of an Old Testament prophet and, in the words of the baroness,

> warned solemnly, and more in sorrow than in anger, that, so sure as she forsook God for man, the retributory Hand would rest upon her and her fellow-sinner to the end of their days. Undeterred by her spiritual father's prophetic words, Lizzie Meek married the dusky object of her affections, and within one month of the wedding-day both husband and wife were dead and in their graves.

It was during his time at the St George's Mission that Lyne first felt the specific call to revive the Benedictine Order within the Church of England. It came during a chance visit he paid while on holiday to the Roman Catholic priory of Belmont, near Hereford. The monks received him with kindness and courtesy, and presented him with a copy in Latin of the Rule of St Benedict. A few days later he visited the ruins of Llanthony Abbey in the Black Mountains. Inspired by its beauty and sanctity, he resolved to restore it as a centre for a revived Anglican Benedictinism. On his return to London he substituted for his cassock and biretta a monastic habit and hood made on the lines of those he had seen at Belmont. He went about in his new garb, barefoot or in sandals and with a rosary. He also began calling himself Brother Ignatius of Jesus, after the founder of the Jesuits, Ignatius Loyola. His ambition soon became known in the Church at large, and he received encouragement from Bishop Forbes of Brechin, who wrote: 'I thank God for putting it into the heart of a deacon of our Church to restore the Rule of St Benedict of Nursia in our midst.'

Others were not so happy. They included Charles Lowder, who, while not personally worried if his assistant went about the streets dressed as a monk, was very concerned indeed when some of the mission's patrons threatened to withdraw their subscriptions if he continued to do so. Luckily Ignatius – as he may now be called – solved Lowder's dilemma by deciding to resign his curacy and found a Benedictine community. He was still only twenty-five – and without financial resources, as his father, incensed at his decision, refused to subsidize his new venture. As he puts it in his autobiography:

> I realized that I should be penniless . . . but I had made up my mind to break away from every tie. Relatives, except my mother, would have nothing to say to me. My bright prospects in the Church would be for ever ruined; the world would say I was mad; the Church would regard me as most dangerous, a kind of ecclesiastical Ishmael. I should have to face persecution of every kind – want, suffering, poverty. Yet I firmly believed God was calling me, and I must obey.

* * *

Ignatius's first monastic headquarters were in Suffolk: at Claydon, three miles outside Ipswich. The rector of Claydon, George Drury, was a keen Tractarian who had known him since his Plymouth days and was sympathetic to his desire to found a monastic order. He offered him a wing of his large rectory in return for assistance in the parish, and Ignatius took up residence there with two postulants on Shrove Tuesday, 1863. Poor Drury, however, had taken on more than he could chew. For one thing he was under the illusion that Ignatius had come to stay only until he could obtain permanent accommodation in Ipswich, a more convenient centre for the fledgling community. It soon transpired, however, that their funds were insufficient to purchase or lease a suitable property in the town, so Ignatius decided that it was God's will that Claydon rather than Ipswich should be the headquarters of 'the English Order of St Benedict'. The rector and his wife were soon resigning themselves to the permanent presence of their guests; and it was Mrs Drury's cook who provided them with their meals. In return for their keep Ignatius and his colleagues supplemented their monastic duties with teaching in the village school and playing with the Drury children. But they cannot have had a great deal of time for such duties, as the monastic regime which Ignatius instituted was one of extreme rigour.

The day began at two a.m. with Mattins and Lauds (or 'Nocturns') in the parish church, a service which could last up to two hours. The monks then staggered back to bed until five-thirty, when it was time to rise for Prime. At eight they would be back in church again for a celebration of the Eucharist by the rector, followed by Terce. The morning and most of the afternoon were taken up with manual work – but no food was allowed until after Sext, recited at noon. Nones followed at three p.m., Vespers at five and Compline at nine. The Rule, however, was less stringent for the Superior than for his subordinates, as he could always find excuses for not observing it too meticulously. He could, for instance, plead the necessity of writing some more begging letters as a reason for non-attendance at one or other of the daily services. His companions, compelled to observe the full rigours of the Rule, began to crack under the strain of too little sleep and food and too much work and prayer. The first Prior, Charles Walker, soon gave up. His legacy to the community was *Three Months in an English Monastery*, a vivid account of the life at Claydon published in 1864.

If it had been merely a question of raising sufficient funds to pay for their upkeep and gradually acclimatizing themselves to the punishing monastic routine, the community might conceivably have made a go of it at Claydon. But Ignatius made no attempt to adopt a low profile, and his powerful preaching was soon having a dramatic effect in the neighbourhood. Moreover, he had not bothered to seek permission from the Bishop of

Norwich, J. T. Pelham, to preach in the first place – a precaution which he ought of course to have taken in view of the conditions laid down at the time of his ordination. His hell-fire sermons, steeped in Catholic dogma, impressed the yokels but infuriated the Protestant farmers of the district. They nicknamed him 'Father Blazer' and warned him: 'If you would not tell us we are going to Hell we would leave you alone. We won't be told that by no man.' Complaint was made to the bishop, who summoned Ignatius to his palace at Norwich.

> He tried to induce me to give up my 'peculiarities' – he had no thought whatever that it might be a call from God that I was obeying. I could not give up. He then forbade my preaching in churches. On my return to Claydon I had to preach in the rectory barn. The Protestant party now stirred up active violence against me, and several times my life was in danger.

The persecution certainly took an ugly form. Ignatius was constantly jostled in the streets and assailed with missiles. On one occasion he was attacked by drunken farm labourers, stoned, and only narrowly escaped an attempt to roast him alive over a bonfire. But he had his local defenders. The *Suffolk Mercury*, for instance, despite its disapproval of Ignatian rites which, 'if not identically Popish, are in in no slight degree similar', saw no reason why he should be 'insulted, pelted with garbage of the street, with rotten eggs or equally offensive missiles'. And, further afield, the Anglo-Catholic *Church Times* (which had been founded only a week or two before Ignatius's arrival at Claydon) judged his work commendable and the assaults on him unjustified. Nevertheless, the paper (like Lowder's rich patrons) was uneasy on one particular score: Ignatius's monastic garb. Pointing out that the original monastic habit had been the dress of the ordinary peasant of the period, the *Church Times* observed:

> If Mr Lyne wishes to follow the *intention* of St Benedict he will forthwith attire himself in homely corduroy or moleskin, a smock frock, a belcher neckerchief and a billy-cock hat. . . . We believe his serge garment rather hinders than helps him. We honestly think so, and we are candid enough to say so. . . .

He may be a true monk who never wore a leathern girdle, a
garment of serge or a hair-shirt.

Needless to say, Brother Ignatius declined to take such well-
meaning advice to exchange serge for moleskin. What finally
caused his departure from Claydon was the rector's insistence
that he needed the rooms occupied by the monks for the use of
his own family. No doubt both he and his wife were tired of
providing free board and lodging for a handful of monks who
stirred up nothing but trouble. So Ignatius, it was decreed, had
to go; and the only question was, where?

After exploring various possibilities Ignatius decided to stay in
the same diocese but to move farther north – to Norwich itself.
He had the offer of dilapidated premises on Elm Hill which
stood on the site of a pre-Reformation Dominican friary. The
premises were leased as a warehouse by a ragman, but the freehold belonged to the cathedral. The only problem was how to
pay for them. The price of the lease was £400 and that of the
freehold £146. Ignatius himself had no capital of his own. He
managed to raise £13 through a lecture in Ipswich, and a further
£300 came in via a series of addresses he gave in London and the
West Country. But he put down only £50 of this amount as a
deposit on the house and spent the rest of the money on necessary repairs and renovations. He moved in with nine companions
on 30 January 1864, less than a year after his arrival in Claydon.
He was to stay there rather longer – but was to experience even
greater vicissitudes.

For one thing, the monks' new quarters were far less comfortable than the rectory. Indeed conditions to begin with were
appalling, and they lived almost literally from hand to mouth.
The warehouse had been unheated for years, and the glass had
vanished from most of the windows. Snowflakes drifted in and
mice scampered around. Food and fuel were both in short
supply. 'This morning', Ignatius wrote to a friend, 'just as our
firing was nearly all spent, a gentleman sent us two chaldrons
of coke. One of the Brothers fainted away in choir on Wednesday last, and some ladies who were present in chapel sent,
about an hour afterwards, a hamper of fish and seven and six-

pence; and so we had a good dinner that day.' The monks lived almost entirely on what was brought them in kind. Offerings came in daily from the town. One person would bring a basket of eggs, another a loaf and cake, a third some coffee, a fourth some butter, and so on. 'Another', a visitor reported, 'seems to consider it her mission to bring pots of jam. She manages to bring one daily, or nearly so; so that the brothers are rolling in jam at present, without overmuch bread to spread it on.'

The locals rallied round in other ways. Carpenters, plasterers and glaziers helped repair the building and keep out the ravages of the weather without payment. Women volunteered to act as laundresses, and a doctor gave his services free if any of the monks were ill. Elm Hill abounded in Good Samaritans.

But of course it was the spiritual rather than the material which took precedence at the monastery – souls before bodies. Three large rooms on the ground floor of the warehouse were turned into a chapel; and here the punishing ritual of the daily offices went on as at Claydon. The Bishop of Norwich continued to take a dim view of the monks and their goings-on. However, as the chapel was on private property, he had no power to prevent Ignatius from conducting services or preaching from its pulpit. 'He can do what he likes with a congregation; his oratory is of the very highest order,' wrote the Rev. Gerard Moultrie in a letter to the *Church Times*. 'There is a real turning of the heart from the world to God. It is a genuine Catholic revival.' Moultrie reported that the monks had converted more than thirty Dissenters, as well as Roman Catholics. Ignatius also developed the Third Order of St Benedict, which he had founded while at Claydon. This was made up of laypeople who were pledged to assist the monks by their prayers and alms. The latter provided a large part of the monastic income. It was about now that Ignatius assumed the professed monk's title of 'Father'.*

---

*According to Peter Anson, in *The Call of the Cloister*, Ignatius made his profession to Pusey, though Anson admits that there is no mention of this in the official biography. Pusey began by admiring Ignatius's work, but grew less enthusiastic as time went on. After the Bristol Church Congress of 1865 he remarked that it was a blessing that Ignatius had not been made a priest. And in 1870 he told the future Lord Halifax: 'Father Ignatius is a most impracticable man.'

It was during his time at Norwich that he approached the Bishop of Oxford, 'Soapy Sam' Wilberforce, with a view to obtaining from him the episcopal recognition which he was unable to secure from the Bishop of Norwich. He had no joy in this quarter, however – indeed quite the reverse. Wilberforce, in his reply to Ignatius's appeal (dated 5 June 1865), minced no words. He accused Ignatius of flinging away the greater part of his usefulness to the Church by the adoption of a form of dress '*never* suited to English habits and now pre-eminently unsuitable'. Such a form of self-advertisement was, said the bishop, 'a sacrifice of the kernel to the shell such as I have hardly ever seen equalled'. He went on:

> You are sacrificing everywhere the great reality for which you have sacrificed yourself to the puerile imitation of a past phase of service which it is just as impossible for you to revive in England as it would be for you to resuscitate an Egyptian mummy and set it upon the throne of the pharaohs. . . . If you persist in your present line you will indeed make it practically impossible that for another generation such efforts should succeed.

Ignatius's imprudence was not confined to the wearing of a monastic habit. His eccentricities began to alienate some of his closest supporters. Because he was not yet a priest, he and his fellow-monks relied for their celebrations of the Eucharist on a neighbouring priest, the Rev. E. A. Hillyard, vicar of St Lawrence's. This was a church which instead of chairs had pews, for which rents were charged – a fruitful source of revenue, but a discouragement to the poorer worshippers. The pew-rents, however, could only be abolished if incumbent and congregation were united in their desire to do so. Ignatius took it into his head that the pews of St Lawrence's must go; and, when Hillyard hesitated to take so drastic a step (to which many of his parishioners were opposed), local members of Ignatius's Third Order ripped out the pews themselves and reduced them to firewood.

If such an act of organized vandalism was not bad enough, Ignatius went one step – a big step – further. He forbade any of the members of his Third Order from attending a dance in a particular church hall because, before the Dissolution, it had been the Church of the Black Friars; and a secular function in such a sacred place appeared to him a blasphemy. Disregarding the inhibition, Hillyard himself and other members of his congregation who were also members of the Third Order attended the dance. Ignatius took their names and, on the following Sunday, summoned the offenders to the altar-rail in the middle of the service. After lecturing them on the enormity of their 'sacrilege' he laid down appropriate acts of penance. The women were to lie prostrate in ashes on the chapel floor; the elder men were to present themselves before the congregation carrying in their right hands a stinking candle made of 'tallow dip'; and the younger men were to be publicly caned by Ignatius on the altar steps. The alternative to undergoing the appropriate penance was excommunication from the priory chapel. Incredible as it may seem, a few members of the congregation actually agreed to undergo the prescribed punishment rather than risk such 'excommunication'. But the majority of the malefactors, including the vicar, chose to break with Ignatius. If they could now no longer attend his chapel, he and his monks would likewise be cut off from the ministrations of St Lawrence's. When they attended another church in Norwich its incumbent complained to the bishop and was told: 'If these Monks present themselves for Communion in their ridiculous dress, you have my permission to pass them over.' Ignatius, by his folly, had now alienated both Catholics and Protestants in Norwich. It is hardly surprising that, when he attended the Church Congress at Bristol in 1865 to plead his cause, the feeling among those attending was that unspectacular 'colleges' of monks such as that which Fr Benson had just founded at Cowley were much more in keeping with the ethos of the Church of England than a medieval revival like Elm Hill.

Protestant opposition to Ignatius's Norwich ministry soon took the same ugly turn as it had at Claydon. Hired rowdies organized demonstrations against him, and his meetings were picketed. Ignatius himself was often absent on money-raising expeditions, and on one occasion narrowly escaped in a hansom cab from a mob who were all set to beat him up. But, on the credit side, his disciples grew in numbers to such an extent that admission to services in the monastery was restricted to ticket-holders and the chapel was enlarged to accommodate three hundred worshippers. His goings-on attracted increasing attention in the world outside East Anglia. A scornful paragraph in *Punch* (15 July 1865) concluded sarcastically: 'It is not true that Br. Ignatius and the monks his associates have removed from their monastery at Norwich to the Zoological Gardens, Regent's Park, and there taken up their abode in the Monkey House.'

The community's reputation was not helped by a minor scandal which broke out over the relations between the choirmaster, Brother Augustine, and one of his choristers. Augustine had written the lad a foolish but ostensibly harmless letter into which, when its contents were made public, the prurient read undertones of homosexuality. Ignatius successfully defended the community's reputation in letters to the press, but expelled the offender. A less public but potentially more serious row erupted nine months later in June 1865, when Ignatius was in London conducting a mission. Towards the end of his stay one of the monks (described by Baroness de Bertouch as an 'execrable villain' and by Ignatius's mother as an 'unmitigated scamp') arrived at his lodgings to tell him that he had been deposed as Superior and a rival elected in his place. The ostensible cause of the 'mutiny' was anger at an absurd penance for breaking the Solemn Silence which Ignatius had imposed on his fellow-monks just before leaving for London: they had been ordered to trace a cross on the ground with their tongues. Anger at the nature of the penance, coupled with dislike at being ordered about by a Superior twenty years his junior, had led one of the older monks, Brother Marcus, to denounce Ignatius in his absence and to persuade the others to elect a more pliable substitute. Ignatius acted swiftly to quell the mutiny. He at once left London for Norwich, stormed into the monastery and reasserted his authority. Marcus and another of the ringleaders were expelled from the community. The remaining transgressors received a free pardon. Ignatius told the baroness that the mutineers had planned to seize him, shut him in a cellar and leave him to die of starvation. If this was true, he had indeed had a narrow escape. The flavour of the rebellion was captured in a set of doggerel verses printed in a local broadsheet of which a typical stanza reads:

> This Father Ignatius who was thought such a Saint
> Has turned out a devil without any paint,
> And those who obey such a tyrant's rules
> Must be poor simple people or very great fools.

Added to all this cloak-and-dagger business was increasing anxiety over money – and the ownership of the Elm Hill monastery. Ignatius, it will be recalled, had only had sufficient funds to put down a £50 deposit before moving in; but the rest of the purchase money had somehow to be found. The proceeds of the Superior's money-raising forays went on the day-to-day living expenses of the community and could provide nothing extra towards the purchase of the house. In the end some sort of a solution was found through the agency of an anonymous well-wisher who agreed to lend £500 for the purpose. The property was registered in the name of George Drury, the rector of Claydon, as patron of the project, and bought with the well-wisher's loan. In August 1865 Ignatius signed a lease agreeing to pay an annual rent until the mortgage had been repaid. The arrangement, though solving his short-term problem, was to store up trouble for the future.

Meanwhile, however, his health had again been put in jeopardy by his accumulating burdens. He suffered a cataleptic fit during a chapel service and, when sufficiently recovered, was advised to take a prolonged holiday on the Continent. He left early in 1866. His travelling companions were a strangely assorted crew: Brother Philip, one of the dimmer but more devoted of his associates; Sister Ambrosia, an elderly widow whose chief duty was to act as nurse to the invalid; and the 'Infant Samuel'. The last-named, a child of four, had been adopted by Ignatius fifteen months earlier as an oblate, to be brought up to the monastic life in accordance with the Rule of

St Benedict.* He went about dressed in a miniature white habit and cowl, which added the finishing touch to a party of tourists who must have struck the wondering Continentals as more than a little bizarre. The party travelled overland to Marseilles and thence by steamer to Civitavecchia, from where they went on to Rome. Their appearance created a minor sensation at the Vatican, but the Pope, Pius IX, agreed to receive Ignatius in audience. He gave him a medal of the Immaculate Conception and told him (in Latin) that the cowl didn't make the monk, whereupon Ignatius allegedly quipped back (also in Latin): 'True, most reverend father, but it is the *life* which makes him.' After sight-seeing in Rome and Naples the party passed on to Sicily and thence took ship to Malta. They had hoped to catch up there with Pusey, who, accompanied by Mother Lydia, was on a pilgrimage to Jerusalem; but, when they reached Valletta, they discovered, to their chagrin, that the pair had already sailed for the Holy Land. Ignatius and his party spent a month in Malta before returning to Marseilles and thence to England. On his arrival, however, they were faced with a shock beside which a mutiny of monks must have seemed a mere bagatelle: they learned to their horror that the community at Elm Hill had been dispersed and the house itself put up for sale.

*   *   *

The events that had led up to such an unfortunate dénouement were complex. The baroness, in her biography, claims that Ignatius was the victim of a deliberate fraud perpetrated by his erstwhile associate Drury and two local solicitors, who should have been subject to criminal proceedings. The truth was, of course, rather different. Until recently Ignatius had supposed that the £500 which had been used to purchase the Elm Hill property was a gift rather than a loan. It was the knowledge that he was head over ears in debt which had helped precipitate the nervous illness

---

*Also known as the Infant Oblate and Baby Ignatius, he was the son of a member of the Third Order who had been deserted by her husband. The adoption was not a success, as the young man failed to take kindly to his 'vocation'. He ran away to sea at the age of seventeen and later married a Glasgow girl.

that had led to his convalescent trip abroad. He now found himself having to face up to reality. While overseas he had been in correspondence with both Drury and the two solicitors in an attempt to persuade them to take on his financial responsibilities. Not unnaturally, they declined to do so. They pointed out that they had been themselves raising money on his behalf, but that they could not expect members of the Third Order to under-write his remaining debts (as he had suggested). If he wanted to keep the monastery going, he must come back and raise the necessary funds himself. Ignatius's response to this ultimatum was to go into another nervous decline. Drury took over the Elm Hill premises and provided the three remaining monks with the wherewithal to return to secular life. Meanwhile Francis Lyne, in whose house at Hambleden his son was now convalesc-ing, advertised in the Norwich papers that Father Ignatius had dispersed his Norwich community and abandoned all thoughts of re-establishing monasticism in the Church of England. The latter claim roused Ignatius from his sickbed to publish an emphatic denial. But he had undoubtedly lost Elm Hill for good.*

It was at this stage that the Archbishop of Canterbury, C. T. Longley, was unwillingly drawn into the fray. He had already been approached by Mrs Lyne on behalf of her son, and had rashly promised to find him a suitable curacy and (assuming he performed his duties satisfactorily for a year) to advance him to the priesthood. Longley now wrote to the vicar of Margate, Canon Bateman, asking him to take on what he hoped was a penitent deacon and keep him gainfully occupied in 'common clerical duties' for the next twelve months. Bateman agreed reluctantly; but the experiment soon came to grief. At his own interview with the Archbishop, Ignatius had agreed to don the ordinary 'clericals' worn by the secular clergy; but, in conver-sation with Bateman, he disclosed that, though he might have

---

*Attempts to regain it through a long-drawn-out lawsuit lasting ten years and costing £10,000 – money which would have been better spent on Llanthony – came to nothing. They involved Ignatius in bitter quarrels first with his erstwhile patron, George Drury, and later with his own father.

temporarily abandoned the habit, he still hankered after the Benedictine life and had every intention of resuming it. As Bateman put it many years afterwards:

> He [Ignatius] had no idea of living a curate's life – he meant eventually to have a house and grounds of his own – he would call 'good monks' around him, and establish rules and discipline: for all which he needed and sought priest's orders. . . . It was plain enough that I should soon lose all authority over him and his monks; and I expressed undisguised astonishment at what he now said, as contrasted with what I had heard from the Archbishop.

The good canon was beginning to lecture his would-be curate on the folly of such proceedings when 'he turned pale and faint' and had to be led into the open air. 'He was unfit for evening service and spent the time writing to the Archbishop. We met at breakfast: and, without further discussion, he left by an early train and I saw him no more.'

*   *   *

After this there was of course no question of Longley admitting Ignatius to priest's orders. Once again he was thrown into the depths of depression, and this time it was Pusey who came to the rescue. He invited Ignatius to join him at Black Gang Chine, in the Isle of Wight, where he was working on his *Eirenikon*. It was there, during the temporary absence of his host, that Ignatius underwent the conversion experience that was profoundly to affect his future life. His own account of the experience, as dictated to Baroness de Bertouch, occupies eight pages of her biography and includes a vision he had of Mary, Joseph and the infant Jesus. A summary of this account takes up only a few sentences of his own brief 'autobiography' (one of the 'Llanthony Tracts' intended for sale in mission halls). The key section of this abridgement reads:

> Broken down entirely, and in shattered health – from a worldly standpoint a ruined young man – God's great mercy was manifested to me. One Sunday evening on the sea-shore

God showed me, by the Holy Spirit's power, that what I had been trying all my life to do, and in vain, *viz*., to save my soul, Jesus had done eighteen hundred years ago for me on the cross; and that if I would, with a simple faith, accept Jesus in His fulness as God's free gift to me, I should receive in Him wisdom and righteousness, sanctification and redemption. I cannot tell the joy, the new life, the strength that came to me.

'Up to my twenty-ninth year', Ignatius says elsewhere, 'I had found no personal *comfort* in my religion.' The experience on the sea-shore replaced the fear of hell that had dominated his life and ministry up till then with a conviction of the saving power of Jesus. He had been born again; and thenceforward he believed passionately that no one could find God who had not experienced a sudden conversion similar to his own. However ornate the outward trappings of the monasticism which he practised, he preached salvation in the manner of an Evangelical missioner.

Meanwhile, however, he had to pick up the pieces of his failed monastic venture and begin again. His initial solution was to be a monk during the week and a missioner at weekends. His base was London. From Monday to Friday he lodged in a villa at Stoke Newington, the community over which he ruled having been reduced to two members of his Elm Hill band who were still loyal to him, plus the reluctant oblate, the Infant Samuel. On Saturdays and Sundays he acted as curate to the Rev. William Denton, vicar of St Bartholomew's, Cripplegate, in the City, with the blessing of the Bishop of London, A. C. Tait. Denton was a High Churchman but not a ritualist. He had been sufficiently impressed by Ignatius's powers as a preacher to wish to secure his services on a regular basis. The new curate became a star attraction, lecturing in the church on Sunday evenings and drawing huge crowds who stayed behind after the service in the hope of exchanging a word with the lecturer. Needless to say, Denton soon became jealous of his assistant, whose drawing power was so obviously superior to his own – and resorted to such petty expedients as turning out the lights immediately after Evensong on the plea of not wasting gas, but in reality to deprive

Ignatius of the chance to hold court at what Denton called his 'levées'. Tait had agreed to ordain him priest provided that he served a year at St Bartholomew's, but he failed by six weeks to stay the course. The growing tension between the vicar and curate erupted one Sunday evening, when they almost came to blows as Denton tried to prevent Ignatius from attending a triumphant meeting with his fans. Ignatius left in a huff – and without any prospect of becoming a priest.

But he was not through with London. He continued to devote his weekends to city missions. He established his headquarters in Hunter Street, Bloomsbury, and preached regularly in St Edmund's, Lombard Street, and St Paul's, Bunhill Row. He again attracted enormous congregations, not hesitating to denounce Mammon as represented by the rich City bankers – but suggesting that they could assuage their guilt by contributing to his appeal for funds with which to build a new permanent monastery. Money (and even personal jewellery) poured on to the collection-plate, and Ignatius's reputation as a preacher went from strength to strength. His denunciation of the City grandees attracted widespread popular support.

In March 1867 he moved his community from Stoke Newington to a small house at Laleham-on-Thames, near Staines, Middlesex. A three-year lease was taken out. The coach-house was made into a chapel, and a cottage in the garden converted into a shelter for 'waifs and wayfarers'. A Bavarian Roman Catholic priest agreed to say Mass daily for the community, in spite of the disapproval of Archbishop Manning. The number of brothers increased to eight. A companion community of Benedictine nuns was established at Feltham, six miles from Laleham, under a prioress seconded from Mother Lydia's community at Plymouth. With his growing community and his success as a mission preacher, all seemed set fair for Ignatius. But he still lacked the priesthood. He again approached Tait to see if he would relent, but was again rebuffed. As a typical pillar of the Establishment, Tait could hardly approve of such a tiresomely unorthodox character as Ignatius, whatever his achievement as a popular preacher. He wrote to tell him so:

Let me earnestly beg you to be contented that God has given you powers whereby you are able greatly to influence those whom you address in your pastoral character.... Let me earnestly beg you to be contented with such means of influence, and to give up the attempt to engraft on the Church of England parts of the Roman system which are disapproved of by the whole body of our Church governors. I am greatly interested in what I hear of your zeal and of the earnestness of your preaching, but you must suffer me to remind you, as set over you in the Lord, that the course which you pursued in Norwich, and which I fear you are anxious to pursue again, seems to have so much self-will in it that it cannot be expected to be followed by God's blessing.

The tide now turned against Ignatius in other ways. Protestant opposition to his community began at Laleham, gangs of rowdies being sent from London to disrupt the monastic devotions. They camped outside the coach-house-chapel and played their mouth-organs and hurdy-gurdies at solemn moments during the Mass. They attempted to break into the house itself and wrought havoc in the garden. Life for the inmates became extremely fraught. On top of all this came a damaging attack on Ignatius's personal character, master-minded by Brother Stanislaus, one of the ringleaders in the Norwich mutiny. At a series of meetings in Hanover Square Stanislaus and others testified to the allegedly unsavoury activities that had taken place on Elm Hill. There were dark hints of homosexual practices; and Ignatius's reputation suffered as a result.

A more sustained attack on him took place during one of his appearances at St Edmund's, Lombard Street. A crowd led by Protestant toughs and estimated at sixty thousand gathered outside the church. The lunch-hour traffic was disrupted, and the police had difficulty in preventing a full-scale riot. Paradoxically the incident increased Ignatius's reputation for a while, but nemesis was at hand. Its humble instrument was a certain Sister Gertrude, whom Ignatius had installed as prioress of the Third Order sisterhood attached to his mission headquarters in Bloomsbury. She wanted to be entitled 'Mother' like the prioress at Feltham. Ignatius refused her request on the ground that she was a tertiary, not a professed nun. Sister Gertrude began to spread gossip about his favouritism and lack of understanding. He ordered her to resign and, when she declined to do so, 'excommunicated' her from the Order. Sister Gertrude, under the impression that he had excommunicated her from the Church of England, complained to the Bishop of London, who inhibited Ignatius from preaching in any church in the diocese. This was a blow which struck at the heart of his activities. At an interview with the bishop he attempted to get him to change his mind, but without success. All Tait offered to do was to release him from his monastic vows. 'What you ask of me', Ignatius retorted, 'is tantamount to asking me to go to Hell!' Gladstone intervened on his behalf, but Tait was unrepentant. When he succeeded Longley at Canterbury at the end of 1868 his successor, John Jackson, continued the inhibition. If Ignatius wished to continue conducting missions in London, he would have to do so in future in public halls rather than churches. But at least he could charge for admission.

In fact Ignatius decided at this juncture to move out of London. An unexpectedly generous gift from a member of the Third Order enabled him to purchase a site for a monastery in the remote Vale of Ewyas, nestling beneath the Black Mountains of South Wales. In such a secluded spot, he felt, he and his fellow-monks would be safe from the unkind attentions of Protestant toughs and other opponents, and there would be no worldly distractions to tempt members of the community away from the path of virtue. Ignatius's original ambition had been to restore the ruins of Llanthony Abbey – but they were not for sale. The owner, a son of the writer Walter Savage Landor, refused to consider any offers, and Ignatius was reduced to retreating five miles further up the valley. There, at Capel-y-ffin, he was able to purchase thirty-four acres of land on which to build his monastery. He could have chosen no lonelier location. It was five miles from a post-office, ten miles from a railway station, fifteen miles from Abergavenny, the nearest market town. But its very solitude suited Ignatius, and there he decided to pitch his camp. Accompanied by a single postulant, he took up residence in a hut on the site in November 1869, their purpose being (as he put it afterwards) 'to serve the Lord God apart from this most wicked age in solitude, self-denial, labour and prayer'.

The foundation-stone of the new monastery was laid on 17 March 1870; and, as it happens, we have an eye-witness glimpse of those early days from the pen of the Rev. Francis Kilvert, the Victorian diarist. Kilvert first visited Capel-y-ffin in April 1870, when work had been in progress a bare couple of weeks. On that occasion Ignatius himself was away, but two of his fellows were at work on the foundations. They were dressed, Kilvert noted, in long black habits which they appeared to find irksome in the heat of the sun. Kilvert observes censoriously: 'It does seem very odd at this age of the world in the latter part of the 19th century to see monks gravely wearing such dresses and at work in them in broad day.'

On his second visit to Capel-y-ffin on 2 September 1870 Kilvert was able to meet both Ignatius himself and members of his family.* His description of Ignatius (who was then thirty-two) is worth quoting:

> His head and brow are very fine, the forehead beautifully rounded and highly imaginative. The face is a very saintly one and the eyes extremely beautiful, earnest and expressive, a dark soft brown. When excited they seem absolutely to flame. He wears the Greek or early British tonsure all round the temples, leaving the hair of the crown untouched. His manner gives you the impression of great earnestness and single-mindedness.

Kilvert reports that the building work ought to have been finished by now, but that Ignatius was 'perfectly unworldly, innocent and unsuspicious' and, as a result, had been 'imposed upon, cheated and robbed right and left'. He had a long conver-

---

*Seven weeks earlier the susceptible Kilvert had met Ignatius's sister Harriet and had been much taken by her. 'Shall I confess', he confides to his diary, 'how I longed to kiss that beautiful white little hand, even at the imminent risk that it would instantly administer a stinging slap on the face of its admirer?'

sation with Ignatius, in the course of which the latter spoke frankly about his community and its problems. The monks, he said, were supported entirely by his preaching, which brought in £1000 a year. He got on much better with Low Church than with High Church people, and best of all with the Dissenters, 'who consider and call him a second Wesley'. Kilvert goes on:

> He allows that a man must be of a very rare and peculiar temperament to become and remain a monk. A monk he says must either be a philosopher or a 'holy fool'. He also allows that monkery has a strong tendency to drive people mad. Out of 50 novices he could only reckon on making 3 monks. The rest would probably be failures. One in seven was a large percentage.

Mindful of his feelings on his April visit to the monastery, Kilvert asked Ignatius if he would not find an ordinary dress more convenient and practical and less open to insult. 'He scouted the idea of abandoning his distinctive monastic dress. He said he had once given it up for a few days, but he felt like a deserter and traitor till he took to the habit again.' Ignatius told Kilvert that the Bishop of Gloucester and Bristol (C. J. Ellicott) had suggested the same thing, but that he had turned the tables on the bishop by asking him why *he* did not discard his own 'foolish and meaningless' dress. 'The Bishop laughed and said there was a good deal in what Father Ignatius said. He thinks the Bishops are coming round to his side.' After which over-optimistic observation Ignatius took leave of Kilvert, though he called out to him as he left: 'Father! Will you remember us the next time you celebrate the Holy Communion?' 'Yes,' replied Kilvert, 'I will.'

The situation of the monastery was unfortunate, in that it was on the shady side of the Vale of Ewyas. Very little sunshine reached it, and the damp and chill which crept into the building both harmed the fabric and depressed many of its inmates. But Donald Attwater, who lived there in the 1920s after it had been acquired by Eric Gill, denies that the house was as desolate and forbidding as some people made out, though he admits that it had been designed with a 'masterly eye for inconvenience'.

Nearly all the rooms opened into one another and several of the fireplaces smoked. Attwater claimed that few who had lived there for any length of time could deny its attraction – 'an attraction which is as potent to some as the personality of its builder was to others'. Certainly Ignatius himself must have found the place attractive, for he stuck it out there for thirty-eight years – though admittedly he was away for quite long stretches at a time on money-raising expeditions.

Peter Anson discusses the Ignatius experiment at length in his *The Call of the Cloister* and says that it is hard to understand how such a life could have been maintained for so long a period as thirty-eight years. There was a continual stream of novices coming and going, some staying for years and others for only a few weeks. Many, says Anson, would never have been admitted by a more experienced judge of character, while others might have made good monks if they had received proper training and direction. Some of those familiar with the Llanthony* set-up considered that the real cause of its failure was the lack of a monk of the right type to act as novice-master. An even more potent reason, however, lay in the frequent absence of the Superior, whose forceful personality was the mainspring behind the enterprise. On average he spent almost half the year away from Llanthony, leading missions or giving addresses to raise funds for the monastery. Such long sabbaticals may have been inevitable if the community was to survive, but they certainly made things difficult for those who had to carry on in his absence.

Ignatius himself was only too well aware of the problem. He told an interviewer in 1896, by when he had been established at Llanthony for over a quarter of a century: 'While I am there things go on pretty straight and comfortably, but when I am away no one hardly stays. They cannot keep the rule without spiritual help.' Later in the year, in the course of a speech at Bath, he complained that the community was a failure as he was saddled with the double duty of supporting it both financially

---

*Technically, of course, Capel-y-ffin. But Ignatius himself and most contemporary commentators usually referred to the monastery as being at Llanthony.

and spiritually. When he was absent from Llanthony the spiritual work suffered, and when he was present he was unable to raise money to keep the place going. But of course, vital as Ignatius was to the smooth running of Llanthony, he made sure that it was run in a highly idiosyncratic manner. Though he professed to follow the Rule of St Benedict, he interpreted that Rule according to his own whims and fancies. The Rule thus became an eclectic one devised by the Superior himself. The parts of the genuine Rule that failed to appeal to him he would ignore, replacing them with unBenedictine traditions and customs that happened to tickle his fancy.

The monastic regime at Llanthony was as rigorous as it had been at Claydon and Elm Hill: a mixture of devotional observance and manual labour. The canonical hours were recited daily, the brethren being roused in time for Mattins at two a.m., followed by Lauds. Between the end of Lauds at three-thirty and Prime at five they were not allowed back into bed but were allocated various domestic duties. Prime was followed by a period of private reading in the common-room. Breakfast of coffee and dry bread was available for the weaker brethren, but abstinence was encouraged ('Offer up your fast to Jesus for poor sinners'). After Terce there was a celebration of the Mass if a priest was available. The monks then dispersed to their various manual jobs in the house or garden or on the farm – though they had to break off whatever they were doing to attend a compulsory Bible-reading at ten o'clock, each brother reciting a verse at a time. Sext was said at noon, and after it was over the brethren could settle down to their one good meal of the day – dinner. This normally consisted of thick soup; tinned salmon, sardines or lobster, or eggs, with fresh vegetables; and pudding followed by cheese. Fresh fish was served once a week, poultry on Sundays, and cider or perry during the summer.*

---

*St Benedict frowned on the eating of the flesh of four-footed animals, but beef was served at Christmas and lamb at Easter. During Lent the main meal was postponed until five p.m. On Ash Wednesday the choir floor was covered with cinders and ashes, the monks lying prostrate on the ashes and reciting the whole psalter at intervals. On Good Friday, they lay flat on the hard pavement of the choir from noon to three p.m.

None at three p.m. was followed by an hour's siesta, recreation (out-of-doors whenever possible) and more manual work. Then came a light supper and sung Vespers. At eight there was a meeting in the sacristy to discuss a chapter of the Rule and listen to readings from Scripture and from Butler's *Lives of the Saints*. The day ended with Compline, and at nine the brethren could at last retire to bed – and the allotted five hours of slumber. Ignatius liked to stress the importance of maintaining such an austere regime. 'We don't want any more namby-pamby, nine-teenth-century-hearted men,' he once wrote; 'we want only downright, brave, faithful, medieval-souled Welshmen and Eng-lishmen who can leave all and give all to Jesus only.'

He certainly expected a great deal of his subordinates, which may help to explain why so few of them stayed for any length of time. And, as if the Benedictine Rule (as amended by the Superior) was not punishing enough, breaches of it were pun-ished by absurd forms of penance or mortification. On one occasion, for instance, a monk who had served to his fellows meat intended for guests in case it should go bad in the summer heat was made to hold a piece of meat in one hand throughout Vespers and in the other hand a copy of the Rule. A monk who spoke to anyone outside the monastery had to wear an article of lay clothing, such as a top hat or a coloured tie, for days at a time. And, if he was late for meals, he was made to eat off the floor. Children attached to the monastery also had to mind their behaviour. A priest who celebrated Mass at Llanthony in 1894 was served by a boy dressed in a sailor suit instead of the customary cassock and cotta as a penalty for some childish misdeed.

If speech outside the monastery was a forbidden luxury, within the monastery it was restricted to cases of absolute necessity or to the periods of 'recreation'. And even then the speaker had to whisper, kneeling, with his hood over his head and his hands folded beneath his scapular. From Compline at night until after breakfast the next morning there had to be unbroken silence (apart from saying the offices). The penalty for talking was to recite the entire psalter aloud – a three-hour chore.

One problem for Ignatius in his early days at Llanthony was retaining control of the community of nuns which he had set up at Feltham under Mother Hilda (Emily Stewart) in 1868. She had a certain amount of delegated authority, but would have liked to have been made an abbess in her own right. She felt that it was impracticable for Ignatius to try to run the convent from a distance. The growing disagreement between two equally autocratic characters came to a head in 1878, when, on a visit to the convent, Ignatius found it in a state of schism. Mother Hilda and the majority of the nuns now broke away in open rebellion and were solemnly 'excommunicated' by Ignatius. They stayed on at Feltham until 1889 and eventually, after successive moves to Twickenham, Malling Abbey in Kent and St Bride's, Milford Haven, went over as a body to the Church of Rome in 1913. Four nuns remained loyal to the Superior, who first set them up in a house at Slapton, Devonshire. When, in 1881, the lease of the house fell in, they joined the monks at Llanthony. The establishment of a 'mixed' community might have caused problems considering the odd characters whom Ignatius attracted, but there appears to have been no case of scandal. The monks and nuns occupied adjoining buildings and shared the same church. But the two wings of the community kept strictly apart from each other; and even in church the nuns, being segregated from the monks, were heard but not seen. The Superior alone was entitled to enter the nuns' enclosure, and only when he had official business to transact. Otherwise all contacts between the two wings was strictly forbidden. A monk who so far forgot himself as to speak briefly to a nun through the church grille was at once dismissed. But the nuns' life cannot have been an easy one. Their numbers never ran beyond single figures; and in 1891, during Ignatius's absence in America and a consequent lack of spiritual ministrations, the three remaining nuns defected in a body to Rome. Two and a half years later, however, he admitted another novice to the reopened convent wing, though there were never thereafter more than a handful of nuns in residence.

Indeed, numbers at Llanthony as a whole were scarcely impressive. Between 1870 and 1907 only forty names appear in the monks' register (though the list is probably incomplete). Fourteen of these are recorded to have been 'sent away', usually for bad conduct. Twelve walked out of their own accord. Six left by agreement with the Superior, and one was returned to his parents after a legal battle. Three of the remaining seven were still there at the time of Ignatius's death. One of the reasons why so few of those who came stayed for more than a short while was the extreme rigour of the life at Llanthony. Donald Attwater, who talked to many of those who had known Ignatius, recorded one man as saying that 'such sacrifice was required that only those who generously made complete oblation were able to endure the regime'. Ignatius himself took the view that it was better to be highly selective in allowing solemn professions than to risk broken vows. In May 1896, when his novices were seven in number, he expressed doubts as to whether he should ever again let anyone take the life vow 'unless it pleases God to send us someone who has the vocation and would be able to take my place in my absence'. As Kilvert had been told when he visited Llanthony, Ignatius was a notoriously poor judge of character – which was the reason why such a large proportion of those he admitted to the community turned out to be unsatisfactory. Dom Cyprian Alston, once a novice at Llanthony and later a Roman Catholic, testified that 'anyone who could talk glibly about conversion and salvation and so forth found no difficulty in making him [Ignatius] believe any plausible tale they might choose to invent for their own advantage. . . . His limitation, if such it may fairly be called, was an apparent inability to conceive malice or meanness in another.'

The maximum number of adult male members of the community at any one time appears to have been twelve. That was in the summer of 1890. But numbers fluctuated, and two years earlier there had been only three novices and three boys beside the Superior.* Numbers were to decline again immediately after

---

*According to B. G. A. Cannell (Brother Gildas) in *From Monk to Busman* (1935), there was a mass expulsion of monks and novices about this time for alleged breaches of the Rule – which led Gildas to exclaim to Ignatius: 'Dear Father, perhaps it would be easier if you asked me the Rules I *have* kept. As the Abbot does not keep *any* strict Rules, how can he expect us to?'

the 1890 high-spot, for it was then that Ignatius left on his longest absence – a trip to the USA that lasted for just over a year. The trip was intended to give him a chance to recoup his health, but developed into a full-scale mission tour. He returned, however, to a sadly depleted community. In addition to the nuns all the monks save two had left – fed up, no doubt, with the dreadful monotony of the life and without the charismatic presence of their Superior to revive them.

If they were kept at full stretch both physically and spiritually, any mental initiative was strictly discouraged. 'We never allow ourselves to think,' Ignatius told an interviewer on one occasion. 'It is all decided for us.' Exactly what his subordinates might read was of course 'decided' by the Superior – and a dreary diet it must have been. Apart from the Bible and the Rule of St Benedict, the only form of literature to which unrestricted access was allowed was Butler's multi-volume *Lives of the Saints*. The key of the library was retained by Ignatius, who doled out such treasures as there were with a sparing hand. Only recognized religious classics were normally allowed, such as Montalembert's *Monks of the West*, or biographies of figures such as Fénélon or Bossuet. No novels were permitted – and certainly no 'religious' novels as potentially dangerous as Mrs Humphry Ward's *Robert Elsmere*, with its advocacy of the detested modernism. No period of the day was allowed for study as such, either sacred or secular. There was no regular religious instruction and no proper ascetical training. The only 'teaching' the monks received took place during the daily Bible-reading sessions, when Ignatius would comment on the particular passage being read.

His remark about the monks not allowing themselves to think was made in response to a suggestion that they ought to be well up in the thought of the day. He went on: 'If we doubt one thing, the whole thing must go. . . . I hate [the 'New Criticism'] and, if [Mr Gore] came into this room now, I feel as though I could tear him limb from limb.' This was at the time when Charles Gore's editorship of *Lux Mundi* had shaken the faith of many of his erstwhile supporters such as Denison. But Ignatius's obsessive hatred of anything that could be associated with the 'New Criticism' went beyond even Denison's. It was said that he kept a large Bible in the chapel at Llanthony which he invited visitors to kiss – but only on the condition that they disclaimed belief in Gore. He even went so far as to hire a hall in Oxford and issue posters announcing that he would address a meeting in order to denounce 'the man Charles Gore'. Although, at the meeting, he roundly abused Gore, the latter consoled himself with two 'profound convictions': first, that he was not guilty of the faults with which he was charged; and, secondly, that he deserved far greater punishment for sins of which his accusers knew nothing.

Ignatius's campaign against Gore reached its apogee at the Birmingham Church Congress of 1893, when Gore was down to read a paper on Christian reunion. When he was about to begin, Ignatius, who was sitting in the front row of the audience, jumped to his feet and exclaimed: 'In the name of Jesus Christ, I say that Charles Gore has no right to speak.' On being over-ruled by the Bishop of Worcester, who was in the chair, Ignatius held up a copy of *Lux Mundi* and declared: 'It is a denial of Jesus Christ.' Later in the proceedings he advanced towards the platform and demanded the right to address the meeting. He was ruled out of order by the chairman but refused to leave, declaring that he would be taken out by the police and nobody else. He was eventually calmed down with the offer of a seat on the platform, and the meeting was able to resume its business. But his unruly behaviour on this occasion gave ammunition to those who claimed that it went beyond mere eccentricity and that he was definitely mad.

He was far, of course, from being alone in his hatred of modernism (Denison must have run him a close second), but he carried his opposition to extreme lengths. During his trip to America in 1890–91 he denounced all the New York clergy as preachers of rationalism as against revelation, dubbing individual ministers 'impostor', 'lunatic' or 'brute'. His heresy-hunting offended many Americans. One Boston newspaper dubbed him 'a singular mixture of the mediaeval monk, the Methodist Revivalist, the Modern Churchman and the Catholic devotee who has held hundreds of listeners in rapt attention'. Back home he carried on a particular vendetta against the Dean of Ripon,

W. H. Fremantle. 'Fremantle is not a heretic,' he inveighed in
1900. 'He is an absolute and entire infidel. He believes in neither
God nor Devil, Creeds or Bible, Heaven or Hell. And yet he
uses the expressions and phrases of the Christian religion for
the express object of deceiving unsuspicious hearers.' For years
Ignatius harassed the unfortunate dean in pamphlets, sermons
and letters to the newspapers.

Paradoxically he came to regard with respect and even affection one particular opponent with whom he must have had less
in common theologically even than with Fremantle. This was
the atheist MP, Charles Bradlaugh, whom he had challenged in
1872 to a debate on the subject 'Is Jesus Christ an Historical
Reality?' Bradlaugh was impressed in spite of himself by the
burning faith of his opponent. He is alleged to have said later:
'Father Ignatius is the only man whose influence I fear for my
followers.' Ignatius, for his part, could recognize a 'fine, brave
soul' with whom you always knew where you were. 'I should
be happy if my Protestant fellow Christians would receive me
with equal fairness,' he declared.

It is hardly surprising that the combination of a flamboyant
character like Ignatius and the wild and romantic scenery of
the Black Mountains should give rise to allegedly supernatural
manifestations. The chief of these were the so-called Apparitions
of Our Lady, which occurred on 30 August 1880 and subsequent
days and were solemnly commemorated on each anniversary
thereafter. Various witnesses claimed to have seen a dazzling
light near the monastery within which they discerned the form
of a woman (presumed to be the Virgin Mary), with her hands
raised as if in blessing or in prayer. Ignatius collected a number
of eye-witness accounts in a Llanthony pamphlet published in
1885. There is no space in which to discuss the reliability or
otherwise of these accounts. Sceptics would obviously be suspicious, but it is too easy to dismiss the evidence out of hand.
A former editor of the *Church Times*, Ernest Hermitage Day,
examining it with a journalist's cool objectivity, could write:
'About the apparitions I have always kept an open mind. There
are one or two little bits of good evidence which seem to me to
have importance. . . . There is no reason why the utter simplicity

and ardent faith of the old man [Fr Asaph, Ignatius's successor at Llanthony] might not have had its supernatural rewards.' Certainly 30 August, the anniversary of the first apparitions, immediately took its place as one of the two high-spots of the Llanthony year (the other was Ascension Day). Crowds of pilgrims and sightseers made their way up the valley on these two days for the celebratory services, at which Ignatius was able to indulge to the full his flair for the flamboyant. In recent years the 30 August pilgrimage has been revived, and hundreds of admirers of Ignatius make their way to Llanthony for the annual commemoration.

*   *   *

A major difficulty at Llanthony was the absence of a resident priest to say Mass. None of the few clergymen who came as novices stayed long, and the community had to rely mainly on the ministrations of the occasional visiting priest. Such visits were rare in winter, so a large number of hosts would be consecrated at a time to enable Ignatius to give communion from the tabernacle. But the situation was obviously unsatisfactory. As we have seen, Ignatius, because he was not a university graduate, had been told on being made deacon that he would have to wait three years for the priesthood. By the time the three years were up, however, he was going around Claydon dressed as a monk and had already fallen foul of his nominal diocesan, Bishop Pelham of Norwich. Priesting was automatically ruled out while he remained in East Anglia. There had been a glimmer of hope when Archbishop Longley had half-promised him the priesthood if he would serve for a year as curate to the vicar of Margate. But it had soon come to nothing, as had the similar half-promise by Bishop Tait in respect of the London curacy. By then Ignatius had hopelessly blotted his copy-book with the Church of England hierarchy. Successive Bishops of St Davids, the diocese (then in the province of Canterbury) in which Llanthony stood, were completely unsympathetic to the community and its founder. Not only did Bishop Jones refuse Ignatius the priesthood himself, but in 1883 he even declined the offer of a colonial bishop to confer it on his behalf. If the bishops' attitude seems harsh, it was shared by some who at least sympathized with Ignatius's aims. Pusey, for instance, in a letter to Mrs Lyne written in 1867, had remarked:

> I appreciate, as you know, your son's gifts and good qualities, but with the disposition which I have seen and *watched* for several years I should dread the priesthood for him. If it comes in God's Providence He will, I trust, give him grace for it; but I *dare not* take part in trying to obtain it for him.

It is to Ignatius's credit that he seems never to have contemplated obtaining the priesthood by irregular means – until an opportunity presented itself to him in 1898 which he felt unable to resist. He had by then been in deacon's orders for thirty-eight years, and presumably thought that it was a case of now or never. The irregular episcopal avenue through whom he was to obtain the priesthood was a certain Joseph Rene Vilatte, a Frenchman by birth who had migrated to Canada as a young man. Described by one American Episcopalian bishop as 'morally rotten, a swindling adventurer and a notorious liar', Vilatte was of highly dubious ecclesiastical pedigree. Indeed, he had gone the rounds in such a remarkable manner that, by the time of his death in 1929, he had been five times a Roman Catholic, once an Anglican, twice a Methodist, once a Congregationalist and twice a Presbyterian. The great thing about him from Ignatius's point of view was that he could arguably be considered a true bishop in the apostolic succession. Under a bull obtained from the Patriarch of Antioch he had been consecrated in Colombo in 1892 by the self-styled Archbishop of the 'Independent Catholic Church of Goa and Ceylon'. He now claimed to be 'Primate of the Old Catholic Church in America' and styled himself Mar (i.e., Lord) Timotheos. This was the exotic if questionable character who turned up at Llanthony one summer day in 1898, armed with suitable recommendations, and bestowed the priesthood on both Ignatius and another monk – possibly for a cash consideration, though this has never been proved.

The deed was done, but it was to have unfortunate repercussions. Ignatius no doubt considered Vilatte's visit to Llanthony a clear call from God. He defended his action on the ground that in ancient times the Church had allowed the superiors of monasteries to invite any bishop they chose to ordain within the monastic enclosure without having to obtain the consent of the diocesan. Few people agreed with him, and the effect of his action was to distance Llanthony even further from the Church of which it still regarded itself as nominally a part. The *Church Times* spoke for many sympathizers when it accused Ignatius (28 July 1898) of having made a 'sad mistake':

> We cannot see that the boycott of thirty-eight years to which Father Ignatius has been subjected is any valid reason for so irregular a proceeding as his ordination by a Bishop fetched from the ends of the earth. . . . We admire the plucky and faithful way in which he has stuck to his convictions for so many years, but we cannot approve of this last attempt to right one wrong by another.

Nor did Ignatius's ambitions end at the priesthood. He saw himself as a monastic bishop on the Celtic precedent. Shortly after his visit to Llanthony, Vilatte had been received back again into the Roman Catholic Church, so was no longer available to supply what was wanting. Ignatius therefore appealed to the man who had consecrated Vilatte, Mar Julius, to see if he would act himself in the matter:

> I had been very anxious that the Archbishop Mar-Timotheos should give us the episcopate in our monastery, that we might thus have secured a continuation of the priesthood among us in future years. But now this cannot be. . . . Would it appear right and opportune to your grace, if an occasion permitted, to give us the episcopate in our monastery, in view of future emergencies which might arise from the toleration of Dean Fremantle and his teaching in our Church?

Nothing came of this, however – though it was subsequently rumoured that Mar Julius was proposing to establish an Independent Catholic diocese of Great Britain, with Ignatius as its first metropolitan. Such an alarming possibility led one commentator ironically to remark: 'Should Ignatius develop into a full-blown Archbishop of the line of Antioch, the position of both

Archbishop Temple and Cardinal Vaughan will be seriously undermined.'

The rest is soon told. In spite of age and weariness Ignatius still maintained a frantic round of activities, though to less and less effect. He still continued to alternate between Llanthony and the outside world, though the outside world was beginning to regard him, however affectionately, as a figure of fun. He was always hankering after new causes. He was a keen supporter of Evan Roberts's Welsh Revival Campaign. He was also an enthusiastic Zionist, a convinced British Israelite and a believer in the 'Flat Earth' theory. For two years he collaborated with the Baroness de Bertouch over her flamboyant biography, *The Life of Father Ignatius, O.S.B.*, published in 1904. The result was a work of pure, albeit colourful, propaganda, the image presented being that which Ignatius wished to bequeath to posterity. The reviewers of this unintentionally hilarious work, the style of which matched its approach to its subject,* had a field-day – the more serious notices expressing regret that Ignatius should not have been more fortunate in his biographer.

His race was now almost run. The last four years of his life were years of rapidly declining health and achievement. In March 1908 he had a stroke. Six months later he suffered two further strokes in quick succession. He died in his sister's house at Camberley, Surrey, on 16 October, a few weeks short of his seventy-first birthday. His last recorded words were, 'Praise be Jesus for ever and ever.' His body was conveyed to Llanthony, where the funeral took place on 23 October. He lies buried beneath the choir of the monastery church (now open to the skies) in which for so many years he had reigned supreme.

*   *   *

Ignatius has been called the Don Quixote of the Catholic Revival, a figure of both fun and tragedy. His eccentricities are

---

*The baroness was an Englishwoman married to a Danish nobleman. Her literary style lent itself to easy mockery, typical sentences reading: 'In the twinkling of an eye he floated a Sunday school'; or 'Father Ignatius, by a retrograde inspiration, holds the reins of the primitive mediaeval Benedictinism of the early centuries.'

continually tripping him up and robbing him of the dignity which his devotion deserves. His career exhibited many inconsistencies, the greatest of which was that which allowed him to combine the profession of a preaching friar with that of a cloistered monk. As an orator he was in a class of his own. An actor once said of him: 'Look at his hands! Just look at the emotion in them! What would not some of us actors give to possess hands like those!' And an observer recalls him at the Town Hall at Oxford in 1879 preaching on the snares of the Devil and stopping suddenly, pointing with his arm over the heads of the audience and saying in a low and solemn voice, 'I see him now!' At least half the people in the hall turned round to look. It was a feat of oratory beyond compare. Of theological learning he had little, though he was an adept at translating the thought of others into terms which a popular audience could understand. His intense if narrow piety gave his sermons a force which many found irresistible. As a London maid-of-all-work put it: 'Dear Father, I feel I must tell you that it is through you I have heard the Master's voice calling to me!' And the *Church Times* justly affirmed in its obituary of Ignatius: 'He wielded such a power as few have exercised since John Wesley ceased from his labours, and by his power to sway men's emotions he was the means of bringing many to God and the Faith.'

Fr Charles Hopkins, founder of the Order of St Paul at Alton and a friend of Ignatius, commented perceptiently after his death: 'The most prominent peculiarity about Father Ignatius was the way in which he embraced the spirit and form . . . of two seemingly opposite extremes – Protestantism and Catholicism. . . . The seeming peculiarity was, I am sure, the result of a dual love. A love for souls . . . and a love for . . . the beauty of worship expressed in the ritual of the old historic Church.'

The power to convert souls was his great achievement. Yet, in what he would have regarded as the mainspring of his career, his attempt at reviving Benedictinism within the Church of England, he was seemingly a total failure. That he failed was not wholly his own fault. He lacked proper guidance in the pursuit of his vocation; and he failed to attract support or sympathy from members of the hierarchy, with some of whom he found himself in active conflict. But he lacked that spirit of obedience which should be the first duty of a monk. He would not even obey the letter of his own Benedictine Rule, interpreting it as he chose and adding to it as the fancy took him. The offices in the chapel at Llanthony were an eclectic jumble said partly in English, partly in Welsh, partly in Latin. The number of his monks never rose above a pathetic handful who often turned out to be rogues or misfits. As the *Church Times* observed in its obituary: 'In those long years of energetic striving nothing tangible, nothing established, remains, save the forlorn shell of a monastery in the Black Mountains.'

Yet was his life such a total failure? C.P.S. Clarke, in *The Oxford Movement and After*, concedes that Ignatius might be condemned for having put the monastic revival on the level of comic opera. Yet, he adds, other communities 'of the strictest orthodoxy and unimpeachable correctness . . . may nevertheless owe their very existence to the publicity which he gave to the religious life as a possible vocation for men.' Donald Attwater, who makes no attempt in his biography to paper over the cracks in Ignatius's character, makes the same point when he maintains that the 'real and permanent achievement' of his life *was* as a religious. 'Every monk, friar and clerk regular in England today owes gratitude to him for all he did to familiarize the people of England and Wales with the forgotten, misjudged or vilified idea of monasticism. . . . He gave England the vision of a good, loving man who was nevertheless a monk. The path of all monks has been easier for the life and sacrifice of Ignatius.' Another writer, Desmond Morse-Boycott, who was almost as colourful a character as Ignatius himself, was prepared to go further and award him a positive halo. In *Lead, Kindly Light* he dubbed him 'a fool like St Francis, a hero like St Benedict, a revivalist like Moody, a lover of souls like General Booth, an ascetic like St Anthony the hermit, an orator as golden as Lacordaire, but withal a poor theologian and as simple as a child, of whom his Church was unworthy. Alas! She is awkward in her handling of saints, and her saints cannot breathe in "Establishment".'

*   *   *

The story of Llanthony after the death of its founder is a sad one. Five monks and two nuns survived him. In his will he left the monastery and its lands jointly to Fr Asaph Harris, the senior monk, and to Mother Tudfil (Jessie Dew), the senior nun. However, in a separate document, he provided that, if they were unable to continue at Llanthony, they were to hand the premises over to the abbot of the Roman Catholic monastery at Buckfastleigh, Devon, 'for his absolute personal use and benefit'. The paper ended: 'This wish is expressed simply to guard our beloved Monastery from the "Higher Criticism", supported as it is by the traitorous Bishops of our beloved and cruelly wronged English Church.'

At first all promised well. At a chapter meeting the surviving members of the community elected the Rev. Richard Courtier-Forster, curate of St Giles's, Cambridge, and a long-time friend of the community, as their new abbot. He was happy to accept, and entered into negotiations with the Bishop of St Davids, John Owen. But these broke down when Owen discovered that two of the Llanthony monks had been ordained irregularly in America. He refused to recognize them as priests, and, as a result, Courtier-Forster withdrew his acceptance of the abbacy. After struggling along on their own for the next eighteen months Fr Asaph and two of the other monks decided to throw in their lot with the Benedictine community on Caldey Island, near Tenby, Pembrokeshire, which had been founded by Aelred Carlyle in 1891 and had a certain amount in common with Llanthony. The remaining two monks returned to secular life. Mother Tudfil relinquished her rights in the estate, which remained in the sole possession of Fr Asaph. It was at this point that the Abbot of Buckfast went to law to establish his right to the property under the terms of the will. He was unsuccessful, on the ground that a mere 'wish' attached to a will but not technically forming part of it had no legal effect. Llanthony thus passed, through Fr Asaph, into the hands of the Anglican Benedictines of Caldey. But that was by no means the end of the story. To begin with, all went smoothly. A Caldey oblate acted as caretaker at Llanthony and looked after parties of monks from Caldey who visited it from time to time for periods of rest and relaxation. But in 1913 almost all the members of the Caldey community (including Fr Asaph*) went over to Rome and the monastery at Llanthony therefore passed into the possession of the Roman Catholic Church. For a time the property was maintained, but soon shortage of money led to the outlying farm buildings and land being sold and the monastery itself being left empty. From 1924 to 1928 it was leased to Eric Gill, the leader of the community of artists and craftsmen associated with Ditchling in Sussex, and he wrote his autobiography there. Among others who lived there during this period was Donald Attwater, whose own biography of Fr Ignatius was published in 1931. The main monastery buildings passed into private hands; but the ruined abbey church (containing Ignatius's tomb) is now owned by the Father Ignatius Memorial Trust, founded in 1967. Essential repairs have been carried out and the tomb re-tiled.

The main achievement of the Trust has been to revive the annual pilgrimage to Llanthony on or around 30 August each year, the anniversary of the first Apparition of Our Lady. After separate Anglican and Roman Catholic celebrations of the Eucharist the pilgrims walk in procession up the lane from the hamlet of Capel-y-ffin for a service of Evensong and an address in the ruined abbey church. It is all very low-key compared to the flamboyant rites one associates with the man being commemorated. But at least it helps to keep green the memory of a man whose strange life has earned him a place among the Church's most enigmatic eccentrics.

---

*Fr Asaph lived on until 1959. In an article published in the *Church Times* of 20 November 1987 S. G. A. Luff, who had known him, recalled: 'I asked him once: "Fr Asaph – those miracles one hears about so much at Llanthony – what do you think of them?" He replied quite simply: "All I can say is – I saw them." It could be that the "miracles" . . . were the attestation of what was valid in [Ignatius's] work and mission.'

'THE HIGH CHURCHMAN HAS, as I think, deserved to win. Very patiently, very courageously has he worked. Most of the opposition he has met with has been fatuous to the last degree. The High Church position is largely warranted by our Church's formularies. It is, so it seems to me, only malice and ignorance that can determine otherwise.'

Roger Lloyd, in his *The Church of England 1900–1965*, quotes this testimonial from a Broad Church incumbent to the growing strength of the Anglo-Catholic Movement. The incumbent, the Rev. H. L. Jackson, vicar of St Mary's, Huntingdon, at the turn of the century, made the comment in the course of an 1899 pastoral letter to his parishioners on the 'Ritual Controversy'. Although by no manner of means a ritualist by inclination, he was sufficiently convinced by now of the strength of the High Church position to be prepared to indulge in many of the High Church practices for which men like Mackonochie had suffered in the past. He expressed, for instance, his 'perfect willingness' to wear eucharistic vestments (on condition that they were provided by the parish). Lloyd considers that Jackson's attitude was not peculiar to himself. 'His pronouncement meant that the average and fair-minded opinion in the Church had in 1899 come to the point when it was ready to admit the victory of the Anglo-Catholics. . . . The Anglo-Catholics had won, and in 1899 it was evident that they had won. They had out-thought, out-lived, and out-suffered all their opponents.'

This was not to say that they were necessarily popular with their fellow-churchmen. The very fact that they had triumphed in so many ways tended to make them uneasy bedfellows. Many of them seemed intemperate and even arrogant in the hour of victory. As Hensley Henson put it, they were in 'an exasperated and exasperating mood'. At the start of a new century, however, they could rest on their laurels and survey the English ecclesiastical scene with quiet satisfaction.

The statistics tell their own tale. According to the *Tourists' Church Guide* published by the English Church Union, the number of churches in England and Wales in which vestments were worn had increased from 336 in 1882 to 2158 by 1901. In 1882 candles had stood on the altars of a mere 581 churches: by 1901 that figure had risen to 4765. Incense was still the exception rather than the rule, but over the same twenty-year period the number of churches in which it was used had grown from nine to 393. The eastward position, by contrast, was that now normally adopted in the Church of England – in 7397 churches in 1901, as opposed to 1662 churches in 1882. Although Hensley Henson, no friend to the ritualists and their Anglo-Catholic successors, assured Lord Halifax in an open letter of 1898 that only one clergyman in six was a High Churchman (and only one layman in twenty), the fact remained that many of the practices formerly stigmatized as ritualistic had penetrated into many churches of far more moderate hue.

How and why had this mass ceremonial conversion experience come about? The primary cause was undoubtedly the revulsion of feeling in favour of the ritualists as a result of the imprisonments brought about by the Public Worship Regulation Act. Archbishop Davidson made this point in the course of his evidence to the Royal Commission on Ecclesiastical Discipline of 1904–6. 'It is impossible in my judgment to exaggerate the importance of those imprisonments,' he told the commissioners. 'I believe that they did more than any single thing that has occurred in the ritual controversy to change public opinion upon the whole question of litigation of this sort; it may have been changed for good or evil, but that the change was largely due to those imprisonments I personally have no doubt.' Others were of the same opinion. The Hon. J. C. Dundas declared that, though he had voted in the Commons for the Public Worship

Regulation Act, he was now horrified at the way in which it outraged civil and religious liberty. The *Pall Mall Gazette* thought that the prolonged resistance of the ritualists had brought the alteration or abandonment of the Act within the range of practical politics. Archbishop Tait, towards the end of his life, admitted that the Act had been a failure – and, as has been seen, endeavoured to act as a peace-maker in the case of Martin v. Mackonochie.

The Church Association fought on as long as it could, but the heart had gone out of its efforts to put down Ritualism by law – and many of its supporters were beginning to doubt its effectiveness. The last dying flickers of its campaign came in 1888, when it accused the saintly Bishop Edward King of Lincoln of conniving in various ritualistic practices during a visit to a church in his diocese. The case was tried not by Lord Penzance but by Tait's successor as Archbishop of Canterbury, Edward Benson, sitting in his own court at Lambeth with five episcopal assessors. His judgment, delivered on 21 November 1890, was basically favourable to the bishop. It affirmed (with minor qualifications) the lawfulness of the eastward position, the mixed chalice, altar lights and the singing of the *Agnus Dei*. It forbade only the sign of the cross at the absolution and at the blessing. The Church Association appealed as usual to the Judicial Committee of the Privy Council, but for once the Committee declined to overturn the verdict. In a judgment delivered on 2 August 1892 it upheld Benson. Owen Chadwick, in *The Victorian Church*, claims that the Evangelical party was more damaged by the prosecution of the Bishop of Lincoln than by any other circumstance in the entire controversy over ritual, even the imprisonments of clergymen, since all Evangelicals suffered for the sins of the Church Association. 'The committee of the Church Association saw the judgment in Read v. the Bishop of Lincoln as a rout.'

The King case marked a watershed in the attitude of the authorities to Ritualism. After 1890 no further attempts were made to put down its practitioners through the courts. The bishops (most of them) might not find Ritualism to their taste, but they were fair-minded (most of them) or prudent enough to realize that the law was too uncertain an ally to be worth invoking in future. This was the heart of the matter, and it was fully brought out in the report of the Royal Commission on Ecclesiastical Discipline, published in 1906. When it came to consider the Judicial Committee of the Privy Council as a final court of appeal in ecclesiastical cases the report shrewdly observed: 'A Court dealing with matters of conscience and religion must, above all others, rest on moral authority if its judgments are to be effective. As thousands of clergy, with strong lay support, refuse to recognize the jurisdiction of the Judicial Committee, its judgments cannot practically be enforced.' This was a pronouncement which, though glaringly obvious with hindsight, was nevertheless of profound significance as coming from a body as prestigious as a royal commission. As Roger Lloyd observes:

> ... the leading laymen were at last brought to see that the objections of the Church at large to recognizing the Judicial Committee of the Privy Council as the ultimate authority in matters and causes spiritual were so wide, so deep, and so determined that it would never be possible to overcome them. This mute recognition meant a final abandonment of the old attempt to force conformity and stamp out variety in public worship by the threats of secular courts for deprivation and imprisonment. Since 1906 these threats have never again been seriously made, and in part we owe it to the realism of these royal commissioners.

Of course this did not mean that the Anglo-Catholic clergy were in future to be left entirely at peace. Individual bishops might (and from time to time did) endeavour to dissuade incumbents from indulging in practices held to be against the Church's law; but they could no longer count on the State to bail them out when they got into difficulties. Davidson himself, at the start of his Winchester episcopate, incurred much odium by attempting (as it seemed) to winkle Dolling out of his Portsmouth cure; but there was no question of Dolling's being hauled before the courts by some minion of the Church Association as a prelude to his being carted off to gaol.

For that measure of relief the successors of the old-guard ritualists could give thanks. The veterans had not suffered to no avail. They had fought against the odds for what they considered to be the truth. They had endured persecution and obloquy. In some cases they had died before the fruits of victory could be garnered. But what they had been denied their successors now enjoy, and so their battle was not fought in vain.

BIBLIOGRAPHY

————•◄••►•————

Anson, Peter F., *The Call of the Cloister*, SPCK, 4th edn. 1964.

Ashwell, A. R., and Wilberforce, R. G., *Life of the Right Reverend Samuel Wilberforce, D. D.*, John Murray, 3 vols., 1880–82.

Attwater, Donald, *Father Ignatius of Llanthony: A Victorian*, Cassell 1931.

Baring-Gould, Sabine, *The Church Revival*, Methuen 1914.

Bateman, Josiah ('Senex'), *Clerical Reminiscences*, Seeley, Jackson & Halliday 1880.

Bell, G. K. A., *Randall Davidson: Archbishop of Canterbury*, Oxford University Press, 3rd edn. 1952.

Bentley, James, *Ritualism and Politics in Victorian Britain*, Oxford University Press 1978.

Calder-Marshall, Arthur, *The Enthusiast: An Enquiry into the Life, Beliefs and Character of the Rev. Joseph Leycester Lyne*, alias *Fr Ignatius, O.S.B., Abbot of Elm Hill, Norwich, and Llanthony, Wales*, Faber and Faber 1962.

Cannell, B. G. A., *From Monk to Busman*, Skeffington 1935.

Chadwick, Owen, *The Victorian Church*, Parts I and II, A. & C. Black 1966, 1970.

Clayton, J., *Father Dolling: A Memoir*, Wells Gardner, Darton 1902.

Coombs, Joyce, *George Anthony Denison, The Firebrand: 1805–1896*, Church Literature Association and Society of Saints Peter & Paul 1984.

Coombs, Joyce, *Judgement on Hatcham: The History of a Religious Struggle 1877–1886*, Faith Press 1969.

Croom, F. G., *Arthur Tooth*, Catholic Literature Association 1933.

Crouch, W., *Bryan King and the Riots at St George's-in-the-East*, Methuen 1904.

Crowther, M. A., *Church Embattled: Religious Controversy in Mid-Victorian England*, David & Charles, 1970.

Davidson, R. T., and Benham, W., *Life of Archibald Campbell Tait, Archbishop of Canterbury*, Macmillan, 2 vols., 1891.

De Bertouch, Baroness Beatrice, *The Life of Father Ignatius, O.S.B, The Monk of Llanthony*, Methuen 1904.

Denison, G. A., *Notes of My Life 1805–1878*, James Parker 1878.

Denison, L. E., *Fifty Years at East Brent: The Letters of George Anthony Denison 1845–1896, Archdeacon of Taunton*, John Murray 1902.

Dolling, Robert R., *Ten Years in a Portsmouth Slum*, Swan Sonnenschein 1898.

Donovan, Marcus, *After the Tractarians*, Philip Allan 1933.

Ellsworth, L. E., *Charles Lowder and the Ritualist Movement*, Darton, Longman & Todd 1982.

Flindall, R. P., *The Church of England 1815–1948: A Documentary History*, SPCK 1972.

Hart, A. Tindal, *Some Clerical Oddities in the Church of England from Medieval to Modern Times*, New Horizon, 1980.

Hubbuck, Rodney, *Portsea Island Churches*. 'Portsmouth Paper' No. 8, Portsmouth City Council, revised edn. 1976.

Kitchin, G. W., *Edward Harold Browne, D. D., Lord Bishop of Winchester: A Memoir*, John Murray 1895.

Lee, C. E., *Father Tooth: A Biographical Memoir*, Truslove & Bray 1931.

Lloyd, Roger, *The Church of England 1900–1965*, SCM Press 1966.

Lockhart, J. G., *Charles Lindley, Viscount Halifax*, Geoffrey Bles, Centenary Press, 2 vols., 1935–6.

Luff, S. G. A., *The Monastery at Capel-y-Ffin: A History and Guide*, Father Ignatius Memorial Trust 1992.

Lyne, J. L. (Fr Ignatius), *Autobiography*, 'Llanthony Tract No. 2' 1896.

Lyne, J. L. (Fr Ignatius), *Brother Placidus and Why He Became a Monk*,* Richard Bentley 1870.

Lyne, J. L. (Fr Ignatius), *Leonard Morris or the Benedictine Novice*,* Richard Bentley 1871.

Macdonnell, J. C., *The Life and Correspondence of William Connor Magee, Archbishop of York, Bishop of Peterborough*, Isbister, 2 vols., 1896.

Marsh, P. T., *The Victorian Church in Decline: Archbishop Tait and the Church of England 1868–1882*, Routledge & Kegan Paul 1969.

Morse-Boycott, Desmond, *They Shine Like Stars*, Skeffington 1947.

Ollard, S. L., *A Short History of the Oxford Movement*, Mowbray, revised edn. 1963.

Osborne, C. E., *The Life of Father Dolling*, Edward Arnold 1903.

Palmer, Bernard, *Gadfly for God: A History of the Church Times*, Hodder & Stoughton 1991.

Penhale, Francis, *The Anglican Church Today: Catholics in Crisis*, Mowbray 1986.

Brother Placidus and its sequel, *Leonard Morris* (the first originally appeared under the pseudonym 'A Monk of Llanthony Abbey'), were novels in which Ignatius allowed his lurid imagination over-free rein.

Pickering, W. S. F., *Anglo-Catholicism: A Study in Religious Ambiguity*, Routledge 1989.

Plomer, William, ed., *Kilvert's Diary: Selections from the Diary of the Rev. Francis Kilvert*, Jonathan Cape, 1960 edn.

Prestige, G. L., *The Life of Charles Gore: A Great Englishman*, Heinemann 1935.

Purcell, E. S., *The Life of Cardinal Manning*, Macmillan 1896.

Reynolds, Michael, *Martyr of Ritualism: Father Mackonochie of St Alban's, Holborn*, Faber & Faber 1965.

Russell, G. W. E., *Arthur Stanton: A Memoir*, Longmans 1917.

Russell, G. W. E., *St. Alban the Martyr: A History of Fifty Years*, George Allen 1913.

Simpkinson, C. H., *The Life and Work of Bishop Thorold*, Isbister 1896.

Towle, Eleanor, *Alexander Heriot Mackonochie: A Memoir by 'E.A.T.'*, Kegan Paul, Trench, Trubner 1890.

Voll, Dieter, *Catholic Evangelicalism: The acceptance of Evangelical traditions by the Oxford Movement during the second half of the nineteenth century*, Faith Press 1963.

Walker, Charles, *Three Months in an English Monastery*, 1864.

Walsh, Walter, *The Secret History of the Oxford Movement*, Charles J. Thynne, 5th edn. 1899.

Woodward, F. J., *The Doctor's Disciples: A Study of Four Pupils of Arnold of Rugby*, Geoffrey Cumberlege, Oxford University Press 1954.

Yates, Nigel, *The Anglican Revival in Victorian Portsmouth*, 'Portsmouth Paper' No 37, Portsmouth City Council 1983.

INDEX

Aberdeen, George Hamilton
Gordon, 4th Earl of, 42
Agnus Dei, 97, 122, 247
Allen, Rev. W. Hugh, 75–6
Alston, Dom Cyprian, OSB, 233
Altar lights, 6, 9, 11, 51, 74, 86,
87, 89, 91–2, 93–4, 97,
120, 122, 246, 247
Altar Steps, The (C.
Mackenzie), 196
Ambrosia, Sister (Mrs A.
More), 219
Amphlett, Lord Justice, 13
Andrewes, Lancelot, Bishop of
Winchester, 44
Anglo-Catholic Congresses,
118, 155–6
Anglo-Catholicism: see
'Ritualism, growth of'
Anne, Queen, 70
Anson, Peter F., 215*n*, 229
Anthony, St, The Hermit, 242
'Apparitions of Our Lady',
236–7, 244
Arches, Court of, 8, 9–10, 11,
33, 34–5, 46, 91–2, 95,
127, 146–7
Arnold, Thomas, 22
Articles of Religion, Thirty-
Nine, 39, 40, 44–6, 55, 175
Athanasian Creed, 48, 54–7
Attwater, Donald, 203, 228–9,
233, 242, 244
Auckland, Robert John Eden,
3rd Baron, Bishop
successively of Sodor &
Man and of Bath & Wells,
42–3, 52
Augustine, Brother, OSB, 218
'Autobiography' of Fr Ignatius,
222

Bagot, Richard, Bishop
successively of Oxford
and of Bath & Wells, 23,
27–8, 29, 37–8, 40–2
Baptism, conflicting theories
of, 34–7
Baring-Gould, Sabine, 76
Bateman, Canon Josiah, 221–2

Becket, St Thomas, Archbishop of Canterbury, 156
Bellairs, H.W., 31
Belmont, Priory of, 211
Benedict, St, 211, 213, 230n, 242
Bennett, Rev. William James Early, 8–9
Benson, Edward White, successively Bishop of Truro and Archbishop of Canterbury, 111, 247
Benson, Fr Richard Meux, ssje, 201, 217
Bickersteth, Edward Henry, Bishop of Exeter, 15–16
Birmingham Church Congress, 235
Book of Common Prayer, 6, 26, 39, 53, 55–7, 65, 78, 93, 97, 123, 145, 150, 175–8, 184, 186, 190, 206
Booth, William, 242
'Bordesley Sacrilege', 14n
Bowles, Rev. Thomas, 68–9
Bradlaugh, Charles, 236
Bread, wafer, 6, 9, 13, 14, 51, 87, 97
Bright, Rev. William, 205–6
Bristol Church Congress, 215n, 217
British Weekly, 197
Broadwindsor (Dorset), G.A. Denison at, 23–5
Browne, Edward Harold, Bishop successively of Ely and of Winchester, 160, 164, 176–80, 181, 188
Browne, Rev. William Henry, 128

Bull, Fr. Paul, CR, 190
Burgon, John William, Dean of Chichester, 4
Butler, William John ('Butler of Wantage'), 69, 78–9, 81

Cairns, Hugh MacCalmont, 1st Earl, 92
Calder-Marshall, Arthur, 204, 208
Caledon, James Alexander, 1st Earl of, 160
Camberwell and Peckham Times, 133
Cameron, 'Granny', 206
Candles: see 'Altar lights'
Cannell, B.G.A. (Brother Gildas), 233n
Canterbury Cathedral, 156
Capel-y-ffin: see 'Llanthony Monastery'
Carlyle, Benjamin Fearnley (Fr Aelred, osb), 243
Carnarvon, Henry Howard Molyneux, 4th Earl of, 49
Carter, Canon Thomas Thellusson, 16–17
Cassock, suspicion of, 4, 81–2
Chambres, Rev. Richard, 132, 134
Charles I, King, 11
Cheese, Cheddar, 48
Chinnery-Haldane, James Robert Alexander, Bishop of Argyll & the Isles, 111–12
Christian Social Union, 178
Chubb's (locksmiths), 135
Church Association, x, xi, xii, 9–10, 12, 14n, 15–17, 248;

behind Mackonochie prosecutions, 51, 65, 90, 92–7, 100–4, 107–9; opposes Tooth at Hatcham, 122, 125, 127–31, 133, 138, 139; prosecutes Bishop King, 247

Church Discipline Act, 16, 42, 44, 91, 97, 100, 102

Church of England Working Men's Society, 127, 136–7

Church Patronage Society, 150

Church, Richard William, Dean of St Paul's, 3, 8, 13

Church Times: and Purchas case, 9–10; and Ridsdale Judgment, 13; and gaoling of S.F. Green, 15; and Archdeacon Denison, 20, 53–4, 61; and A.H. Mackonochie, 78, 92, 99, 103, 105–6, 107, 109; and Arthur Tooth, 126, 129, 133–4, 135–6, 137–8, 142, 146, 152, 156; and R.W.R. Dolling, 188; and Fr Ignatius, 213–14, 215, 239, 241, 242, 244n; mentioned, 127, 145, 236

Claughton, Thomas Legh, Bishop successively of Rochester and St Albans, x, 121–4, 127, 129, 132, 133, 135, 138, 140, 142

Claydon, Suffolk, as HQ for Fr Ignatius, 211–14, 217, 230, 237

Clerical Vestments Bill, 6

Cockshut, A.O.J., 37

Colenso, John William, Bishop of Natal, 69n

Coles, Rev. Charles William, 198

Commons, House of, 31, 36, 246

Community of St Mary the Virgin, 69n

Community of the Paraclete, 120, 153, 156

Community of the Resurrection, 201

Comper, Sir Ninian, 156

Confession, sacramental, 72–3, 85, 87, 88, 97, 120, 142

Convocation of Canterbury, 6, 49, 50, 56, 58–9, 142–3

Convocation of York, 57

Cook's Guide to London, 152

Cosin, John, Bishop of Durham, 44

Court of Appeal, 17, 101, 102

Courtier-Forster, Rev. Richard, 243

Cox, Rev. James Bell, 14

Cranmer, Thomas, Archbishop of Canterbury, 27, 91

Croom, Edmund Frederick, 121–2, 128, 138, 139, 141

Croom, Rev. Frederick Goldsworthy, 156

Cross, sign of the, 79, 97, 98n, 114, 122, 247

Daily Mail, 197

Daily Telegraph, 94, 136

Dale, Rev. Benjamin, 134–40

Dale, Rev. Thomas Pelham, 14

Dampier, Thomas, Bishop of Ely, 34

Davidson, Randall Thomas, successively Bishop of Rochester and of Winchester and Archbishop of Canterbury: 1, 6, 8, 104–5, 106, 110, 143, 159–60, 161, 173, 183–9, 246, 248

Day, Rev. Ernest Hermitage, 236

Dead, prayers for the, 52, 178, 184, 186–7

de Bertouch, Baroness Beatrice, 203, 208, 210, 218, 220, 222, 240

Denison, Alfred (G.A.D.'s brother), 21

Denison, Charles (G.A.D.'s brother), 20

Denison, Charlotte (née Estwick; G.A.D.'s mother), 20, 46

Denison, Edward, Bishop of Salisbury (G.A.D.'s brother), 20, 23, 25, 29, 67, 68

Denison, Frank (G.A.D.'s brother), 20

Denison, George Anthony: character of, 19–20, 33, 61–2; childhood, 21–2; at university, 22; Oriel fellowship and Cuddesdon curacy, 22–3; marriage, 23; at Broadwindsor, 23–5; educational campaigning, 24–5, 28–33; appointed to East Brent, 25; examining chaplain to Bishop Bagot,

27; Archdeacon of Taunton, 27–8, 37; and Gorham controversy, 33–7; deteriorating relations with Bagot, 37–8; brush with Bishop Spencer over Eucharistic doctrine, 38–41; controversial sermons in Wells Cathedral, 41; accused of heresy, 41–4; trial and acquittal, 44–8; concern for welfare of parish, 48–9; and Essays and Reviews, 49; and Irish disestablishment, 49–50; and growth of Ritualism at East Brent, 50–4; and Athanasian Creed, 54–7; and Lux Mundi, 57–60; and Welsh disestablishment, 60; last years of, 60–1; mentioned, ix, x, xii, 8, 9, 118, 123, 124–5, 234, 235

Denison, Georgiana (née Henley; G.A.D.'s wife), 23, 46, 47–8, 52, 58

Denison, Henry (G.A.D.'s brother), 20

Denison, Rev. Henry Phipps (G.A.D.'s nephew), 26, 50, 52–4

Denison, John Evelyn, 1st Viscount Ossington (G.A.D.'s brother), 20

Denison, John (Wilkinson) (G.A.D.'s father), 20

Denison, Maria (née Horlock;

G.A.D.'s father's first wife), 20

Denison, Stephen (G.A.D.'s brother), 20

Denison, William (G.A.D.'s brother), 20, 21, 52

Denton, Rev. William, 223–4

Disraeli, Benjamin, Earl of Beaconsfield, 5–6, 11, 78, 92, 142, 144

Ditcher, Rev. Joseph, 20, 41–4, 46–8, 61

Dolling, Elise (R.W.R.D.'s sister), 190

Dolling, Eliza (née Alexander; R.W.R.D.'s mother), 160, 161

Dolling, Geraldine (R.W.R.D.'s sister), 190

Dolling, Josephine (R.W.R.D.'s sister), 191, 195

Dolling, Robert Holbeach (R.W.R.D.'s father), 160, 161

Dolling, Robert William Radclyffe: character of, 159–60, 196–8; childhood, 160–1; early manhood, 161–2; training for ordination, 162; London ministry, 163; appointed to St Agatha's, Landport, 163–4; character of the parish, 164–5; daily timetable, 166; dealings with parishioners, 167–8; relations with Winchester College, 168–70; 'money-grubbing', 170–1; 'battles civil' as social reformer, 171–4; attitude to ritualism, 174–6; complaint to Bishop Browne, 176–8; row over Stewart Headlam lecture, 178–81; relations with Bishop Thorold, 181–3; showdown with Bishop Davidson, 183–7; resigns, 187–9; anti-climactic final years, 190–1; writes *Ten Years*, 191; vain efforts to obtain new post, 191–2; trip to USA, 192–3; Poplar cure, 193–4; final illness and death, 194–6; mentioned, ix, 2, 144, 248

Dominic, St, 188

Dorling, Henry, 152

Drake, Capt., 120

Drury, Charles, 21, 22

Drury, Rev. George, 211–12, 219, 220, 221n

Dundas, Hon. J.C., 246

East Brent (Somerset), G.A. Denison as incumbent of, 19, 25–7, 48–9, 50–4, 60–1; united to South Brent, 62

East London Observer, 75

'Eastward position', 2, 6, 9, 12–13, 51, 74, 87, 92, 97, 120, 246, 247

Ecclesiastical Commissioners, 110

Ecclesiastical Discipline, Royal Commission on, 1, 8, 11, 246, 248

Eddy, Mary Baker, 193

Eden, Robert, Bishop of

Moray, Ross and
   Caithness, 205–7
Education Act (1870), 28, 31–3
Educational issues, G.A.
   Denison's views on, 24–5,
   28–33
Edward VI, King, 6
Egg (or Hatch), Mrs, 208
Elevation of paten and chalice,
   91–5, 97–8
Elizabeth I, Queen, 45, 91
Ellicott, Charles John, Bishop
   of Gloucester & Bristol,
   50, 228
Elm Hill, Norwich, as HQ for
   Fr Ignatius, 214–21, 225,
   230
English Church Union, 6, 10,
   11, 13, 15n, 57, 59–60, 110,
   122, 127, 129–30, 144, 155,
   246
Enraght, Rev. Richard William,
   14
Essays and Reviews, 49
Eucharistic doctrine,
   conflicting views on, x, 3,
   8–9, 38–47, 50–1, 87–8,
   123–5, 182; see also 'Dead,
   prayers for the'
Evangelical Alliance, 43
Everett, Mr, 45

Father Ignatius Memorial
   Trust, 244
Fearon, William Andrewes,
   successively Headmaster
   of Winchester College and
   Archdeacon of
   Winchester, 159, 164, 168,
   169, 180, 185–6, 189

Fisher, Rev. W.F., 39–40
Forbes, Alexander Penrose,
   Bishop of Brechin, 211
Forster, William Edward, 31
Francis of Assisi, St, 175, 188,
   197, 242
Fremantle, William Henry,
   Dean of Ripon, 235–6,
   239
Froude, Richard Hurrell, 22
Fry, T.W., 139–42, 148

Gee, Canon Richard, 127–8
Genuflection (under any other
   name), 91–5, 101
George III, King, 102
Gertrude, Sister, 225–6
Gilbert, Ashurst Turner,
   Bishop of Chichester, 3–4
Gill, Eric, 228, 244
Gladstone, William Ewart, 13,
   29, 43, 49, 52, 205, 226
Gore, Charles, Bishop
   successively of Worcester,
   Birmingham and Oxford,
   xii, 57–8, 85, 201, 234–5
Gorham, Rev. George
   Cornelius, 33–5
Gorham Judgment, 35–7, 38,
   43, 67
Grant, William, 145
Granville, Rev. Augustus,
   119–20
Green, Rev. Sidney Faithhorn,
   12, 14–15, 117
Gregory, Robert, later Dean of
   St Paul's, 118, 133
Guardian, The (Church
   newspaper), 44, 143–4
Guest, Lady Charlotte, 4

Guild of St Barnabas for Nurses, 85
Guild of St Matthew, 178

Halifax, Charles Wood, 1st Viscount, 130
Halifax, Charles Lindley Wood, 2nd Viscount: see 'Wood'
Hampden, John, 11, 134
Hampden, Renn Dickson (later Bishop of Hereford), 22
Hannah, Rev. John (later Archdeacon of Lewes), 205
Hardy, Gathorne, 32
Harris, Dom Asaph, OSB, 236–7, 243, 244n
Harvest-home, 48–9
Harward, Lt-Gen. Thomas Netherton, 180
Hatcham and Peckham Protestant League, 137
Hatcham and Protestant Defence Committee, 130
Hatcham Defence Committee, 122, 125, 130, 140, 145
Hawkins, Rev. C.J., 52–4
Headlam, Rev. Stewart Duckworth, 178–80, 189
Henson, Herbert Hensley, Bishop successively of Hereford and of Durham, 246
Hervey, Lord Arthur Charles, Bishop of Bath & Wells, 52–4, 61
Hilda, Mother (Emily Stewart), 232
Hillyard, Rev. E.A., 216–17

Holland, Canon Henry Scott, 57
Holloway, Richard Frederick, Bishop of Edinburgh, 114
Holy Trinity, Bordesley, 14
Holy Trinity, Stepney, 163
Hopkins, Fr. Charles Plomer, OP, 241
Horsemonger Lane Gaol, 117, 132–4, 155
How, William Walsham, Bishop successively of Bedford and of Wakefield, 163, 164
Howley, William, Archbishop of Canterbury, 27
Hubbard, John Gellibrand, 1st Baron Addington, 78–80, 81–2, 89
Hubbard, Maria Margaret (née Napier), 80–1
Hume, Joseph, 36

Ignatius, Fr: see 'Lyne, Joseph Leycester'
Ignatius Loyola, St, 188, 211
Incense, 6, 9, 11, 51, 85, 86, 89, 91, 122, 177, 246
Infant Samuel ('Baby Ignatius'), 219–20, 223
Ireland, Church of, disestablishment of, 49–50
Irish Times, 121

Jackson, Rev. Henry Latimer, 245
Jackson, John, Bishop of London, 16, 79, 97, 99, 101, 102–3, 104–5, 109, 110, 226
Jacob, Edgar, successively

Vicar of Portsea and Bishop
of Newcastle and of St
Albans, 173–4, 179, 184,
186

John Bull, 134

Jones, William Basil Tickell,
Bishop of St Davids, 237

Julius, Dr, 16

Kay-Shuttleworth, James, 24

Keate, John, 21

Keble, Rev. John, 22, 37, 43,
44, 46, 68

Kelly, Sir Fitzroy, 13

Kennion, George Wyndham,
Bishop of Bath & Wells,
60–1

Kilvert, Rev. Francis, 227–8,
233

King, Rev. Bryan, 71, 74–7

King, Edward, Bishop of
Lincoln, 1, 247

Kneeling, excessive: *see*
'Genuflection'

Knightsbridge Judgment, 7, 74

Knollys, Francis, 1st Viscount
Knollys, 130

Kynaston, Herbert, 203

Lacordaire, Henri Dominique,
209, 242

Lambeth Palace, 125, 131, 136,
142, 144, 146

Landor, Walter Savage, 226

Lang, Cosmo Gordon,
successively Bishop of
Stepney and Archbishop
of York and of Canterbury,
195–6

Law, George Henry, Bishop of
Bath & Wells, 25, 27

Law, Rev. William, 26

Layman, Thomas, 132, 156

Lee, Rev. Godfrey B., 179–80,
189

Leigh, William Henry, 2nd
Baron, 78

Liddell, Rev. and Hon. Robert,
7–8

Liddon, Canon Henry Parry,
13, 46, 56, 69, 79, 81, 133

Linklater, Rev. Robert, 163–4,
166, 167

Llanthony Abbey, 210, 221n,
226

Llanthony Monastery (Capel-
y-ffin), 226ff

Llanthony Tracts, 222, 236

Lloyd, Roger, 245, 248

Local Government Act, 61

Longley, Charles Thomas,
successively Bishop of
Ripon and of Durham and
Archbishop of York and
of Canterbury: 22, 53, 69n,
118, 176n, 221–2, 226, 237

Lords, House of, 6, 15, 17, 37,
50, 77, 102–3, 108

Loscombe, Louisa, 205

Lowder, Rev. Charles Fuge, 2,
7n, 16, 71–7, 107, 209,
211, 213

Ludlow, J.M., 74

Luff, Rev. S.G.A., 244n

Lushington, Chancellor
Stephen, 7–8, 45, 91

Lux Mundi (ed. C. Gore), 55,
57–60, 234–5

Lyne, Francis (J.L.L.'s father), 202–5, 209, 221

Lyne, Harriet (J.L.L.'s sister), 227*n*

Lyne, Joseph Leycester (Fr Ignatius, OSB): character of, 201–2, 240–2; childhood and youth, 202–5; studies for orders, 205–6; Scots ministry, 206–7; Plymouth curacy, 207–9; in Belgium, 209; Wapping curacy, 80, 209–10; dons monastic habit, 210–11; establishes Benedictine house at Claydon, 211–14; moves camp to Elm Hill, Norwich, 214–19; trip to Continent, 219–20; Elm Hill community dispersed, 220–1; abortive scheme for Margate curacy, 221–2; 'conversion' on Isle of Wight, 222–3; missioner in London, 223–6; move to Llanthony, 226–7; meeting with Kilvert, 227–8; Llanthony regime, 228–34; hostility to New Criticism, 234–6; trip to USA, 234–5; Apparitions of Our Lady, 236–7; controversial ordination as priest, 237–40; final years, 240; mentioned, ix, xii

Lyne, Louise Genevieve (née Leycester; J.L.L.'s mother), 202–3, 205, 207, 218, 221, 238

MacColl, Canon Malcolm, 148

MacColl, Rev. Malcolm, 147–9, 157

Mackarness, John Fielder, Bishop of Oxford, 16–17, 54

Mackenzie, Sir Compton, ix, 196

Mackonochie, Alexander Heriot: character of, 65–6, 113–15; childhood, 66–7; at university, 67; serves title at Westbury, 67–8; curate of Wantage, 69–70; with Lowder at Wapping, 71–7; accepts St Alban's, Holborn, 77–80; early ministry at St Alban's, 80–8; physical appearance and characteristics, 82–4; first taken to court, 90–3; harassed by Church Association, 93–6; fresh lawsuit instituted, 96–8; suspended for six weeks, 98–9; final round in Martin v. Mackonochie, 99–103; dramatic intervention of Tait, 103–7; vain exchange of livings, 107–10; decision to quit St Peter's, 109–10; final years, 111; death in blizzard, 111–13; mentioned, ix, 1, 2, 9, 10, 45, 51, 122, 127, 131, 133, 149, 196, 209, 245, 247

Mackonochie, George (A.H.M.'s father), 66

Mackonochie, Isabella (née

Alison; A.H.M.'s mother), 66–7, 70

Magee, William Connor, later Bishop of Peterborough and Archbishop of York, 88, 132, 133

Magi, 86

Manning, Henry Edward (later Cardinal), 29–30, 33, 37, 224

Mar Julius (Archbishop Alvarez), 239

Mar Timotheos: see 'Vilatte, Joseph Rene'

Marcus, Brother, OSB, 218

Marriott, Rev. Charles, 67

Martin, John, 90–3, 96–8, 100–3, 108–9, 247

Maurice, Rev. Frederick Denison, 31

Maurice, Rev. Peter, 3

Meek, Lizzie, 210

Methodist Recorder, 191

'Miracles' associated with Fr Ignatius, 207–8, 210, 236–7, 244n

Mission services, 52, 175–6

Mixed chalice, 6, 9, 51, 87, 91, 247

Moberly, George, Bishop of Salisbury, 162

Moberly, Canon Robert Campbell, 57

Monks of the West (C.R.F. Montalembert), 234

Moody, Dwight Lyman, 242

Morning Post, 135

Morse-Boycott, Rev. Desmond, 133, 155, 242

Moultrie, Rev. Gerard, 215

National Society (for Promoting Education of Children of Poor), 29–30, 32

Neale, Rev. John Mason, 4, 46

'New Criticism', 57–60, 234–6, 243

Newman, John Henry (later Cardinal), 2, 22, 67

Nonconformist, The, 136–7

Northcliffe, Alfred Charles William Harmsworth, Baron, 165–6

O'Connor, T.P., 161

Ollard, S.L., 11

On Eucharistical Adoration (J. Keble), 46

Order and Rule of St. Benedict, 210–11, 212, 215, 216–17, 220–1, 226, 230–1, 233n, 242

Order of St Paul, 241

Ornaments Rubric, 6, 8, 14

Osborne, Rev. Charles Edward, 163, 165, 168

Ottley, Rev. Edward Bickersteth, 162

Owen, A.J., 180

Owen, John, Bishop of St Davids, 243

Oxford Dictionary of the Christian Church, 35

Oxford Movement, 2, 3, 197

Oxford Movement, The, and After (C.P.S. Clarke), 242

Pall Mall Gazette, 247

Palmer, George Josiah, 127

Paradise Lost, 22

Pares, John, 189
Pastoral Measure, 62
Peel, Sir Robert, 27
Pelham, John Thomas, Bishop
of Norwich, 212–13, 215,
216, 217, 237
Penances, monastic, 217, 218,
231
Penzance, James Plaisted
Wilde, Baron: 13–14, 15,
247; and A.H.
Mackonochie, 100–1,
102–4, 108–9; and Arthur
Tooth, 125–7, 129, 131,
134, 136, 140, 144, 146–7
Perowne, John James Stewart,
Bishop of Worcester, 191
Pew rents, 82, 120, 151, 216
Philip, Brother, OSB, 219
Phillimore, Charlotte (née
Denison), 20n, 58
Phillimore, Sir Robert, 9–10,
13, 20n, 45, 91–2, 97–8,
100
Phillimore, Sir Walter, 46–7,
48, 53, 97
Phillpotts, Henry, Bishop of
Exeter, 33–4, 67, 207
Pius IX, Pope, 220
Plimpton, Joseph, 122, 138, 139
Popery of Oxford, The (P.
Maurice), 3
Poplar Board of Guardians, 194
Postmen's League, St Martin's,
162
Privy Council, Educational
Committee of, 24–5, 28, 30
Privy Council, Judicial
Committee of: and
Westerton v. Liddell, 8;

and Bennett case, 9; and
Purchas Judgment, 10–11;
and Ridsdale Judgment, 13;
and Gorham case, 33,
35–7; and Ditcher v.
Denison, 46; and Martin v.
Mackonochie, 92–5, 98,
102–3, 108; and Tooth
case, 129; and King case,
247; mentioned, 7, 248
Protestant Alliance, 182–3
Prynne, Rev. George Rundle,
207
Public Worship Regulation
Act, x, 6–7, 11–12, 13,
14–17, 97, 100, 106, 108,
117, 122ff, 246–7
Punch, ii, 4–5, 7n, 85, 218
Purchas, Rev. John, 9–10
Purchas Judgment, 9–11, 12, 99
Purgatory, doctrine of, 184
Pusey, Canon Edward
Bouverie, 3, 9, 22, 37, 44,
46, 52, 56, 67, 77, 119, 127,
202, 209, 215n, 220, 222,
238
Pusey House, 57

Real Presence, doctrine of the,
conflicting views on, x, 3,
8–9, 38–47, 50–1, 79, 123–5
Real Presence, The (E.B.
Pusey), 46
Record, The, 96
Requiem Masses: see 'Dead,
prayers for the'
Ridding, George, Bishop of
Southwell, 185
Ridsdale, Rev. Charles Joseph,
12–14, 142–3

Ridsdale, Judgment, 13, 124

Ritualism, growth of, ix–xiii, 2ff, 245–9; at East Brent, 26, 50–4; at Wapping, 72–4; St George's riots, 73–7; at St Alban's, Holborn, 79ff; at St James's, Hatcham, 120ff; at St Agatha's, Landport, 166, 174ff; in Glen Urquhart, 206–7

'Ritualistic Reporters', 87

Robert Elsmere (Mary Ward), 234

Roberts, Evan, 240

Rock, The, 134

Roman Catholicism, distrust of, 3–6, 49, 128, 139–40, 145, 206–7, 225

Rosebery, Archibald Philip Primrose, 5th Earl of, 197

Runcie, Robert Alexander Kennedy, Archbishop of Canterbury, 114

Russell, Rev. Edward Francis, 82–6, 108, 112–13, 114, 115

Russell, George William Erskine, 82, 93

Russell, Lord John, 36, 84–5

Sackville College, 4

St Agatha's, Landport, 159, 163–90, 193, 198–9

St Alban's, Holborn, 9, 51, 70, 77–107, 109–11, 115, 122, 149, 162, 209

St Andrew's, Holborn, 78

St Augustine's, Bermondsey, 148

St Barnabas's, Pimlico, 7

St Bartholomew's, Cripplegate, 223–4

St Edmund's, Lombard Street, 224–5

St George's-in-the-East, 70–7, 78, 209

St James's, Brighton, 9

St James's, Hatcham, 14, 119ff

St John's, Miles Platting, 15

St Lawrence's, Norwich, 216–17

St Margaret's, Toxteth Park, 14

St Mary Magdalene's, Chiswick, 119

St Mary-the-Less, Lambeth, 118

St Mary the Virgin, Oxford, 4

St Mary's, Folkestone, 118

St Mary's, Somers Town, 191

St Michael's School, Woodside (then Otford), 151–5

St Nicholas's, Deptford, 119, 192

St Paul's, Bunhill Row, 224

St Paul's Cathedral, 99, 163, 191, 194

St Paul's, Knightsbridge, 7–8

St Paul's, Middlesbrough, 192

St Paul's School, 203–4

St Paul's, Walworth, 132, 139

St Peter's, Folkestone, 12–14, 124

St Peter's, London Docks, 16, 71, 104–5, 107–10, 139

St Peter's, Plymouth, 207–8

St Raphael's, Bristol, 192

St Saviour's, Leeds, 77, 119

St Saviour's, Poplar, 192–4

St Stephen's, Lewisham, 139

St Vedast's, Foster Lane, 14, 99
Saints, Lives of the (Alban
    Butler), 231, 234
Salisbury Theological College,
    162
Sanders, William Henry, 148–9
Saturday Review, 189
Scott, Adrian Gilbert, 115
Sellon, Caroline, 209
Sellon, Priscilla Lydia (Mother
    Lydia), 208–9, 210, 220,
    224
Selwyn, Rev. Sydney Augustus,
    150
Shaftesbury, Anthony Ashley
    Cooper, 7th Earl of, 6,
    87–8
Ship money, 11
Sinclair, William Macdonald
    (later Archdeacon of
    London), 101
Six Points, the, 6, 11
Socialism, Christian, 179
Society of St John the
    Evangelist (Cowley
    Fathers), 201, 217
Society of the Holy Cross, 71,
    72
Society of the Love of Jesus,
    209
Society of the Most Holy
    Trinity, 208–9
Solicitors' Journal, 128
Spencer, George T., former
    Bishop of Madras, 38–41
Spiller, C.C., 89
'Spy' cartoon, 116, 121
Standard, The, 129
Stanislaus, Brother, OSB, 225
Stanley, Arthur Penrhyn, Dean

of Westminster, 5, 55–6,
    88
Stanton, Rev. Arthur Henry,
    84–6, 95–6, 99, 108, 112,
    113, 115, 118–19, 149, 162
Stations of the Cross, 176, 177
Suckling, Rev. Robert Alfred
    John, 107, 111, 115
Suffolk Mercury, 213
Sumner, Charles Richard,
    Bishop successively of
    Llandaff and of
    Winchester, 118
Sumner, George Henry,
    Bishop-Suffragan of
    Guildford, 177
Sumner, John Bird,
    successively Bishop of
    Chester and Archbishop of
    Canterbury, 27, 29, 37,
    42–6
Sutton, Charlotte (née
    Denison), 20n

Tait, Archibald Campbell,
    successively Bishop of
    London and Archbishop
    of Canterbury: and PWR
    Act, 5–6, 11–12, 15–16;
    and Ridsdale case, 12–14;
    upholds Denison against
    Hervey, 53–4; and
    Athanasian Creed, 56; and
    ritual at Wapping, 86–7;
    and A.H. Mackonochie,
    74–5, 77, 79, 81, 85, 88,
    89, 91, 97, 98–9, 103–7,
    108, 109, 110; and Arthur
    Tooth, 125, 142–4, 147,
    154; and Fr Ignatius,

223–6, 237; mentioned,
14n, 176n, 247

Tait, Rev. Craufurd, 143

Talbot, Fr Edward Keble, CR,
169n

Talbot, Edward Stuart, Bishop
successively of Rochester
and of Winchester, 57

Temperance reform, R.W.R.
Dolling and, 172–4

Temple, Frederick, successively
Bishop of Exeter and of
London and Archbishop
of Canterbury, 49, 163,
178, 240

*Ten Years in a Portsmouth
Slum* (R.W.R. Dolling),
164, 166, 169, 171, 176,
178, 188, 190, 191

Tertullian, 91

Thirlwall, Connop, Bishop of
St Davids, 1

Thomson, William,
successively Bishop of
Gloucester & Bristol and
Archbishop of York, 92,
145, 146

Thorman, A.J., 150

Thorold, Anthony Wilson,
Bishop successively of
Rochester and of
Winchester, 144–5, 149,
150, 160, 181–3, 188

Thynne, Rev. Lord John, 38

Times, The, 37, 59, 94, 134, 136,
197

Tinling, E.D., 31

Tolstoi, Count Leo, 179

Tooth, Arthur: character of,
117–18, 156–7; childhood

and youth, 118; early
ministry, 118–19;
appointed Vicar of St
James's, Hatcham,
119–21; physical
appearance, 121; first
complaint against, 121–2;
accused under PWR Act,
122–6; defies sentence of
inhibition, 126–8; under
increasing pressure,
128–31; pronounced
contumaceous, 131; taken
into custody, 132–4;
released from gaol, 136–7;
leaves for Continent, 138;
returns and makes forced
entry into St James's,
140–1; interviewed by
Tait, 142–4; cleared of all
charges on technicality,
144–7; resigns benefice,
147–8; subsequent
ministry at Woodside,
151–4; and at Otford,
154–5; final years, 155–6;
mentioned, ix, x, xi, 14

Tooth, Mary Anne (A.T.'s
mother), 118

Tooth, Robert (A.T.'s father),
118

Tooth, Robert (A.T.'s brother),
119–20, 147, 150

Tremenheere, Rev. George
Herbert, 190, 198

Trent, Council of, 91

Trinity College, Glenalmond,
205–6

Trinity, doctrine of the, Young

R.W.R. Dolling's analogy
of, 161
Truth, 198
Tudfil, Mother (Jessie Dew),
243
Tufnell, Rev. Edward W. (later
Bishop of Brisbane), 24

United States: Fr Dolling in,
192–3; Fr Ignatius in,
234–5

Vanity Fair, xi, 64, 121
Vaughan, Herbert, Cardinal, 240
Vespers of the Blessed
Sacrament, 177, 178
Vestments, eucharistic, 4, 6, 9,
12–13, 51, 72, 74–5, 79,
89, 97, 114, 122, 246
Victoria, Queen, 5–6, 11, 50,
89, 133, 148, 176n, 202
Vilatte, Joseph Rene (Mar
Timotheos), 238–9
Villiers, Henry Montagu (later
Bishop of Carlisle and of
Durham), 204–5
Virgins, Wise, 86

Waistcoats, 'Mark of the Beast',
4
Wales, Church in, attempted
disestablishment of, 55, 60
Wales, Prince of (later Edward
VII), 89, 129–30
Walker, Charles, 212
Walker, Rev. Henry Aston 148,
149–52, 157
'Wantage System', 69, 83
Water supply, problems of, 26,
48, 61, 194

Webb, Robert A., 139–42
Weekly Dispatch, 128
Wells Cathedral, 40–1, 45, 46,
59
Wells Theological College,
27
Welsh Revival Campaign, 240
Wesley, John, 175, 197, 228,
241
Westcott, Brooke Foss, Bishop
of Durham, 190–1
Westerton, Charles, 7–8
Whately, Richard (later
Archbishop of Dublin),
22
Wilberforce, Samuel ('Soapy
Sam'), Bishop successively
of Oxford and of
Winchester, 29, 42, 70,
176n, 216
Williams, Rev. Isaac, 46
Wilson, Thomas, Bishop of
Sodor & Man, 44
Winchester College, relations
of with R.W.R. Dolling,
168–70, 179–81, 189, 197
Winchester College Mission:
see 'St Agatha's,
Landport'
Winnington-Ingram, Arthur
Foley, Bishop of London,
195
Wood, Charles Lindley, 2nd
Viscount Halifax, 110,
129–30, 133, 155, 215n,
246
Wright, Rev. George, 204
Wright, Valentine, 152

Young, G.M., 9